PLAY THERAPY

THE ART OF THE RELATIONSHIP

GARRY L. LANDRETH

Regents Professor
Department of Counselor Education
Director, Center for Play Therapy
University of North Texas
Denton, Texas

ACCELERATED DEVELOPMENT
A member of the Taylor & Francis Group

Play Therapy: The Art of the Relationship

Technical Development: Tanya Dalton
                         Marguerite Mader
                         Angelia Marlett
                         Sheila Sheward

Library of Congress Cataloging-in-Publication Data

Landreth, Garry L.
    Play therapy : the art of the relationship / Garry L. Landreth.
        p.   cm.
    Includes bibliographical references and index.
    ISBN 1-55959-017-3
    1. Play therapy.   I. Title.
    RJ505.P6L26   1991
    618.92'16--dc 20   91-70335
                                                            CIP

LCN: 91-70335

ACCELERATED DEVELOPMENT
A member of the Taylor & Francis Group

1900 Frost Road, Suite 101 • Bristol, PA 19007 • 1-800-821-8312

The most important task God can give is the opportunity to be a parent. This book is dedicated to Monica for sharing the process with me and to Kimberly, Karla, and Craig for the satisfaction gained from being a father. Being a parent is much more important than writing a book.

ACKNOWLEDGEMENTS

The writing and completion of this book was made possible by the loving support and encouragement of the most important people in my life, my wife and three children who did a wonderful job of shielding me from distractions. My wife, Monica, shared a major burden by typing and having me rewrite sections that were perfectly clear to me but to no one else! A special fatherly appreciation to my three children, Kimberly for her patient understanding when she came home for vacation and found her bedroom had been taken over by an office computer, three tables and stacks of books; Karla for her exuberance about Dad writing another book; Craig for his expressed sensitivity by bringing me snacks late at night when I was tired.

Dr. Emily Oe's assistance in reading and editing the manuscript was invaluable. A special thanks to Dr. Bobbie Wilborn, my department chairperson, for her support and working out the details for my faculty development leave to write. The photographs in this book are of volunteers and not of clients. I am especially grateful to the children and their parents for their cooperation.

Acknowledgement and appreciation is extended to editors of journals for permission to reproduce all or parts of my articles which initially appeared under the titles listed: "Who is this Person They Call a Counselor Who Has a Playroom?" (1982) *The School Counselor, 29,* 359-361 (Reprinted by permission of the American Association for Counseling and Development); "The Uniqueness of the Play Therapist in a Child's Life," (1982) *Texas Personnel and Guidance Association Journal, 10,* 77-81; "Play Therapy: Facilitative Use of Child's Play in Elementary School Counseling," (1987) *Elementary*

School Guidance and Counseling Journal, 21, 253-261 (Reprinted by permission of the American Association for Counseling and Development).

PREFACE

My struggle in writing this book is that I cannot possibly communicate what I know, believe, and have experienced about the dynamic world of children through such an inadequate means as a few words written on a few pages of unresponsive paper. Feelings and experiences cannot adequately be conveyed through the medium of the written word and yet that is the structure I am restricted to using in this part of my effort to impact the way adults interact with children. Trying to communicate what I believe in my mind about children and have experienced to be true in my heart is for me an awesome task. Will I be able to make contact with the reader? Will I be understood? Will my excitement for children be felt? Will the reader see children any differently? Will the dynamics and characteristics of the child's world be better understood? Will what I write make any difference in how the reader approaches and interacts with children? At this point, it is probably quite obvious to the reader that I ventured forth in this process with some apprehension.

Perhaps I should state first that I have experienced play therapy to be a dynamic approach to counseling with children which allows the therapist to fully experience the child's world as the therapist ventures forth in the process of presenting the person he or she is and opening self to receive the delicate and subtle messages communicated by the child which declare the uniqueness of the personality of the child. The process of play is viewed as the child's effort to gain control in the environment. The problems children experience do not exist apart from the persons they are. Therefore, play therapy matches the dynamic inner structure of the child with an equally dynamic approach.

The emerging growth in the number of mental health professionals who use play therapy in their efforts to be helpful to children underscores the increased societal awareness and acceptance of the significance of the stage of development referred to as childhood. Our society may very well be on the threshold of recognizing children as people, not as play things, not as impersonal objects, not as sources of frustration to be tolerated until they mature, but real people who possess unlimited potential and creative resources for growing, coping, and developing. Children are quite capable of teaching adults about themselves if adults are willing, patient, and open to learning. Children are real people and are not simply appendages of those adults around them. They have feelings and reactions independent of their parent's reactions. The assumption of nervous mother, nervous child doesn't hold true. Can we assume that if the house is blown up and mother remains calm, the child will not be affected? No. Children are personalities in their own right and experience feelings and reactions independent of significant adults in their lives.

This book is about significant learnings from children as they have taught me about themselves and their world. Children are much more than I have been able to describe in this book. Likewise, the relationship and experience referred to as play therapy is infinitely more complex than this book portrays. The process of relating to a child who is experiencing permissiveness to be himself or herself is indescribable and can only be known in the actual shared moments of the relationship together. My intent has been to open the door to the child's world of being, experiencing, exploring, appreciating, and creating—a world of wonder, excitement, joy, sadness, and the vivid colors of life.

I also have included in this book an exploration of topics and issues my graduate students have indicated were important in their learning about the process of play therapy and the dynamics of the relationship with children. Therefore, some of the essential topics included in this book are as follows:

- The meaning of play in children's lives and the stages of play in the therapeutic process with adjusted and maladjusted children.

- Unique aspects, key concepts, and objectives of the child-centered philosophy of a therapeutic relationship.

- What children learn in the play therapy process.

- The person of the play therapist, necessary personality characteristics, and the role of the play therapist in the therapeutic experience.

- Characteristics of facilitative responses with specific guidelines on how to help children assume self-responsibility.

- Detailed guidelines for organizing a playroom and recommended toys and materials.

- Specific suggestions on relating to parents and how to explain play therapy.

- Making contact with the reluctant/anxious child and structuring the therapeutic experience in the playroom.

- How children view the play therapy experience.

- When to set limits, steps in therapeutic limit setting, and what to do when limits are broken.

- Typical problems that occur in the playroom and suggestions on how to respond.

- An examination of issues in play therapy such as participating in the child's play, accepting gifts, and who cleans up.

- Transcripts and discussions of children in play therapy: a dying child, an acting out child, a manipulative child, an elective mute child, and a child who had pulled all her hair out.

- Guidelines for determining therapeutic progress in play therapy and termination procedures.

- A description of a program to teach parents basic play therapy skills.

- A comprehensive bibliography of play therapy publications.

Some of this book is about me, my experiences, my reactions, and my feelings. Therefore, I have tried to convey my personal reactions by using the personal pronoun I. Using the customary phrase "the author" just did not convey the personal dimensions I wanted to communicate.

TABLE OF CONTENTS

PLAY THERAPY
THE ART OF THE RELATIONSHIP

CHAPTER 1

ABOUT ME, GARRY LANDRETH

I have always felt that knowing the author or at least knowing something about the author helped me to more clearly understand what the author was trying to communicate. Therefore, I want to let you know something about me. Perhaps this will help you to better understand the meaning of what I write even though my words may not adequately convey the message. Printed words on a page are at best an inadequate method for communicating something important, and what could be more important than talking about children and their world. I experience a very real feeling of apprehension and inadequacy when I think about trying to convey through this medium what I have experienced with children, my feelings for children, my belief in children, my hope for children, and the significance of this process we call play therapy in the lives of children. Perhaps that is why I appreciate so much the opportunities I have to be with children in play therapy relationships, for there we are not limited to words to communicate.

As a child I was scrawny and underdeveloped and attended a one room, all eight grades rural elementary school taught by my mother. In that setting, I developed a genuine appreciation for simple things, a propensity to strive, a love for learning, and a sensitivity for the underdog, the person who doesn't get noticed. Because of those experiences, I am keenly aware of children who do not get noticed.

I have not always been comfortable with children as I suspect many of you who read this text have been, and that I regret for I did not know experientially, emotionally the world of children. Oh, I knew intellectually from books and a university undergraduate course in child development, but I only knew *about* children. I did not *know* children with my heart in a way that touched them and their world. Children were there. I noticed them, but it simply did not occur to me to try to establish communication with them. The child in me had long before been pushed into the background out of my need to be appreciated for being mature, an adult. Being adult for me meant being serious about life, being responsible. I know now that was partially an attempt to overcome some feelings of inadequacy and the fact that, throughout my undergraduate years and my first year as a 21 year old high school teacher, I looked much younger than my chronological age, often being mistaken for one of the high school students.

After four years of teaching, a master's degree, and two years as a high school counselor, I gained my first glimpse into the child's world as a graduate assistant in the Children's Center on the University of New Mexico campus. There a sensitive and perceptive doctoral supervisor, who saw in me qualities I was oblivious to, encouraged me to work with children and introduced me to the exciting multifaceted dimensions of play therapy through which I began to slowly discover and experience the unfolding of the child's world.

Is it possible to truly describe the discovery of a life changing dimension in one's life? If so, then the experience must have been rather small or insignificant or both for most words are small and insignificant. At this moment, I sit here wanting to convey the genuine pleasure of making contact with children and how that added a new depth dimension to my life, and must admit that I am unable to do so. How does one describe children's wonder, excitement in experiencing life, the fresh newness with which they approach living, their incredible resiliency? I feel inept, my mind has suddenly come to a screeching halt. It is no longer active. All the circuits are open and searching. No words come to describe that experience, although I know the feeling well.

Life cannot be described, it can only be experienced and appreciated. Descriptions can always be evaluated. Life cannot. Life is. It unfolds and is in totality at that moment, no more and no less. We do not look at a person and judge or evaluate that person to have too little of life or too much. Indeed, one of my important discoveries was that little children seldom, if ever, evaluate lives of other little children. They interact with each other and accept the other person as enough. In those early years of my professional development, experiencing the unconditional acceptance of children was for me a profound experience. They did not wish I was more or less. I experienced children accepting me for what I was at that moment. They did not try to change me or make me different in some way. They liked me the way I was. I did not have to pretend. I discovered I could just be. What a fantastically freeing experience that was and continues to be as I relate to children. As I related to children on the basis of who they were at that moment and accepted them, their personhood, this became a reciprocal experience of sharing being together and accepting each other.

My early interactions with children in play therapy awakened in me a deep appreciation for the unfolding process of life as experienced by children and in turn a new appreciation for the process of my own life, not something to change, or undo, or overcome, or prove the worth of but to appreciate and live out the excitement of the process of being the person God has created me to be—to be me! Being more fully me means being more fully human, to accept my strengths as well as my weaknesses, for I do have strengths as well as weaknesses, and my mistakes are only a declaration of the fact that I am indeed fallible—human. That was a significant discovery for me, and yet as I look back, it was not a discovery for that seems to indicate an event in time. Like life it was a process which I experienced and gradually became aware of and slowly began to appreciate. What I would like to say to children is wonderfully expressed in Peccei's (1979) "In The Name Of The Children":

> If we were to allow the wonder of the life of a child to reach us fully and truly and to be our teacher, we would have to say: 'Thank you, child of man . . . for reminding me about the joy and excitement of being human. Thank

you for letting me grow together with you, that I can learn again of what I have forgotten about simplicity, intensity, totality, wonder and love and learn to respect my own life in its uniqueness. Thank you for allowing me to learn from your tears about the pain of growing up and the sufferings of the world. Thank you for showing me that to love another person and to be with people, big or small, is the most natural of gifts that grows like a flower when we live in the wonder of life. (p.10)

As I progressed in my relationships with children in play therapy, I made a rather startling discovery about my counseling sessions with adults. The counseling process seemed to be speeding up, and I was becoming more effective. With some adult clients where I had experienced being stuck, little progress, therapeutic movement began to develop and a new depth of sharing and exploring of self occurred for the client. As I examined this development, to me the change could be accounted for by my having become more aware of and responding to the subtle cues in the client that had always been there. I attributed this increased sensitivity to the client's subtle cues to my increased sensitivity to children's subtle forms of communication. I discovered that as I became more effective with children in play therapy, I became much more effective with adults in counseling relationships.

I joined the Counselor Education Department at the University of North Texas in 1966 and taught my first course in play therapy in 1967. Play therapy was not very well known in Texas in those days but from that meager beginning has come tremendous growth. What an exciting adventure that has been. I now teach three sections of that introductory course each year, an advanced course in the theory and practice of play therapy, a group play therapy course, a filial therapy course, supervise play therapy experiences, and direct the Center for Play Therapy. One thing I really enjoy about teaching play therapy is that the child part of me can emerge in the role playing I often do, and that helps to balance my tendency to be too serious about things. I am now able to really prize the child part of the person I am and thus to more fully appreciate and be sensitive to those qualities in children. I have discovered that when I am with children, the person I am is much more important than anything I know how to do in my mind.

I have been working with children in play therapy relationships for over twenty five years, and I am still learning about children and about myself as I experience with them the complex simplicity of their play and the unfolding of the vibrant colors of their emotional inner world. What I have learned and how I have come to incorporate that learning into my relationships with children is perhaps best expressed in the following principles.

Principles for Relationships with Children
Garry L. Landreth

I am not all knowing.
> Therefore, I shall not even attempt to be.

I need to be loved.
> Therefore, I will be open to loving children.

I want to be more accepting of the child in me.
> Therefore, I will with wonder and awe allow children to illuminate my world.

I know so little about the complex intricacies of childhood.
> Therefore, I will allow children to teach me.

I learn best from and am impacted most by my personal struggles.
> Therefore, I will join with children in their struggles.

I sometimes need a refuge.
> Therefore, I will provide a refuge for children.

I like it too when I am fully accepted as the person I am.
> Therefore, I will strive to experience and appreciate the person of the child.

I make mistakes. They are a declaration of the way I am—human and fallible.
> Therefore, I will be tolerant of the humanness of children.

I react with emotional internalization and expression to my world of reality.

Therefore, I will relinquish the grasp I have on reality and will try to enter the world as experienced by the child.

It feels good to be an authority, to provide answers.
Therefore, I shall need to work hard to protect children from me!

I am more fully me when I feel safe.
Therefore, I will be consistent in my interactions with children.

I am the only person who can live my life.
Therefore, I will not attempt to rule a child's life.

I have learned most of what I know from experiencing.
Therefore, I will allow children to experience.

The hope I experience and the will to live come from within me.
Therefore, I will recognize and affirm the child's will and selfhood.

I cannot make children's hurts and fears and frustrations and disappointments go away.
Therefore, I will soften the blow.

I experience fear when I am vulnerable.
Therefore, I will with kindness, gentleness, and tenderness touch the inner world of the vulnerable child.

REFERENCES

Peccei, A. (1979). In the name of the children. *Forum.* May, 10.

CHAPTER **2**

THE MEANING OF PLAY

Children's play is not mere sport. It is full of meaning
and import.

F. Froebel

Children must be approached and understood from a developmental perspective. They must not be viewed as miniature adults. Their world is one of concrete realities, and their experiences are often communicated through play. In seeking to facilitate children's expression and exploration of their emotional world, therapists must turn loose of their world of reality and verbal expression and must move into the conceptual-expressive world of children. Unlike adults, whose natural medium of communication is verbalization, the natural medium of communication for children is play and activity.

Functions Of Play

The universal importance of play to the natural development and wholeness of children has been underscored by the United Nations proclamation of play as a universal and inalienable right of childhood. Play is the singular central activity of childhood, occurring at all times and in all places. Children do not need to be taught how to play, nor must they be made to play. Play is spontaneous, enjoyable, voluntary, and non-goal directed. In order to make children's play more acceptable, some adults have invented a meaning for play by defining it as work. In their push to be successful and to hurry-up the process of growing up, many adults cannot tolerate "the waste of children's time by playing." The attitude is that children must be accomplishing something or working toward some important goal acceptable to adults. Regrettably play has been identified by many writers as children's work. This seems to be an effort to somehow make play legitimate, that play only can be important if it somehow fits what adults consider important in their world. Just as childhood has intrinsic value and is not merely preparation for adulthood, so to play has intrinsic value and is not dependent on what may follow for importance. In contrast to work which is goal focused and directed toward accomplishment or completion of a task by accommodating to the demands of the immediate environment, play is intrinsically complete, does not depend on external reward, and assimilates the world to match the individual's concepts as in the case of a child using a spoon as a car.

Although Sigmund Freud worked very little with children, he had remarkable insight into the meaning of children's play. He wrote:

> We ought to look in the child for the first traces of imaginative activity. The child's best loved and most absorbing occupation is play. Perhaps we may say that every child at play behaves like an imaginative writer, in that he creates a world of his own or, more truly, he arranges the things of his world and orders it in a new way that pleases him better. It would be incorrect to say that he does not take his world seriously; on the contrary, he takes his play very seriously and expends a great deal of emotion on it. (1953, pp. 173-174)

Frank (1982) suggested play is the way children learn what no one can teach them. It is the way they explore and orient themselves to the actual world of space and time, of things, animals, structures, and people. By engaging in the process of play, children learn to live in our symbolic world of meanings and values, at the same time exploring and experimenting and learning in their own individual way.

According to Woltmann (1964),

> The spontaneous and self-generated activities of the child enable him to conceptualize, to structure, and to bring

to tangible levels of activity his experiences and the feelings with which he invests them. Play, in this meaning, furnishes the child with opportunities to 'act out' situations which are disturbing, conflicting, and confusing to him. The small child especially lacks semantic fluency since the development of his apperceptive processes is in a state of growing . . . flux, various types of play materials seem to be ideally suited for the expression of his feelings and attitudes. (p. 174)

Below age ten to eleven, most children experience difficulty sitting still for sustained periods of time. A young child has to make a conscious effort to sit still and thus creative energy is consumed in focusing on a nonproductive activity. Play therapy provides for children's need to be physically active. In play, children discharge energy, prepare for life's duties, achieve difficult goals, and relive frustrations. They get physical contact, discharge their needs to compete, act aggressively in socially acceptable ways, and learn how to get along with others. Play helps children give their imaginations free rein, learn the trappings of their culture, and develop skills (Papalia & Olds, 1986). As children play, they are expressing the individuality of their personalities and drawing upon inner resources which can become incorporated into their personality.

Symbolic Play

According to Piaget (1962), play bridges the gap between concrete experience and abstract thought, and it is the symbolic function of play that is so important. In play, the child is dealing in a sensory-motor way with concrete objects which are symbols for something else the child has experienced directly or indirectly. Sometimes the connection is quite apparent, but at other times, the connection may be rather remote. In either case, play represents the attempt of children to organize their experiences and may be one of the few times in children's lives when they feel more in control of their lives and thus more secure.

The child-centered philosophy considers play essential to children's healthy development. Play gives concrete form and expression to children's inner world. Emotionally significant experiences are given meaningful expression through play. A major function of play is the changing of what may be unmanageable in reality to manageable situations through symbolic representation which provides children with opportunities for learning to cope by engaging in self-directed exploration. The therapist uses play with children because play is the child's symbolic language of self-expression. "Through the manipulation of toys, the child can show more adequately than through words how he feels about himself and the significant persons and events in his life" (Ginott, 1961, p. 51). "A therapist who is too literal minded and who cannot tolerate a child's flight into fantasy without ordering it into adult meaningfulness might well be lost at times." (Axline, 1969, p. 127)

In *War and Children*, Freud and Burlingham (1944) vividly describe differences in the way children and adults expressed their reaction to the bombing of London. Following an air raid, adults told and retold their experience of terror. Children who suffered through the same experience almost never talked about it. Their fearful reactions were expressed through their play. The children built houses out of blocks and dropped bombs on them. Buildings burned, sirens wailed, people were killed and injured, and ambulances took them to the hospital. These enactments continued for several weeks.

Children Communicate Through Play

Children's play can be more fully appreciated when recognized as their natural medium of communication. Children express themselves more fully and more directly through self-initiated spontaneous play than they do verbally because they are more comfortable with play. For children to "play out" their experiences and feelings is the most natural dynamic and self-healing process in which children can engage. Play is a medium of exchange and restricting children to verbal expression automatically places a barrier to a therapeutic relationship by imposing limitations that in effect say to children "You must come up to my level of communication and communicate with words." The therapist's responsibility is to go to the child's level and communicate with children through the medium with which they are comfortable. Why must the child accommodate the adult? The therapist is the one who is supposed to be well adjusted, to have developed coping

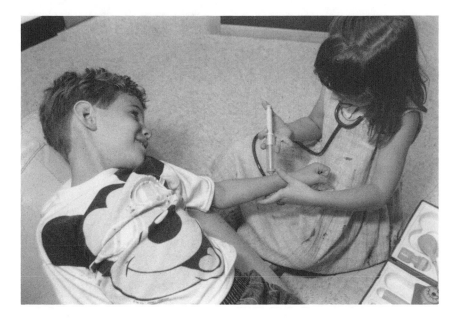

For children to "play out" their experiences and feelings is the most natural, dynamic, and self-healing process in which children can engage.

skills, to know how to communicate effectively at all levels and to possess a developmental understanding of children. When the therapist says "Tell me about it," young children are placed at a disadvantage of having to accommodate the therapist.

A therapeutic working relationship with children is best established through play, and the relationship is crucial to the activity we refer to as therapy. Play provides a means through which conflicts can be resolved and feelings can be communicated. "The toys implement the process because they are definitely the child's medium of expression . . . .His free play is an expression of what he wants to do. . . .When he plays freely and without direction, he is expressing a period of independent thought and action. He is releasing the feelings and attitudes that have been pushing to get out into the open" (Axline, 1969, p. 23). Feelings and attitudes which may be too threatening for the child to express directly can

Feelings and attitudes which may be too threatening for the child to express directly can be safely projected through self-chosen toys.

be safely projected through self-chosen toys. Instead of verbalizing thoughts and feelings, a child may bury in the sand, shoot the dragon, or spank the doll representing baby brother.

Children's feelings are often inaccessible at a verbal level. Developmentally they lack the cognitive, verbal facility to express what they feel and emotionally are not able to focus on the intensity of what is felt in a manner that can be expressed adequately in a verbal exchange. We know from the research of individuals such as Piaget (1962) that children are not developmentally able to engage fully in abstract reasoning or thinking until approximately age eleven. Words are made up of symbols and symbols are abstractions. No wonder then that so much of what we try to communicate verbally is of an abstract nature. The child's world is a world of concretes and must be approached as such if contact is to be made with the child. Play is the concrete expression of the child, and is the child's way of coping with his/her world.

> The most normal and competent child encounters what seem like insurmountable problems in living. But by playing them out, in the way he chooses, he may become able to cope with them in a step-by-step process. He often does so in symbolic ways that are hard for even him to understand, as he is reacting to inner processes whose origin may be buried deep in his unconscious. This may result in play that makes little sense to us at the moment or may even seem ill advised, since we do not know the purposes it serves or how it will end. When there is no immediate danger, it is usually best to approve of the child's play without interfering, just because he is so engrossed in it. Efforts to assist him in his struggles, while well intentioned, may divert him from seeking, and eventually finding, the solution that will serve him best. (Bettelheim, 1987, p. 40)

Play In The Therapeutic Process

Play is a voluntary, intrinsically motivated activity involving flexibility of choice in determining how the item is used. No extrinsic goal exists. The process of play is enjoyed and the end product is less important. Play involves the child's physical, mental, and emotional self in creative expression and can involve social interaction. Thus when the child plays, one can say that the *total* child is present. The term "play therapy" presupposes the presence of some possible *activity* that would be considered play. We do not say of a child who is reading a story, "He/she is playing." In keeping with this description of play, play therapy is defined as a dynamic interpersonal relationship between a child and a therapist trained in play therapy procedures who provides selected play materials and facilitates the development of a safe relationship for the child to fully express and explore self (feelings, thoughts, experiences, and behaviors) through the child's natural medium of communication, play.

Most adults are able to put their feelings, frustrations, anxieties, and personal problems into some form of verbal expression. Play is to the child what verbalization is to the adult. It is a medium for expressing feelings, exploring relationships, and self-fulfillment. Given the opportunity, children will play out their feelings and needs in a manner or process of expression which is similar to that for adults. The dynamics of expression and vehicle for communication are different for children but the expressions (fear, satisfaction, anger, happiness, frustration, contentment) are similar to that of adults. When viewed from this perspective, toys are used like words by children and play is their language. To restrict therapy to verbal expression is to deny the existence of the most graphic form of expression, activity. The goal of some play therapists is to "get the child to talk." When this is the case, it usually reveals the therapist's own state of anxiety or uncomfortableness and a need to be in control by getting the child to talk. Therapy is not limited to a talking cure. If there can be a talking cure, then why not a playing cure? Play therapy offers the opportunity to respond to the total behavior of the child, not just the verbal behavior.

According to Smolen (1959) who analyzed improvement in children who exhibited very little verbal interchange with the therapist,

> We came to the rather obvious conclusion that the "talking cure" was effective only insofar as it represented an adequate substitute for an "acting cure." That words are not always adequate substitutes for actions, even in the therapy of adults, is indicated by the vast amount of literature which

has grown up around the problems of the acting-out patient in therapy. Words, then, as substitutes for and abstractions of behavior can often be quite meaningful to adults who have had many years of experience. But how much less true is this of children who, by virtue of the maturational process alone, have not yet attained a capacity to utilize adequately abstractions or symbolic forms of speech or thinking. This point alone imposes on the therapist the necessity of assuring the consensual validity of the language exchanged with the child. Even though many children may have the vocabulary, they do not have the rich background of experience and associations which would render these words meaningful condensates of emotional experiences in terms of their potential usefulness in therapy. (p. 878)

Children may have considerable difficulty in trying to tell what they feel or how they have been affected by what they have experienced, but if permitted, in the presence of a caring, sensitive, and empathic adult, will show what they feel through the toys and material they choose, what they do with and to the materials, and the story acted out. Children's play is meaningful and significant to them for through their play they extend themselves into areas which they have difficulty entering verbally. Children are able to use toys to say what they cannot say, do things they would feel uncomfortable doing, and express feelings they might be reprimanded for verbalizing. Play is the child's symbolic language of self-expression and can reveal (1) what the child has experienced; (2) reactions to what was experienced; (3) feelings about what was experienced; (4) what the child wishes, wants, or needs; and (5) the child's perception of self.

Play represents the child's attempt to organize her experiences, her personal world. Through the process of play, the child experiences a feeling of being in control even though in reality circumstances may dictate otherwise. This attempt by the child to gain control is explained by Frank (1982).

> The child in his play relates himself to his accumulating past by continually reorienting himself to the present through play. He rehearses his past experiences, assimilating them into new perceptions and patterns of relating . . . . In this way the child is continually discovering himself anew, revising his image of himself as he can and must, with each alteration in his relations with the world. Likewise, in his play the child attempts to resolve his problems and

conflicts, manipulating play materials and often adult materials as he tries to work through or play out his perplexities and confusions. (p. 24)

An understanding of children's play behavior provides cues to help the therapist to enter more fully into the inner life of the child. Since the child's world is a world of action and activity, play therapy provides the therapist with an opportunity to enter the child's world. The selection of a variety of appropriate toys by the therapist can facilitate a wide range of feeling oriented expressions by children. Thus, children are not restricted to discussing what happened, rather they live out at the moment of the play the past experiences and associated feelings. Therefore, the therapist is allowed to experience and participate in the emotional lives of children rather than reliving situational happenings. Since children thrust their total being into their play, expressions and feelings are experienced by children as being specific, concrete, and current, thus allowing the therapist to respond to their present activities, statements, feelings, and emotions rather than past circumstances.

In play therapy children are able to use toys to say what they cannot say and express feelings they might be reprimanded for verbalizing.

If the reason for referral of a child to the therapist is aggressive behavior, the therapist is provided with an opportunity to not only experience the aggression first hand as the child bangs on the Bobo or attempts to shoot the therapist with a dart gun, but also to help the child learn self control by responding with appropriate therapeutic limit setting procedures. Without the presence of play materials, the therapist could only talk with the child about the aggressive behavior the child exhibited yesterday or last week. In play therapy, what ever the reason for referral, the therapist has the opportunity to experience and actively relate to that problem in the immediacy of the child's experiencing. Axline (1969) viewed this process as one in which the child plays out feelings, thus bringing them to the surface, getting them out in the open, facing them, and either learning to control them or abandon them. This process was readily evident in four-year-old Kathy's play in her play therapy experiences. At first glance, Kathy appeared to be just a four-year-old playing pretend. As she became agitated about the panties on the doll, placed a blanket over the doll, took the doll to the doctor for a detailed examination, and expressed the need for the dolls legs to be down, a pattern or theme began to emerge. Although she was quite young when she was abused, it appeared that she was working through some of those experiences.

Stages In The Play Therapy Process

Stages in the play therapy process are the result of shared interactions between the therapist and the child, experienced in the nonevaluative, freeing environment of the playroom, facilitated by the genuinely caring for and prizing of the child as communicated by the total person of the therapist. In this unique living relationship in which the unique nature and individuality of the child is accepted and appreciated, the child experiences permission to expand the horizons of self in keeping with the degree of acceptance inwardly felt and communicated by the therapist. This experiencing and expanding of the possibilities of self are often manifested in identifiable stages of change in the developing play therapy process.

From Moustakas' (1955a) analysis of case studies of disturbed children in play therapy, he observed that children progress through the following identifiable stages of the therapeutic process:

(a) diffuse negative feelings, expressed everywhere in the child's play.

(b) ambivalent feelings, generally anxious or hostile.

(c) direct negative feelings, expressed toward parents, siblings, and others, or in specific forms of regression.

(d) ambivalent feelings, positive and negative, toward parents, siblings, and others.

(e) clear, distinct, separate, usually realistic positive and negative attitudes, with positive attitudes predominating in the child's play. (p. 84)

As viewed by Moustakas (1955a), the disturbed child's attitudes, whether anger, anxiety, or other negative attitudes, all follow this process as play therapy progresses. He contended that the interpersonal relationship allows the child to express and explore the various levels of the emotional process and thus to achieve emotional maturity and growth.

In one of the most comprehensive studies of the process of play therapy, Hendricks (1971) reported a descriptive analysis of the process of client-centered play therapy. She found that children in sessions:

1-4 expressed curiosity, engaged in exploratory, noncommittal, and creative play, made simple descriptive and informative comments, and exhibited both happiness and anxiety.

5-8 continued exploratory, noncommittal, and creative play, generalized aggressive play increased, expressions of happiness and anxiety continued, and spontaneous reactions were evident.

9-12 exploratory, noncommittal, and aggressive play decreased, relationship play increased, creative play and happiness were predominant, nonverbal checking with the therapist increased, and more information about family and self was given.

13-16 creative and relationship play predominated, specific aggressive play increased, expressions of happiness, bewilderment, disgust, and disbelief increased.

17-20 dramatic and role play predominated, specific aggressive statements continued, increased relationship building with the therapist, expression of happiness was predominant emotion, and continued to offer information about self and family.

21-24 relationship play and dramatic and role play predominated, incidental play increased.

A second major comprehensive study of the play therapy process was completed by Withee (1975). She found that during the first three sessions, children gave the most verbal verification of counselors' reflections of their behaviors, exhibited the highest levels of anxiety, and engaged in verbal, nonverbal and play exploratory activities. During sessions four through six, curiosity and exploration dropped off while aggressive play and verbal sound effects reached their peaks. During sessions seven through nine, aggressive play dropped to the lowest point, and creative play, expressions of happiness and verbal information given about home, school, and other aspects of their lives were at their highest. During sessions ten through twelve, relationship play reached its highest point, and noncommittal play sank to its lowest level. In sessions thirteen through fifteen, noncommittal play and nonverbal expressions of anger peaked, anxiety rose over its previous level, and verbal relationship interactions and attempts to direct the therapist were at their highest levels. Differences also were found between boys and girls. Boys expressed more anger, aggressive statements, aggressive play, and sound effects. Girls exhibited more creative and relationship play, happiness, anxiety, verbal verification of therapist responses, and verbalizations of positive and negative thoughts.

These studies illustrate that discernable patterns are evident in the process of children's play in the therapeutic relationship established in the playroom. As the play therapy process develops, children begin to express feelings more directly and realistically and with more focus and specificity. Children initially engage in exploratory, noncommittal, and creative play. In the second stage, children exhibit more aggressive play and verbalizations about family and self. In latter sessions, dramatic play and a relationship with the therapist becomes important. Anxiety, frustration, and anger are expressed.

Play Of Adjusted And Maladjusted Children

The play of adjusted and maladjusted children as described by Moustakas (1955b) differs in several areas. Adjusted children are conversational and prone to discuss their world as it exists for them, whereas some maladjusted children may remain completely silent in their first few play sessions speaking only with great difficulty to the therapist. Other maladjusted children may keep up a rapid-fire flow of questions and conversations during the first sessions. The initial reactions of maladjusted children are cautious and deliberate. Adjusted children are free and spontaneous in their play.

Adjusted children will examine the whole play setting and use a large variety of play materials in contrast to maladjusted children who use a few toys and play in a small area. Maladjusted children often want to be told what to do and what not to do. Adjusted children use various strategies to discover their responsibilities and limitations in the therapeutic relationship.

When bothered or annoyed, adjusted children use a concrete way to bring out their problem. Maladjusted children are more likely to express their feelings symbolically with paints, clay, sand, and water. Maladjusted children are often aggressive and want to destroy the play materials and sometimes the therapist. Aggression also is seen in adjusted children, but it is clearly expressed without massive destruction and responsibility is accepted for the expression. Adjusted children are not so serious and intense in their feelings about themselves, the therapist, or their play as are maladjusted children.

Moustakas (1955b) concluded from his experiences with adjusted and maladjusted children in play therapy that all children, irrespective of the quality of their adjustment, express similar types of negative attitudes. The difference between well adjusted and maladjusted children lies not primarily in the type of negative attitudes they demonstrate, but rather in the quantity and intensity of such attitudes. Adjusted children express negative attitudes less often and with more focus and direction. Maladjusted children express negative attitudes frequently and intensely with less focus and direction.

Howe and Silvern (1981) identified differences in the play therapy behaviors of aggressive, withdrawn and well-adjusted children. Aggressive children presented frequent play disruptions, conflicted play, self-disclosing statements, high levels of fantasy play, and aggressive behavior toward the therapist and toys. Withdrawn boys were identified by their regression in response to anxiety, bizarre play, rejection of the therapist's intervention, and dysphoric content in play. Well-adjusted children exhibited less emotional discomfort, less social inadequacy, and less fantasy play. Withdrawn girls could not be differentiated from well-adjusted girls.

Perry (1988) studied the play behaviors of adjusted and maladjusted children in play therapy and found that maladjusted children expressed significantly more dysphoric feelings, conflictual themes, play disruptions, and negative self-disclosing statements than did the adjusted children. The maladjusted children also spent a larger portion of their play time feeling angry, sad, fearful, unhappy, and anxious than did the adjusted children. Maladjusted children talked and played out their problems and conflicts during more of the play session than did the adjusted children. No significant differences existed between the adjusted and maladjusted children in the area of social inadequacy play or the use of fantasy play.

The initial session play therapy behaviors of maladjusted and adjusted children were compared by Oe (1989) to investigate the value of children's play for diagnostic purposes. Maladjusted children exhibited significantly more self-accepting and nonacceptance of environment behaviors as well as more intense dramatic or role behaviors and acceptance of environment behaviors than did adjusted children. Maladjusted girls expressed dramatic or role behaviors more often and more intensely than maladjusted boys. Maladjusted boys showed more self-accepting and nonacceptance of environment behaviors than maladjusted girls. Maladjusted boys exhibited more self-accepting behaviors than adjusted boys, and adjusted girls expressed more positive attitudinal behaviors than adjusted boys. Adjusted boys engaged in more exploratory play and were more intense in negative attitudinal play than adjusted girls.

The play therapist is cautioned about unrestrained inferences as to the meaning of children's play. Neither the toys the child uses nor the manner in which the child plays with the toys is always an absolute indication of an emotional problem area. Environmental factors, recent happenings, and economic depravation may be structuring factors.

REFERENCES

Axline, V. (1969). *Play therapy.* Boston: Houghton-Mifflin.

Bettelheim, B. (1987). The importance of play. *The Atlantic Monthly.* March, 35-46.

Frank, L. (1982). Play in personality development. In G. Landreth (Ed.), *Play therapy: Dynamics of the process of counseling with children* (pp. 19-32). Springfield, IL: Charles C. Thomas.

Freud, A., & Burlingham, D. (1944). *War and children.* New York: International University Press.

Freud, S. (1953). The relation of the poet to daydreaming. In *Collected papers.* London: Hogarth Press.

Ginott, H. (1961). *Group psychotherapy with children: The theory and practice of play therapy.* New York: McGraw-Hill.

Hendricks, S. (1971). A descriptive analysis of the process of client-centered play therapy (Doctoral dissertation, North Texas State University, 1971). *Dissertation Abstracts International, 32,* 3689A.

Howe, P., & Silvern, L. (1981). Behavioral observation during play therapy: Preliminary development of a research instrument. *Journal of personality Assessment, 45,* 168-182.

Moustakas, C. (1955a). Emotional adjustment and the play therapy process. *Journal of Genetic Psychology, 86,* 79-99.

Moustakas, C. (1955b). The frequency and intensity of negative attitudes expressed in play therapy: A comparison of well adjusted and disturbed children. *Journal of Genetic Psychology, 86,* 309-324.

Oe, E. (1989). *Comparison of initial session play therapy behaivors of maladjusted and adjusted children.* (Doctoral dissertation, University of North Texas, 1989).

Papalia, D., & Olds, S. (1986). *Human development.* New York: McGraw-Hill.

Perry, L. (1988). Play therapy behavior of maladjusted and adjusted children (Doctoral dissertation, North Texas State University, 1988).

Piaget, J. (1962). *Play, dreams, and imitation in childhood.* New York: Rutledge.

Smolen, E. (1959). Nonverbal aspects of therapy with children. *American Journal of Psychotherapy, 13,* 872-881.

Withee, K. (1975). A descriptive analysis of the process of play therapy (Doctoral dissertation, North Texas State University, 1975). *Dissertation Abstracts International, 36,* 6406B.

Woltmann, A. (1964). Concepts of play therapy techniques. In M. Haworth (Ed.), *Child psychotherapy: Practice and theory* (pp. 20-32). New York: Basic Books.

CHAPTER 3

HISTORY AND DEVELOPMENT OF PLAY THERAPY

Birds fly, fish swim, and children play.

Garry Landreth

Play has long been recognized as occupying a significant place in the lives of children. As early as the 18th century Rousseau (1762/1930) wrote about the importance of observing play to learn about children and to understand them. In *Emile* (1762/1930) he expressed his ideas on the training and education of children and observed that they are not tiny adults. An interesting point to note is that 230 years later we are still struggling against this concept of children. Although Rousseau's comments on the play and games of children were more in accord with educative purposes than with the therapeutic uses of play, his writings reveal a very sensitive understanding of the world of children. "Hold childhood in reverence, and do not be in any hurry to judge it for good or ill . . . Give nature time to work before you take over her business, lest you interfere with her dealings . . . Childhood is the sleep of reason" (Rousseau, 1762/1930, p.71).

Froebel, in 1903, in his book *The Education of Man*, emphasized the symbolic components of play. He proposed that play has a definite conscious and unconscious purpose regardless of the nature of the play, and therefore can be looked to for meaning. "Play is the highest development in childhood, for it alone is the free expression of what is in the child's soul . . . Children's play is not mere sport. It is full of meaning and import" (Froebel, 1903, p. 22).

The first published case describing a psychological approach to working with a child was Sigmund Freud's report in 1909 of the classic case of "Little Hans," a 5-year-old little boy with a phobia. Freud saw Hans only one time for a brief visit and conducted the treatment by advising Hans's father of ways to respond with suggestions based on the father's notes about Hans's play. "Little Hans" is the first case, of record in which a child's difficulty was attributed to emotional causes. Today, emotional factors are so readily accepted that it is perhaps difficult to appreciate the magnitude of what was then a new concept of psychological disturbance in children. Reisman (1966) pointed out that at the dawning of the twentieth century, professionals generally believed childhood disorders were the result of deficiencies in the child's education and training.

Kanner (1957) concluded from his research that when the twentieth century began, no procedure or approach was being utilized with children that could in any sense be regarded as child psychiatry. Play therapy developed from efforts to apply psychoanalytic therapy to children. Considering how little was known about children in the early 1900's, one may be a bit surprised to realize that the formal and often highly structured approach utilized in adult analysis to obtain material for interpretation, primarily through the process of recall and recollections of the client, was so quickly recognized as being inadequate and inappropriate for child analysis.

Psychoanalytic Play Therapy

Following Freud's work with Hans, Hermine Hug-Hellmuth (1921) seems to have been one of the first therapists to emphasize play as essential in child analysis and to provide children in therapy with play materials to express themselves. Although her work predates that of Anna Freud and Melanie Klein, she did not formulate a specific therapeutic approach. She did, however, call attention to the difficulty of applying methods of adult therapy to children. It seems that the same problem we face now existed then, that of attempting to apply established methods with adults to children and discovering that child analysis was distinct and different from adult psychoanalysis. Analysts found that children were unable to describe their anxieties verbally as adults did. Also, unlike adults, children seemed not the least bit interested in exploring their past or discussing their developmental stages and many times refused to attempt to free associate. Consequently most therapists who worked with children in the early 1900s resorted to indirect therapy contact by collecting observations of the child.

In 1919 Melanie Klein (1955) began to employ the technique of play as a means of analyzing children under six years of age. She assumed that the child's play was as motivationally determined as the free association of adults. Analysis was carried out by substituting play for verbalized free association. Thus, play therapy provided direct access to the child's unconscious. She reported that additional material was exhibited in the child's play as a result of her interpretations. During this same period, Anna Freud (1946/1965) began to use play as a way to encourage the child to form an alliance with her. Unlike Klein, she emphasized the importance of developing the emotional relationship between the child and the therapist before interpreting the unconscious motivation behind the child's drawings and play. Both Klein and Freud stressed the importance of uncovering the past and strengthening the ego. Both also believed play to be the medium through which children express themselves most freely.

Melanie Klein (1955) utilized play as a way to encourage children to express fantasies, anxieties, and defenses which she then interpreted. A major difference between Melanie Klein and Anna Freud was Klein's heavy reliance on interpretation of preconscious and unconscious meanings of children's play. She saw symbolic meaning, especially sexual, in almost every play activity. She believed exploration of the unconscious was the main task of therapy and that this could best be achieved through analysis of the child's transference relationship with the therapist. Klein stressed taking the desires and anxieties in the therapist-child relationship back to where they originated—to infancy and in relation to the first love objects, the parents, especially the mother. Reexperiencing early emotions and fantasies and understanding them, gaining insight through the therapist's interpretations, diminishes the child's anxieties.

Klein (1955) explained the significance of interpretation by describing a play therapy episode with a child who surrounded a few toy figures with bricks.

> I would conclude and interpret that the child shows a room and that the figures symbolize people. Such an interpretation effects a first contact with the child's unconscious. For through the interpretation he comes to realize that the toys stand in his mind for people and therefore that the feelings he expresses toward the toys relate to people; also that preceding the interpretation he had not been aware of this. He is beginning to gain insight into the fact that one part of his mind is unknown to him, in other words, that the unconscious exists. Moreover, it becomes clearer to him what the analyst is doing with him. (p. 225)

The toys and materials Klein utilized were primarily simple, small, unstructured, and nonmechanical: little wooden men and women, animals, cars, houses, balls, marbles, paper, scissors, clay, paints, glue, and pencils. She kept each child's playthings locked in a drawer which represented the private and intimate relationship between child and therapist. Klein did not allow physical attacks on herself, but provided opportunities for children to act out aggressive fantasies in other ways including verbal attacks on her. She stated that she was usually able to interpret children's deeper motives in time to keep the situation under control.

Anna Freud (1946/1965) used children's play primarily as a means for facilitating children's positive emotional attachment to the therapist as a way to gain access to the child's inner life. A major objective was to influence the child to like her. Direct interpretation of play was minimal, and she cautioned against viewing everything in the play situation as symbolic. She believed some play had little emotional value because it was merely conscious repetitions of recent experiences. Freud believed that children do not form a transference neurosis. She delayed offering direct interpretations to children concerning the real meaning of their play until she had gained extensive knowledge from play observations and interviews with parents.

Since free association as developed by Sigmund Freud was cognitive in nature, Anna Freud modified the structure by involving the child in a feeling level experience. She encouraged the child to verbalize daydreams or fantasies, and when the child had difficulty discussing feelings and attitudes, she encouraged the child to sit quietly and "see pictures." By using this technique, the child was enabled to learn to verbalize his innermost thoughts and, using the interpretations of the analyst, to discover the meaning of these thoughts. Thus the child gained insight into his unconscious. As the relationship with the therapist developed, the emphasis of the sessions was shifted from play to more verbal interactions.

In the psychoanalytic approach to play therapy, no attempt is made to direct, reeducate, or pressure the child toward any predetermined direction or alternate course of action. In this sense, the approach is nondirective. Play is used as (1) a means of establishing contact with the child, (2) a medium of observation and a source of data, and (3) an instrument for interpretative insight.

Klein (1955) visited the United States in 1929 and later reported that play, as a part of the therapeutic procedure with children, was little used here. The work of Hermine Hug-Hellmuth, Anna Freud, and Melanie Klein was revolutionary in changing attitudes about children and their problems.

Release Play Therapy

The second major development in formulating play therapy occurred in the 1930s with the work of David Levy (1938) in developing release therapy, a structured play therapy approach for children who had experienced a specific stressful situation. Levy felt there was no need for interpretation and based his approach primarily on a belief in the abreactive effect of play.

In this approach, the major role of the therapist is to be a shifter of scenes to recreate through selected toys the experience which precipitated the child's anxiety reaction. The child is permitted to engage in free play to gain familiarity with the room and the therapist, and then the therapist uses play materials to introduce the stress producing situation when he feels it is appropriate. The reenactment of the traumatic event allows the child to release the pain and tension it caused. At other times, the child may be allowed to select her own free play. In this process of "playing out" or reenacting the experience, the child is in control of the play and thus moves out of the passive role of having been "done to" and into an active role of being the "doer." As the child plays, the therapist reflects the verbal and nonverbal feelings expressed.

Three forms of activities of release therapy occur in the playroom: (1) release of aggressive behavior in throwing objects or bursting balloons or release of infantile pleasures in sucking a nursing bottle; (2) release of feelings in standardized situations such as stimulating feelings of sibling rivalry by presenting a baby doll at a mother's breast; (3) release of feelings by recreating in play a particular stressful experience in a child's life.

The following case described by Levy (1939) presents the essence of the release therapy approach.

> A girl, aged two years, was referred because of night terrors, onset two days before referral. She awoke frightened and screamed that there was a fish in her bed . . . The night terror was related to a visit to a fish market on that very day. The fish merchant . . . lifted her up to see the fish.
>
> A second complaint was stammering, which had its onset five months before referral, although speech had developed normally up to that time . . . There were ten play sessions. A fish made of clay was introduced in the second session. To the question, why was the doll afraid of the fish, the answer was that the fish would bite, and the fish would go 'in here,' pointing to her eye, her ears, and her vagina. A few days before the night terror the patient had inquired about sex differences after seeing the father naked. Other than the introduction of the fish in various parts of the play sessions, the method was chiefly to facilitate

her own type of play . . . For example, she saw finger paint and wanted to play with it. I showed her how, but she wouldn't touch it, nor let me put a dot of paint on her hand . . . By playing with it myself and getting her to handle it gradually, she got to prefer it . . .

Following her first appointment there was no change in behavior . . . Fear of the fish left after the third or fourth session and the stammering showed improvement after the sixth, disappearing two weeks before the last session. A follow-up was made seven months later. Improvement was maintained. (p. 220)

Gove Hambidge (1955) extended the work of Levy under the title "Structured Play Therapy" and was more direct in introducing events. Following the establishment of a therapeutic relationship, the format consisted of directly recreating the anxiety producing situation, playing out the situation and then allowing the child free play to recover from the intrusive procedure.

Relationship Play Therapy

The emergence of the work of Jesse Taft (1933) and Frederick Allen (1934), referred to as relationship therapy, constituted the third significant development in play therapy. The philosophical basis for relationship play therapy evolved from the work of Otto Rank (1936) who deemphasized the importance of past history and the unconscious and stressed the development of the therapist-client relationship as crucial with a consistent focus on the present, the here and now.

In relationship play therapy, the primary emphasis is placed on the curative power of the emotional relationship between the therapist and the child. As Allen (1934) stated, "I am interested in creating a natural relation in which the patient can acquire a more adequate acceptance of himself, a clear conception of what he can do and feel in relation to the world in which he continues to live . . . I am not afraid to let the patient feel that I am interested in him as a person" (p. 198).

No effort is made to explain or interpret past experiences. Present feelings and reactions are the primary focus of attention and this approach reportedly led to considerable reduction in the length of therapy. Allan and Taft stressed regarding children as persons of inner strength with the capacity to alter their behavior constructively. Therefore, children are given freedom to choose to play or not to play and to direct their own activity. The hypothesis was that children gradually come to realize that they are separate persons with their own strivings and that they can exist in a relationship with other persons with their own qualities. In this approach the child has to assume responsibility in the growth process, and the therapist concentrates on those difficulties which concern the child rather than on those concerning the therapist.

Nondirective Play Therapy

The work of the relationship therapists was studied and expanded by Carl Rogers (1942), who extended these concepts and developed nondirective therapy, later referred to as client-centered therapy (Rogers, 1951) and today as person-centered therapy.

The fourth major development in play therapy was the work of Virginia Axline (1947). She successfully applied non-directive therapy principles (i.e., belief in the individual's natural strivings for growth and the individual's capacity for self-direction) to children in play therapy. Nondirective play therapy makes no effort to control or change the child and is based on the theory that the child's behavior is at all times caused by the drive for complete self-realization. The objectives of nondirective play therapy are self-awareness and self-direction by the child. The therapist has a well-stocked playroom and the child has the freedom to play as she chooses or to remain silent. The therapist actively reflects the child's thoughts and feelings believing that when a child's feelings are expressed, identified, and accepted, the child can accept them and then is free to deal with these feelings.

In summarizing her concept of play therapy, Axline (1950) stated, "A play experience is therapeutic because it provides a secure relationship between the child and the adult, so that the child has the freedom and room to state himself in his own terms, exactly as he is at that moment in his own way and in his own time" (p. 68). This approach was later referred to as client-centered play therapy and in this text is extended to child-centered play therapy.

Play Therapy in Elementary Schools

The establishment of guidance and counseling programs in elementary schools in the 1960s opened the door to the fifth major development in play therapy. Until the 1960s, play therapy was largely the domain of the private practitioner with a focus on treatment of maladjusted children and the literature related to play therapy reflected this condition. However, with the addition of counselors to elementary schools, counselor educators such as Alexander (1964), Landreth (1969, 1972), Muro (1968), Myrick and Holdin (1971), Nelson (1966), and Waterland (1970) were quick to describe their play therapy experiences in the literature. These authors encouraged the use of play therapy in school settings to meet a broad range of the developmental needs of all children not just the maladjusted. This trend toward the preventive role of play therapy has continued.

Dimick and Huff (1970) suggested that until children reach a level of facility and sophistication with verbal communication that allows them to express themselves fully and effectively to others, the use of play media is mandatory if significant communication is to take place between child and counselor. The main question then is not whether the elementary school counselor, school psychologist, or social worker should use play therapy, but rather how play therapy should be utilized in elementary schools.

The ultimate objective of elementary schools is to assist the intellectual, emotional, physical, and social development of children by providing adequate learning opportunities. Therefore, a major objective of utilizing play therapy with children in an elementary school setting is to help children get ready to profit from the learning experiences offered. Children cannot be made to learn. Even the most effective teachers cannot teach children who are not yet ready to learn. Play therapy, then, is an adjunct to the learning environment, an experience which assists children in maximizing their opportunities to learn.

Association for Play Therapy

The establishment of the International Association for Play Therapy in 1982 constitutes the sixth major development in the progressive growth of the field of play therapy. The organization of APT was the brain child of Charles Schaefer and Kevin O'Connor who envisioned an international society dedicated to the advancement of play therapy. The Association for Play Therapy is interdisciplinary and eclectic in orientation. It defines play therapy as "a distinct group of interventions which use play as an integral component of the therapeutic process." The goals of APT are to

> unite and provide a common meeting ground for persons involved or interested in the therapeutic use of child's play,

> promote training, research and the development of materials which further the practice of play therapy, and

> encourage active communication among those involved in play therapy.

The Association publishes an excellent quarterly newsletter and sponsors a conference each year in a different region of the United States or Canada. Membership in APT increased from a total of 450 in 1988 to almost 2,000 in 1990. This rapid increase graphically demonstrates how fast the field of play therapy is developing. For a membership application, write to the Association for Play Therapy, California School of Professional Psychology, 1350 "M" Street, Fresno, CA 93721.

Trends in Play Therapy

University Training. An increasing number of universities are offering courses and supervised experience in play therapy in response to the heightened interest in play therapy training by professionals in the field and preprofessionals in training.

A national survey in 1989 by the Center for Play Therapy at the University of North Texas found that 84 universities offer at least minimal introduction to play therapy in the form of a unit in a course, and 33 of these institutions offer at least a full semester course. The Department of Counselor Education at the University of North Texas offers master's and doctoral level courses and supervised practicum experiences in play therapy each semester.

Conferences and Workshops. The number of advertised conferences and workshops on play therapy has increased dramatically in the past five years as individual leaders in the field extend training opportunities. An indication of the tremendous interest in play therapy can be seen in the mushrooming attendance at these conferences and workshops by the curious and the dedicated professional. The 1990 Annual Play Therapy Conference at the University of North Texas was attended by 700 participants. This is a healthy sign of the developmental growth of play therapy.

Center for Play Therapy. In 1988 a National Center for Play Therapy was established on the University of North Texas campus under the direction of Garry Landreth. The Center serves as a clearinghouse for information regarding play therapy literature, training and research as well as a site for ongoing play therapy training and research. The Center has six fully equipped play therapy rooms, offers several graduate courses in play therapy, provides training workshops, sponsors an annual play therapy conference, provides a monthly Play Therapy Forum, and publishes results of surveys and research including a Directory of Play Therapy Training and a Bibliography of Play Therapy Literature. For information write to the Center for Play Therapy, University of North Texas, P.O. Box 13857, Denton, Texas 76203.

Filial Therapy. One of the most significant trends in the field of play therapy is the training of parents to be therapeutic agents with their children using basic play therapy skills. This innovative approach was developed in the 1960s by Bernard and Louise Guerney, a husband and wife team, and has gained wide spread acceptance as a model for enhancement of the parent-child relationship. Louise Guerney, now at Pennsylvania

State University, continues to be the leader and definitive authority on the filial therapy approach.

The filial therapy model, as conceived by the Guerneys, consists of a highly structured program in which parents are trained in the skills necessary to conduct weekly home play sessions with their own children using client-centered play therapy techniques. Training consists of didactic instruction, observations of the therapist with children, discussion groups and play sessions which the therapist supervises and acts as a consultant to the parent. Typically parents enter the training experience thinking their children are going to be changed and discover along the way that their perceptions of their children have changed and their behavior has become more empathically tolerant and accepting of their children.

Therapeutic skills should be shared with parents. If what the therapist does with children in the playroom is helpful to children, then those same behaviors exhibited by parents should be helpful to children's overall growth and development.

Adult Play Therapy. Although not yet a trend, a developing interest is occurring in the use of play therapy with adults in therapy setting. Since the focus is on the play activity and not the person(s) involved, the adult becomes absorbed in the activity of play itself and thus engages in a kind of awareness that is not possible through mere verbalization. Through play the adult has a conversation with self that is a very personal experience because direct involvement is called for. The doll house, sandbox, paints, and Bobo are very facilitative materials for adults. Some therapists have reported exciting results allowing adults to choose toys freely in the playroom. Other therapists conduct group therapy sessions in the playroom and ask the adult members to choose objects which represent symbols for themselves. These objects then become the point of focus for sharing by the member and for feedback from other members.

Play Therapy Techniques in Family Therapy. Family therapists are beginning to recognize the value of bringing toys and art materials to their sessions to facilitate involvement and expressions of children. Children below the age of nine

The presence of several children in the playroom facilitates the reluctant child's discovery that the therapist is a safe person by observing the other children.

or ten do not possess the verbal facility necessary to participate effectively in family interviews. Without the inclusion of play media, many family therapy sessions consist primarily of verbal interactions between the participating adults with the children either fulfilling the role of spectator or wandering aimlessly around the room in actuality or in their thoughts. To hand a child the family doll figures and ask the child to show what happens at home is far more effective than to ask the child to verbally describe or confirm what an interaction is like at home. At other times involving the whole family in play activity can be very facilitative and quite therapeutic for all involved. When parents are asked to participate with their children in planning play activities, they learn problem solving methods which will be helpful to them in future family interactions. Family play therapy allows the therapist to assume a variety of roles in interacting with the family including play facilitator, role model, participant, and teacher or educator.

Group Play Therapy. Although group play therapy has been used throughout most of the developmental history of play therapy, utilization has been very limited. Haim Ginott's *Group Psychotherapy with Children: The Theory and Practice of Play Therapy* published in 1961 and now out of print is the only text ever published on the topic of group play therapy. It is for these reasons and the rapidly growing interest in group play therapy that it is listed here under trends.

As in group counseling for adolescents and adults, group play therapy is basically a psychological and social process in which children, in the natural course of interacting with each other in the playroom, learn not only about other children but also about themselves. In the process of interacting, children help each other assume responsibility in interpersonal relationships. Children are then able to naturally and immediately extend these interactions with peers outside the setting of group play therapy. Unlike most other approaches to group counseling, in group play therapy there are no group goals and group cohesion is not an essential part of the

In group play therapy, each child plays out his or her story independent of other members.

developing process. By watching other children, a child gains the courage to attempt the things she wants to do.

Play Therapy in Hospitals. Hospitalization can be a frightening and stressful experience for the young child because he is in a strange environment where all sorts of invasive procedures are carried out. Because of these activities and new surroundings children often experience anxiety and a feeling of loss of control. Golden (1983) believed that the play therapist's toys are every bit as important as the surgeon's knife in assisting children to leave the hospital healthier than when they arrived. If children do not have an opportunity to appropriately express and deal with their fears and apprehensions, emotional problems may emerge and healthy adjustment will be altered.

The application of play therapy principles and procedures can be found in hospitals internationally. In the United States, Child Life Programs have been instrumental in incorporating playrooms and play therapy into what would otherwise be a sterile environment. Using hospital equipment, syringe, stethoscope, mask, etc., in combination with dolls or puppets, the therapist can acquaint children with medical procedures through directed play and thereby significantly reduce children's hospital-related anxiety. Positive results also have been achieved by allowing children to choose materials and direct their own play. Children will often act out in their play procedures what they have just experienced. This could be viewed as the child's way of trying to understand what has been experienced or as the child's way of developing control.

Other Settings for Play Therapy

Interdisciplinary Team Approach To Learning Disabilities. An approach which has been found to be effective in intervening in children's learning disability failure patterns is the development of a systematic interdisciplinary team approach (Landreth et al., 1969) which matches the global nature of children's problems by bringing together the teacher, speech therapist, play therapist, remedial reading teacher, and school nurse. Since the play therapist is typically in a better position to conceptualize the dynamic interrelated structure of the child, the play therapist is in a unique position to serve as the catalyst to unite in staffing sessions the disparate units concerned with the child's total learning development. Learning disabilities do not occur in isolation. They reverberate throughout the child's system impacting emotional and social adjustment just as readily as the area of learning difficulty. Consequently, such children are in need of play therapy.

Teachers as Play Therapist. Kranz (1972) reported an innovative approach to meeting the psychological needs of school children in the early grades by initiating a program in which twelve volunteer elementary school teachers were given ten weeks of training in play therapy in preparation for conducting play therapy sessions with children in their own schools but not from their own classroom. Sessions were scheduled before school, during teacher free periods, and after school. All the teachers reported the experience to be positive. Kranz reported positive changes in the children as evidenced by their being more relaxed and open to educational experiences and more adequate peer relationships. Children who had experienced difficulties with adult authority figures were less threatened and more comfortable in the presence of those adults. Guerney and Flumen (1970) and Schiffer (1960) reported similar results from their efforts to train teachers in play therapy skills.

Psychiatric settings. Play therapy has been utilized in a wide variety of psychiatric settings including: psychotherapeutic day camps (Mondell, Tyler, & Freeman, 1981), establishment of wards for entire families in the psychiatric treatment of the child— stressing the importance of family interplay in individual development (Noess & Spurkland, 1983), psychiatric day hospitals (Bettschart, Galland, & Brossy, 1983), and evening psychotherapy units for children at institutional settings (Diatkine, Avram, & Girard, 1982).

Play Therapy Results

Play Therapy has been demonstrated to be an effective therapeutic approach for a variety of children's problems including the following areas:

alleviation of hair pulling (Barlow, Strother, & Landreth, 1985)

amelioration of elective mutism (Barlow, Strother, & Landreth, 1986)

decrease in aggressive, acting-out behaviors (Willock, 1983)

improved emotional adjustment of children of divorced parents (Mendell, 1983)

improved emotional adjustment of abused and neglected children (Mann & McDermott, 1983)

reduction of stress and anxiety in hospitalized children (Golden, 1983)

correction of poor reading performance (Axline, 1947, 1949; Bills, 1950; Bixler, 1945; Mehus, 1953; Pumfrey & Elliot, 1970; Winn, 1959)

increased academic performance in learning disabled children (Axline, 1949; Guerney, 1983; Holmer, 1937; Jones, 1952; Machler, 1965; Moustakas, 1951; Sokoloff, 1959)

correction of speech problems (Axline & Rogers, 1945; Dupent et al., 1953; Reynert, 1946; Winn, 1959)

decreased emotional and intellectual problems of the mentally retarded (Leland, 1983; Leland & Smith, 1962; Miller, 1948; Moyer & Von Haller, 1956; Pothier, 1967)

better social and emotional adjustment (Andriola, 1944; Axline, 1948, 1964; Baruch, 1952; Conn, 1952; King & Ekstein, 1967; Miller, 1947; Moustakas, 1951; Pothier, 1967; Schiffer, 1957; Ude-Pestel, 1977)

amelioration of stuttering (Wakaba, 1983)

relieving psychosomatic difficulties such as asthma, ulcerative colitus and allergies (Dudek, 1967; Jessner, 1951; Miller & Baruch, 1948)

improved self concept (Bleck & Bleck, 1982; Crow 1989)

reduction of separation anxiety (Milos & Reiss, 1982)

Play therapy has been demonstrated to be effective with children of all diagnostic categories except the completely autistic and the out-of-contact schizophrenic. Thus only a few contraindications exist for placing children in play therapy.

REFERENCES

Alexander, E.D. (1964). School centered play therapy program. *Personnel and Guidance Journal, 43,* 256-261.

Allen, F. (1934). Therapeutic work with children. *American Journal of Orthopsychiatry, 4,* 193-202.

Andriola, J. (1944). Release of aggressions through play therapy for a ten-year-old patient at a child guidance clinic. *Psychoanalytic Review, 31,* 71-80.

Axline, V. (1947). Nondirective play therapy for poor readers. *Journal of Consulting Psychology, 11,* 61-69.

Axline, V. (1948). Play therapy: Race and conflict in young children. *Journal of Abnormal and Social Psychology, 43,* 300-310.

Axline, V. (1949). Play therapy: A way of understanding and helping reading problems. *Childhood Education, 26,* 156-161.

Axline, V. (1950). Entering the child's world via play experiences. *Progressive Education, 27,* 68-75.

Axline, V. (1964). *Dibs: In search of self.* Boston: Houghton Mifflin.

Axline, V. & Rogers, C.R. (1945). A teacher-therapist deals with a handicapped child. *Journal of Abnormal and Social Psychology, 40,* 119-142.

Barlow, K., Strother, J., & Landreth, G. (1985). Child-centered play therapy: Nancy from baldness to curls. *The School Counselor, 32,* 347-356.

Barlow. K.. Strother. J.. & Landreth. G. (1986). Sibling group play therapy: An effective alternative with an elective mute child. *The School Counselor. 34*. 44-50.

Baruch. D.W. (1952). *One little boy.* New York: Dell Publishing.

Bettschart. W.. Galland. S.. & Brossy. P. (1983). Therapeutic approaches through daily life in a children's day hospital. *Acta Paedopsychiatrica. 49*(3-4). 163-169. (From *Psychological Abstracts. 1984.* 71. Abstract No. 10353)

Bills. R.C. (1950). Nondirective play therapy with retarded readers. *Journal of Consulting Psychology. 14.* 140-149.

Bixler. R.H. (1945). Treatment of a reading problem through nondirective play therapy. *Journal of Consulting Psychology. 9.* 105-118.

Bleck. R. & Bleck. B. (1982). The disruptive child's play group. *Elementary School Guidance and Counseling. 17.* 137-141.

Conn, J.H. (1952). Treatment of anxiety states in children by play interviews. *Sinai Hospital Journal, 1,* 57-63.

Crow. J. (1989). Play therapy with low achievers in reading. Doctoral dissertation. University of North Texas.

Diatkine. R.. Avram. C.. & Girard. S. (1982). Psychotherapy in evening units. Information Psychiatrique. 58(9). 1145-1156. From *Psychological Abstracts.* 1983. *70.* Abstract No. 8374.

Dimick. K.M. & Huff. V.E. (1970). *Child counseling.* Dubuque. IA: William C. Brown.

Dudek. S. (1967). Suggestion and play therapy in the cure of warts in children: A pilot study. *Journal of Nervous and Mental Disease. 145.* 37-42.

Dupent. J.J.. Landsman. T.. & Valentine. M. (1953). The treatment of delayed speech by client-centered therapy. *Journal of Consulting Psychology. 18.* 122-125.

Freud. A. (1946). *The psychoanalytic treatment of children.* London: Imago.

Freud. A. (1965). *The psycho-analytical treatment of children.* New York: International Universities Press.

Freud. S. (1909/1955). *The case of "Little Hans" and the "Rat Man."* London: Hogarth Press.

Froebel. F. (1903). *The education of man.* New York: D. Appleton.

Ginott, H. (1961). *Group psychotherapy with children: The theory and practice of play therapy.* New York: McGraw-Hill.

Golden, D.B. (1983). Play therapy for hospitalized children. In C.E. Schaefer & K.L. O'Conner (Eds.), *Handbook of play therapy* (pp. 213-233). New York: John Wiley & Sons.

Guerney, L. (1983). Play therapy with learning disabled children. In C.E. Schaefer & K.L. O'Conner (Eds.), *Handbook of play therapy* (pp. 419-435). New York: John Wiley & Sons.

Guerney, B., & Flumen, A. (1970). Teachers as psychotherapeutic agents for withdrawn children. *Journal of School Psychology, 8,* 107-113.

Hambidge, G. (1955). Structured play therapy. *American Journal of Orthopsychiatry, 25,* 601-617.

Holmer, P. (1937). The use of the play situation as an aid to diagnosis, a case report. *American Journal of Orthopsychiatry, 7,* 523-531.

Hug-Hellmuth, H. (1921). On the technique of child analysis. *International Journal of Psychoanalysis, 2,* 287.

Jessner, L., & Kaplan, S. (1951). The use of play in psychotherapy with children. *Journal of Nervous and Mental Disease, 114,* 175-177.

Jones, J.W. (1952). Play therapy and the blind child. *New Outlook for the Blind, 46,* 189-197.

Kanner, L. (1957). *Child psychiatry.* Springfield, IL: Thomas.

King, P., & Ekstein, R. (1967). The search for ego controls: Progression of play activity in psychotherapy with a schizophrenic child. *Psychoanalytic Review, 54,* 25-37.

Klein, M. (1955). The psychoanalytic play technique. *American Journal of Orthopsychiatry, 25,* 223-237.

Kranz, P.L. (1972). Teachers as play therapist: An experiment in learning. *Childhood Education, 49,* 73-74.

Landreth, G.L., Allen, L., & Jacquot, W. (1969). A team approach to learning disabilities. *Journal of Learning Disabilities, 2,* 82-87.

Landreth, G.L. (1972). Why play therapy? *Texas Personnel and Guidance Association Guidelines, 21,* 1.

Leland, H. (1983). Play therapy for mentally retarded and developmentally disabled children. In C.E. Schaefer & K.L. O'Conner (Eds.), *Handbook of play therapy* (pp. 436-454). New York: John Wiley & Sons.

Leland, H., & Smith, D. (1962). Unstructured material in play therapy for emotionally disturbed brain damaged, mentally retarded children. *American Journal of Mental Deficiency, 66,* 621-628.

Levy, D. (1938). Release therapy in young children. *Psychiatry, 1,* 387-389.

Levy, D. (1939). Release therapy. *American Journal of Orthopsychiatry, 9,* 713-736.

Machler, T. (1965). Pinocchio in the treatment of school phobia. *Bulletin of the Menniger Clinic, 29,* 212-219.

Mann, E., & McDermott, J.F. (1983). Play therapy for victims of child abuse and neglect. In C.E. Schaefer & K.L. O'Conner (Eds.), *Handbook of play therapy* (pp. 283-307). New York: John Wiley & Sons.

Mehus, H. (1953). Learning and therapy. *American Journal of Orthopsychiatry, 23,* 416-421.

Mendell, A.E. (1983). Play therapy with children of divorced parents. In C.E. Schaefer & K.L. O'Conner (Eds.), *Handbook of play therapy* (pp. 320-354). New York: John Wiley & Sons.

Miller, H.E. (1947). Play therapy for the problem child. *Public Health Nurse Bulletin, 39,* 294-296.

Miller, H.E. (1948). Play therapy for the institutional child. *Nervous Child, 7,* 311-317.

Miller, H.E. & Baruch, D. (1948). Psychological dynamics in allergic patients as shown in group and individual psychotherapy. *Journal of Consulting Psychology, 12,* 111-113.

Milos, M., & Reiss, S. (1982). Effects of three play conditions on separation anxiety in young children. *Journal of Consulting and Clinical Psychology, 50,* 389-395.

Mondell, S., Tyler, F., & Freeman, R. (1981). Evaluating a psychotherapeutic day camp with psychosocial competence and goal attainment measures. *Journal of Clinical Child Psychology, 10* (3), 180-184.

Moustakas, C.E. (1951). Situational play therapy with normal children. *Journal of Consulting Psychology, 15,* 225-230.

Moyer, K., & Von Haller, G. (1956). Experimental study of children's preferences and use of blocks in play. *Journal of Genetic Psychology, 89,* 3-10.

Muro, J.J. (1968). Play media in counseling: A brief report of experience and some opinions. *Elementary School Guidance and Counseling Journal, 2,* 104-110.

Myrick, R.D., & Holdin, W. (1971). A study of play process in counseling. *Elementary School Guidance and Counseling Journal, 5,* 256-265.

Nelson, R.C. (1966). Elementary school counseling with unstructured play media. *Personnel and Guidance Journal, 45,* 24-27.

Noess, P., & Spurkland, I. (1983). Family day treatment for children and adolescents. *Acta Paedopsychiatrica, 49*(3-4), 133-140. (From *Psychological Abstracts,* 1984, *71,* Abstract No. 10373)

Pumfrey, P.D., & Elliott, C.D. (1970). Play therapy, social adjustment and reading attainment. *Educational Research, 12,* 183-193.

Pothier, P.C. (1967). Resolving conflict through play fantasy. *Journal of Psychiatric Nursing and Mental Health Services, 5,* 141-147.

Rank, O. (1936). *Will therapy.* New York: Knopf.

Reisman, J. (1966). *The development of clinicl psychology.* New York: Appleton-Century-Crofts.

Reynert, M.I. (1946). Play therapy at Mooseheart. *Journal of the Exceptional Child, 13,* 2-9.

Rogers, C. (1942). *Counseling and psychotherapy.* Boston: Houghton Mifflin.

Rogers, C. (1951). *Client-centered therapy.* Boston: Houghton Mifflin.

Rousseau, J.J. (1930). *Emile.* New York: J.M. Dent & Sons.

Schiffer, M. (1957). A therapeutic play group in a public school. *Mental Hygiene, 41,* 185-193.

Schiffer, M. (1960). The use of the seminar in training teachers and counselors as leaders of therapeutic play groups for maladjusted children. *American Journal of Orthopsychiatry, 30,* 154-165.

Sokoloff, M.A. (1959). A comparison of gains in communicative skills, resulting from group play therapy and individual speech therapy, among a group of non-severely dysarthric, speech handicapped cerebral palsied children. (Doctoral dissertation, New York University).

Taft, J. (1933). *The dynamics of therapy in a controlled relationship.* New York: Macmillan.

Ude-Pestel, A. (1977). *Betty: History and art of a child in therapy.* Palo Alto, CA: Science and Behavior Books.

Wakaba, Y. (1983). Group play therapy for Japanese children who stutter. *Journal of Fluency Disorders, 8,* 93-118.

Waterland, J.C. (1970). Actions instead of words: Play therapy for the young child. *Elementary School Guidance and Counseling Journal, 4,* 180-197.

Willock, B. (1983). Play therapy with the aggressive, acting-out child. In C.E. Schaefer & K.L. O'Conner (Eds.), *Handbook of play therapy* (pp. 386-411). New York: John Wiley & Sons.

Winn, E.V. (1959). The influence of play therapy on personality change and the consequent effect on reading performance. (Doctoral dissertation, Michigan State University).

A VIEW OF CHILDREN

To grow up to be healthy, very young children do not need to know how to read, but they do need to know how to play.

Fred Rogers

Although some people have said space is our last frontier to explore, childhood may in fact be our last frontier. We know so little about the complex intricacies of childhood and are limited in our efforts to discover and understand the meanings in childhood because we are forced to allow children to teach us. Many adults don't want to be taught by children, but we can only learn about children *from* children. Children bring to the relationship with the therapist a rich tapestry of emotional possibilities from which they weave the intricacies of their personalities. The direction these emotional possibilities take is affected by the person of the therapist, the kinds of responses the therapist makes, and what children sense in the therapist.

Tenets for Relating to Children

The process of relating to children from a child-centered frame of reference is based on the following tenets about children which are, for the therapist, the framework for an experiential self-projecting attitude about children. The tenets are as follows:

1. ***Children are not miniature adults*** and the therapist does not respond to them as if they were.

2. ***Children are people.*** They are capable of experiencing deep emotional pain and joy.

3. ***Children are unique and worthy of respect.*** The therapist prizes the uniqueness of each child and respects the person they are.

4. ***Children are resilient.*** Children possess a tremendous capacity to overcome obstacles and circumstances in their lives.

5. ***Children have an inherent tendency toward growth and maturity.*** They possess an inner intuitive wisdom.

6. ***Children are capable of positive self-direction.*** They are capable of dealing with their world in creative ways.

7. ***Children's natural language is play*** and this is the medium of self-expression with which they are most comfortable.

8. ***Children have a right to remain silent.*** The therapist respects a child's decision not to talk.

9. ***Children will take the therapeutic experience to where they need to be.*** The therapist does not attempt to determine when or how a child should play.

10. ***Children's growth cannot be speeded up.*** The therapist recognizes this and is patient with the child's developmental process.

Children are persons in their own right. They do not become persons upon the attainment of some predetermined age or after having met certain criteria. Each child is a unique personality and that uniqueness is not dependent on any significant person in the child's life; neither is personal significance limited to or a function of the child's behavior. Therefore, children are worthy of respect because they have worth and dignity as individuals. Their uniqueness is prized and appreciated by the therapist who responds to the child as a person. Some adults refer to a child as "it" as though referring to some inanimate object. That is always most disturbing. Children are people. They do not have to earn that distinction.

The child is not an object for study, but rather is a person to be known in the dynamics of the moment. The child standing before the therapist in the playroom is not a problem to be analyzed but a whole person to be related to and understood. Children, indeed all persons, have a longing to be heard, to be recognized as a person of value. For some children, it is as though they go through their lives day after day tapping out their message, "Hey, up there! Does anyone hear me? Does anyone see me? Does anyone care that no one seems to care about me? My heart aches. Do you see it? Do you care?" And day after day adults in their lives ignore these emotional messages. In the playroom, though, children are noticed, listened to, heard, responded to, and allowed to chart their own lives. This is a freeing process for children which allows them to draw on their inner resources for growth and self-direction. The permissiveness experienced in the playroom allows children to express the fullness of their personalities.

Children Are Resilient

Children possess an inner strength and are resilient. They bounce back. Attempting to explain that they are a product of their home environment seems to be far too simplistic and does not account for the differences and variability in children reared in the same environment. How do we account for some children who seem to be invulnerable to what would appear to be devastating experiences in their lives? Some children experience regular beatings by unloving and insensitive parents but are not beaten down psychologically in the process. Some children are reared in poverty but grow up rich in spirit and outlook on life. Some children have alcoholic parents but unlike so called co-dependent brothers and sisters are themselves independent and well adjusted. Some children are reared by emotionally disturbed parents and are themselves quite successful and well adjusted as teen-agers and adults. A possible explanation seems to be the integration that has occurred within individuals as they have interacted with their environment. Such examples emphasize the capacity and striving of the human organism to grow toward fulfillment and maturity even in the midst of adverse circumstances.

Significant variables which researchers have suggested as contributing factors to making some children invulnerable are high self-regard, self-control, inner motivation, and a sense of personal identity. These children have confidence in themselves. They *feel* capable of exerting control over their environment and are goal directed. Researchers have found that parents of such children have allowed considerable self-direction (Segal & Yahraes, 1979). These findings echo the dynamics and process of the play therapy relationship as experienced by children.

When I think of resilient children, I am reminded of eighteen-month-old Jessica McClure who fell down an abandoned well shaft in west Texas and captured the attention of people around the world. What a horrible and terrifying experience for a small child, surely as frightening as anything an adult could possibly experience. She was stuck in that small shaft for almost two whole days with no one to talk to her, no one to touch her, no one to comfort her. There was no way for her to know where she was or what had happened to her. Those two days must surely have been an eternity for Jessica. When rescue workers first made contact with her after she had been wedged into that dark shaft and all alone for forty-six hours, they heard this tiny little toddler singing softly to herself. What a remarkable demonstration of the inner natural motivation of children to comfort and take care of themselves. We adults are not wise enough to know the capacity and potential of children. Our view of children is typically much too narrow and restrictive. Some adults want to limit children to their finite comprehension. The capacity of the human organism surpasses our level of understanding.

All children should experience some joy in their life every day and this should be the goal of all adults who interact with children on a regular basis. Children are deprived of joy when they are rushed to complete tasks and hurried to grow up. Places of calmness and patience should exist in all children's lives; for in the midst of calmness and patience, children can discover and test their inner resources. Children are basically trusting and are, therefore, vulnerable. Adults must be very careful that they not take advantage of children's trust. Adults must be very sensitive to the inner experiencing of children.

Normally, children have fun. They are exuberant. When provided with opportunities to do so, children approach life with excitement, openness, and wonder. Children do not hold on to yesterdays. The world of the child is now. We cannot say to children "wait" because their world is a world of experiencing now. The world of the child is a world of slow amply punctuated with whirlwind activity. Children appreciate simple things. They do not try to make things more complex. Children are constantly growing and changing inwardly and outwardly and this dynamic process must be matched with an equally dynamic therapeutic approach.

Some Children Are Like Popcorn and Some Are Like Molasses

Anyone who has ever been in the presence of children for any extended period of time is well acquainted with the personality and behavioral variability they exhibit as they go about exploring their world in their own individual, unique ways. Some children are like popcorn; they do everything with great bursts of energy and activity. When something occurs to them, they pop forth with exuberance to activate this new and wonderful idea. They are like bumble bees, capable of seemingly motionless hovering when something captures their attention, and then they zoom off with a great burst of motion and buzz of noise to find something else of interest.

Other children are like molasses and can barely be poured from one place to another. They do everything with great deliberateness and careful consideration, caught up in their own seeming inertia, impervious to activity being generated around them. They are like a gyroscope, everything is functioning and spinning on the inside as it should, but little, if any, movement or change is observable in direction on the outside.

Some children are like mushrooms, they pop forth overnight. Other children are like orchids; they take seven to twelve years to bloom (Nutt, 1971). The effective play therapist is the kind of person who waits for orchids but is patient with mushrooms. Each child has his/her own unique approach to how life should be lived and the solution to problems. Therefore, since the child possesses those qualities necessary for growing and becoming a well adjusted, mature individual, the therapist waits patiently for the child to discover that unique self. The therapist has a sincere belief in the child's ability to work out difficulties and so does not, out of his/her impatience, suggest the child become involved in other activities or talk about more important topics, which, after all, other significant adults have said are important and should, therefore, be explored because this child needs to change. Since the therapist respects the child, he/she does not interrupt or "talk down" to the child, nor does the therapist discount what the child says or the feelings experienced.

REFERENCES

Nutt, G. (1971). *Being me: self you bug me.* Nashville: Broadman.

Segal, J. & Yahraes, H. (1979). *A child's journey: Forces that shape the lives of our young.* New York: McGraw-Hill.

CHAPTER 5

CHILD-CENTERED PLAY THERAPY

The best discovery the discoverer makes for himself.
                                        Ralph W. Emerson

The child-centered philosophy is just that, an encompassing philosophy for living one's life in relationships with children— not a cloak of techniques to put on upon entering the playroom, but a way of being based on a deep commitment to certain beliefs about children and their innate capacity for growth. Child-centered play therapy is a complete therapeutic system, not just the application of a few rapport building techniques, and is based on a belief in the capacity and resiliency of children. Children are the best source of information about themselves. They are quite capable of appropriately directing their own growth and are granted the freedom to be themselves in the process of playing out feelings and experiences. The child creates his/her own history in the playroom, and the therapist respects the direction determined by the child. The child-centered therapist is concerned with developing the kind of relationship which facilitates inner emotional growth and children's belief in themselves. Child-centered play therapy is an attitude, a philosophy, and a way of being.

Personality Structure

What a child knows, some intellectual knowledge or some "important" information the therapist can provide, is not what is important to personality development; how a child feels about self is what makes a significant difference in behavior. Each child possesses a personal perceptual view of self and the world that is reality for the child and this view of self provides a basis for individual functioning in whatever daily experiences occur in the child's life. This view of self and the limitless potentialities within each child are the basis for the theory of personality structure on which the child-centered approach to play therapy is based. These principles provide a framework for understanding the complex intricacies of the therapist's beliefs, motivation and attitude which form a life-style approach to children. At this point, the tendency is to go on writing about children and the wonderfully fresh and exciting way they approach the creative living of life, but a discussion of theory is necessary. An understanding of and adherence to a system of theoretical personality constructs provides consistency to the therapist's approach to children and enhances the therapist's sensitivity to the child's internal world of experiencing.

As I sit here in my home trying to formulate my thoughts into meaningful messages, I have just been struck by an awareness of being surrounded by bean plants in varying stages of growth; my son's science project for school. He has conscientiously watered these plants and placed one group of bean plants in the sunlight each day. They are healthy looking, have rich green colored leaves and some have produced little bean pods. In these plants there has been a natural, forward movement toward growth and maturity. My son has done nothing to make them grow. He has only provided some conditions that encourage growth. The plants have done the growing. A similar striving toward growth and maturity exists within individuals. Two other groups of plants have been grown in dark closets exposed to a red light or a blue light. The difference in these plants and the plants grown in sunlight is significant. Both groups of closet plants are tall, spindly, have a few small yellowish green leaves and no bean pods. Just as plants need a balance of sun, water, and fertile soil for healthy growth, children need the nurturing for healthy growth provided by complete acceptance of self by self and others, the right to make choices, opportunities to develop self-responsibility, and permissiveness to be themselves. The dynamics of inner growth occur in the light of these experiences which are internally integrated as a part of the child's perceptual view of self.

The child-centered theory of personality structure is based on three central concepts: (1) the person, (2) the phenomenal field and (3) the self (Rogers, 1951). The person is all that a child is: thoughts, behaviors, feelings, and physical being. The phenomenal field is everything the child experiences, whether or not at a conscious level, internal as well as external, and forms the basis of internal reference for viewing life. Whatever the child perceives to be occurring is reality for the child. The self is the totality of those perceptions the child has of self.

A basic proposition is that every child "exists in a continually changing world of experience of which he is the center" (Rogers, 1951, p. 483). As the child reacts to this changing world of experience, the child does so as an organized whole so that a change in any one part results in changes in other parts. Therefore, a continuous dynamic intrapersonal interaction occurs in which the child, as a total system, is striving toward actualizing the self. This active process is toward becoming a more positively functioning person, toward improvement, independence, maturity, and enhancement of self as a person. The child's behavior in this process is goal-directed in an effort to satisfy personal needs as experienced in the unique phenomenal field which for that child constitutes reality. Personal needs, then, influence the child's perception of reality. Therefore, the child's perception of reality is what must be understood if the child and his/her behavior are to be understood. Thus, the therapist avoids judging the child's behavior and works hard to try to understand the internal frame of reference of the child. The child's phenomenal world is the point of focus and must be understood if a person to person relationship contact is to be made.

The constantly changing interaction of the person of the child—thoughts, behaviors, feelings, and physical being—with the experiential environment is such that the child's perspective, attitude, and thought is constantly changing. This has great significance for the therapist who may only see the child once a week. The child this week is in some ways different, and the therapist must "catch up" so to speak. Events that were reacted to one way last week may be reacted to differently this week as the child's inner world of reality changes. This constantly changing integration within the child seems to explain the tremendous resiliency within children and the generating effect on hope. Life is a constant process of personal dynamic experiences and children are constantly experiencing an internal reorganization of thoughts, feelings, and attitudes. Therefore, past experiences are not experienced with the same degree of intensity or impact day after day. Thus, the therapist has no need to take the child back to past experiences because the child has grown since those former events, and they no longer have the same impact that they formerly had. Therefore, the therapist allows the child to lead, to take the current playroom experience to where the child needs to be.

The third central concept of the child-centered theory of personality structure is the self. Through interactions with significant others in the environment and from the total phenomenal field, the child, as an infant, gradually begins to differentiate a portion of these experiences as the self. According to Patterson (1974), the child can only become a person and develop a self in interactions with other persons. The self grows and changes as a result of continuing interaction with the phenomenal field. Rogers (1951) described the structure of the self as

> an organized configuration of perceptions of the self which are admissible to awareness. It is composed of such elements as the perceptions of one's characteristics and abilities; the percepts and concepts of the self in relation to others and to the environment; the value qualities which are perceived as associated with experiences and objects; and the goals and ideals which are perceived as having positive or negative valence. It is, then, the organized picture, existing in awareness either as figure or ground, of the self and the self-in-relationship, together with the positive or negative values which are associated with those qualities and relationships, as they are perceived as existing in the past, present, or future. (p. 501)

Awareness of self ushers in the development of the need for positive regard from others. This need for positive regard is reciprocal in that, as an individual satisfies another person's need for positive regard, the individual fulfills the same need. Satisfaction or frustration of the need for positive regard in association with self-experiences contribute to the development of a need for self-regard. This "sense of self-regard becomes a pervasive construct influencing the behavior of the whole organism and has a life of its own, independent of actual experiences of regard from others" (Meador & Rogers, 1989, p. 154).

The basic propositions regarding personality can be summarized as viewing the child as

1. being the best determiner of a personal reality,

2. behaving as an organized whole,

3. desiring to enhance the self,

4. goal directed in satisfying perceived needs,

5. being behaviorally influenced by feelings that affect rationality,

6. best able to perceive the self,

7. being able to be aware of the self,

8. valuing,

9. interested in maintaining a positive self-concept,

10. behaving in ways that are consistent with the self-concept,

11. not owning behavior that is inconsistent with the self,

12. producing psychological freedom or tension by admitting or not admitting certain experiences into the self-concept,

13. responding to threat by becoming behaviorally rigid,

14. admitting into awareness experiences that are inconsistent with the self if the self is free from threat,

15. being more understanding of others if a well integrated self-concept exists, and

16. moving from self-defeating values toward self-sustaining values. (Boy & Pine, 1982, p. 47)

Key Concepts

Child-centered play therapy is both a basic philosophy of the innate human capacity of the child to strive toward growth and maturity and an attitude of deep and abiding belief in the child's ability to be constructively self-directing. It is based on an understanding of the observable natural forward movement of the human organism through developmental stages of growth which are normally progressive and always toward greater maturity. This tendency is innate and is not externally motivated or taught. Children are naturally curious, delight in mastery and accomplishment, and energetically live life in their continual pursuit of discovery of their world and themselves in relation to the world.

Speaking of the process of self-discovery and self-growth, Moustakas (1981) said, "The challenge of therapy is to serve, to wait with interest and concern for the child to activate the will and to choose to act, to dare to pursue what is present in the way of interest and desire. This calls for unusual patience and an unshakable belief in the child's capacity to find the way, to come to terms with the restraints and tensions of living, a belief in the child's powers to listen inwardly and to make choices that are self enhancing" (p. 18).

An inherent tendency exists within children to move in subtle directedness toward adjustment, mental health, developmental growth, independence, autonomy of personhood, and what can be generally described as self-actualization. The basic character or nature of children's lives is activity. Their approach to living is an active process, and this can perhaps best be seen in a close observation of their play which is active and forward moving, not passive, toward enhancing self-sufficiency in the activity of living life. This inherent push toward discovery, development, and growth is readily observable in the developmental stages of infants and young children. When difficulty or frustration is experienced in attempts to accomplish or master a physical developmental task, the infant naturally strives forward toward mastery utilizing his/her own unique coping skills and propensity to try again with renewed vigor, effort, and determination.

The infant is not content to continue crawling from one place to another. An inner urge exists to stand up, followed by a developmental forward-moving continuation of the inner striving which results in the child learning to walk. This is not a conscious decision, a well thought out plan, or the result of some significant adult's efforts to teach walking. It occurs spontaneously as a result of growth and development inherent in the child's nature if the necessary conditions are present. This inherent directional process does not automatically insure a smooth succession of transitional steps. The infant pulls up to a standing position, turns loose, takes a faltering, wobbly step forward, falls, stands up, wobbles forward for a few steps, and falls again. Although some pain may be experienced in this process, the infant continues this forward-striving directional process toward growth. It is not necessary for someone to explain to the infant what causes the pain, what is being done the wrong way, how the behavior affects significant adults, or what behaviors need to be changed in order to achieve the desired goal. This directional striving will occur spontaneously when the infant is ready to take the next step, even though a period of temporary regression to crawling may occur. The infant will try again and again until walking is mastered to the infant's satisfaction. Since, in these experiences, the infant has been responsible for self, the accomplishment and accompanying satisfaction are internalized and strengthen the self. This continual striving for growth makes mature behavior more satisfying than immature behavior.

Although this example may seem to be an over simplification of a very complex process, it does seem to clearly highlight the point that children are capable of self-determination. This propensity to move in the direction of increasing independence, self-regulation, and autonomy and away from control by external forces is not limited to developmental accomplishments in infants or toddlers but can be seen as a primary motivating force of the whole person at all developmental levels and phases of life as persons strive for meaningful interpersonal relationships and enhancement of self. Children have a far greater capacity for self-direction than is readily recognized and are capable of making appropriate decisions. A powerful force exists within every child that strives continuously for self-actualization. This inherent striving is toward independence, maturity, and self-direction. The child's mind or conscious thoughts are not what direct the child's behavior to areas of emotional need but rather the child's natural striving toward inner balance that takes the child to where he/she needs to be. According to Axline (1969),

> The behavior of the individual at all times seems to be caused by one drive, the drive for complete self-realization. When an individual reaches a barrier which makes it more difficult for him to achieve the complete realization of the self, there is set up an area of resistance and friction and tension. The drive toward self-realization continues, and the individual's behavior demonstrates that he is satisfying this inner drive by outwardly fighting to establish his self-concept in the world of reality, or that he is satisfying it vicariously by confining it to his inner world where he can build it up with less struggle. (p. 13)

Adjustment and Maladjustment

The inner drive toward self-realization and affirmation of the worthwhileness of self are basic needs, and each child is striving continually to satisfy these needs. "An adjusted person seems to be an individual who does not encounter too many obstacles in his path—and who has been given the opportunity to become free and independent in his own right. The maladjusted person seems to be the one who, by some means or other, is denied the right to achieve this without a struggle" (Axline, 1969, p. 21). Manifestation of these principles can readily be seen in the lives of some children such as the following case of Matt.

Seven year old Matt walked methodically beside me into the counseling center, hands stuffed into his pockets, shoulders hunched, and a hollow look on his face. He looked older, defeated by the jarring, awful reality of having been locked in a hot, smelly, dark jail cell on the upper floor of a county government office building for four days without anyone with whom he was familiar to comfort him. His parents lived within walking distance of the jail but had not visited him, their reason locked somewhere deep inside and either unknown to them or deliberately withheld. When I saw Matt standing in the cell earlier that morning, he tried hard to appear calm and almost nonchalant, but the fright in his eyes and bright red half circle outlining his bottom lip betrayed his inner anxiety and revealed a frightened little boy, the victim of a system not prepared to understand or provide for the needs of children.

Earlier in the school year Matt had been referred to the counseling center by his second grade teacher for "aggressive behavior, short attention span, frequently tardy, and being moody." Test results were inconclusive but did indicate satisfactory academic progress potential. He was recommended for play therapy and walked the one block from his school to the center, accompanied by a school staff member, once a week for six sessions. When Matt missed his seventh session, I called the school and was informed that he was in jail. Matt had been caught stealing empty soft drink bottles from a grocery store and since this was the second such incident in a month, the county judge, having been given legal jurisdiction over Matt by his parents because "We can't do anything with him," declared Matt to be incorrigible and ordered him sent to jail. I persuaded the court to release Matt to my custody, and now here we were in the play therapy room together again. As he banged out his frustration on Bobo, he said, "Sometimes a guy gets to wondering if his parents really love him, and what you gotta do is go out and do something kinda bad. Then when your parents find out about it, if they beat up on you, you know they love you." Matt was striving to enhance his self and, yet, at the same time, was pushing the very thing he wanted further away because his behavior made him unacceptable to his parents.

Matt wanted to feel that he was a lovable person, to be accepted and included in the family as a worthy member. He found himself, however, in a home environment where the relationships were not lovingly supportive enough to provide the security and sense of belonging necessary for him to demonstrate directly in a constructive way that part of self that longed to be appreciated and responded to as a lovable person. Since Matt was not able to express outwardly his inner drive to enhance self, he resorted to indirect and ultimately self-defeating ways of affirming the worthwhileness of self.

Axline (1969) explained the difference between well-adjusted behavior and maladjusted behavior as

> When the individual develops sufficient self-confidence . . . consciously and purposefully to direct his behavior by evaluation, selectivity, and application to achieve his ultimate goal in life—self-realization—then he seems to be well-adjusted.
>
> On the other hand, when the individual lacks sufficient self-confidence to chart his course of actions openly, seems content to grow in self-realization vicariously rather than directly, and does little or nothing about channeling this drive in more constructive and productive directions, then he is said to be maladjusted . . . The individual's behavior is not consistent with the inner concept of the self which the individual has created in his attempt to achieve complete self-realization. The further apart the behavior and the concept, the greater the degree of maladjustment. (pp. 13-14)

All maladjustments result from an incongruence between what is actually experienced and the concept of self. Whenever a child's perception of an experience is distorted or denied, a state of incongruence between self and experience exists to some degree. As previously stated, children possess the capacity to experience the factors of their psychological maladjustments and the capacity and the tendency to move away from a state of maladjustment toward a state of psychological health.

Therapeutic Conditions for Growth

This forward moving, actualizing tendency previously described is the central tenet of the child-centered approach to play therapy and is succinctly described by Rogers (1980) as "Individuals have within themselves vast resources for self-understanding and for altering their self-concepts, basic attitudes, and self-directed behavior; these resources can be tapped if a definable climate of facilitative psychological attitudes can be provided" (p. 115). The attitudes of the play therapist which form the basis for the therapeutic relationship and which facilitate the release of the child's inner resources for growth are genuineness (being real), nonpossessive warmth (warm caring and acceptance), and empathy (sensitive understanding) (Rogers, 1986).

Being Real. The child-centered play therapy relationship is not an experience in which the therapist assumes a certain role or tries to do things in a prescribed manner. That would not be real or genuine. An attitude is a way of living life, not a technique to be applied when it seems to be needed. Genuineness is a basic and fundamental attitude that is for the therapist a way of being rather than a way of doing. Realness is not something to be "put on" but rather a "living out" of self at the moment in the relationship. The extent to which this is possible is a function of the therapist's awareness of his/her own feelings and attitudes. Genuineness or realness implies that the therapist possesses a high degree of self-understanding and self-acceptance and is congruent in what is being felt and what is being expressed in the relationship. This concept, does not imply that the play therapist must be fully self-actualized but, rather, is a statement regarding the importance and necessity of being congruent in the relationship with the child.

The kind of realness or genuineness discussed here does not entail expressing every immediate feeling or fleeting thought. To do so would be irresponsible and would exhibit a lack of insight on the part of the therapist. Therefore, the play therapist must have great self-understanding and insight into personal feelings of rejection experienced in relation to the child's behavior in the playroom which are a function of personal attitudes and values and that these feelings be directed toward self, rather than the child. This area of self-understanding is especially important for beginning play therapists whose experiences and/or value systems may result in them experiencing feelings of rejection or dislike of a child who exhibits messy behavior, tries to manipulate, or is verbally abusive to the therapist. A play therapist who lacks self-understanding of his/her own motivation in this area may inappropriately project rejection to the child. Realness, then, is being aware of and accepting one's own feelings and reactions with insight into the accompanying motivation and being willing to be oneself and to express these feelings and reactions when appropriate. The therapist is then being real or genuine and can be experienced by the child as a person, rather than as a professional. Children are very sensitive to the play therapist's way of being and are keenly aware of any false front or professional role presented. The experience of being with an adult who is living a life of realness at the moment with the child can be very rewarding for a child. Such an experience was summed up by one child who said, "You don't seem like a counselor. You just seem like a real person."

Warm Caring and Acceptance. A discussion of warm caring and acceptance must first focus on the necessity of the play therapist's acceptance of self. The time with the child is not an objective relationship in which some kind of mechanical acceptance of the child exists but rather an extension occurs of self as being acceptable to self and relating on that basis. Children are nonassuming in their acceptance, and their acceptance is basically unconditional. I have learned from my experiences with children that they like and accept me for the person I am, for the way I am. They do not try to analyze or diagnose me. They accept me, my strengths, and my weaknesses. Experiencing their acceptance has freed me to be more accepting of the person I am. How can a play therapist extend to a child genuine warmth if the therapist does not feel that for himself/herself? How can the therapist be accepting of the child if the therapist experiences self-rejection or nonacceptance of the person they are? How can I respect you if I do not respect myself? Acceptance is, like genuineness, an attitude, a way of being, an extension of the person of the therapist and all that the therapist is at that moment.

This kind of acceptance and warm caring is characterized by a positive respect for the child as a person of worth. The therapist experiences a genuine feeling of warmth and caring for the child that is unconditional. This caring is experientially felt and is not some abstract attitude of respect and acceptance of the worth and dignity of other persons that has been picked up from readings or graduate courses in counseling or psychology. The therapist really cares for the child and experiences a genuine prizing of the person of the child so what occurs is an absence of evaluation or judgment. Experiential caring is based on interactions within a relationship, getting to know the person of the child, and therefore, obviously does not automatically exist at the deepest levels possible within the first few minutes of encountering the child. Neither is it likely, as Rogers (1977) has pointed out, that the therapist will experience unconditional caring at all times. Unconditional caring and acceptance is not an all-or-none characteristic but is best thought of as a matter of degree, experienced in relation to the child out of the play therapist's deep, abiding feeling for, faith in, and appreciation of children's lives. Not only is an attitude of willingness present but also an actual experiencing of acceptance for the child as he/she is in the developing relationship in the playroom. The child is respected and prized just as much when deviant, moody, angry, or resistive as when cooperative, happy, or pleasantly engaging the therapist.

Warm caring and acceptance grant the child freedom and permission to be fully himself/herself in the emerging togetherness of the relationship in the playroom. The therapist does not wish that the child were different in some way. The attitudinal message consistently projected is, "I accept you as you are," not "I'll accept you if . . ." Acceptance does not imply approval of all the child's behavior. As is discussed in the chapter on therapeutic limits, many behaviors are considered unacceptable in the playroom. However, the central concept here is that none of the child's behaviors are evaluated as making the child any more or any less worthy of being accepted or prized as a unique person. Such nonevaluative acceptance is absolutely essential to establishing the kind of climate in which the child feels safe enough to express and, thus, reveal his/her innermost feelings and thoughts.

Most children have a strong desire to please adults and are quite sensitive to even the most subtle cues of rejection by the therapist. Children are keenly aware of and sensitive to whatever the play therapist experiences. Therefore, the importance of therapist self-awareness and self-understanding needs to be emphasized again. Children are egocentric and are likely to internalize the therapist's feelings of boredom, impatience, veiled criticism, or other negative behaviors as

Warm caring and acceptance grant the child freedom and permission to be fully herself in the emerging togetherness of the relationship in the playroom. The therapist really cares for the child so there is an absence of evaluation or judgment.

rejection of themselves. Since children have been developmentally dependent on "reading" nonverbal communication cues of adults, they are sensitive to whatever the therapist is feeling.

If the therapist experiences some inner tenseness as the child takes a fist full of play doh and repeatedly squishes it in the cup of brown tempera paint, that will be sensed by the child and will inhibit further experiential communication and exploration. Impatience with a child who stands in silence in the middle of the playroom and is slow to begin playing may show in a slightly different tone of voice such as, "You don't want to play with any of the toys here?" or a suggestion, "Beth, maybe you would like to play with some of those dolls right there." Beth hears these as messages of rejection, that she is not pleasing the therapist. In response to a ten-year-old boy filling the nursing bottle with water and sucking on it at length, the therapist's reaction may be, "Now what! He's too big to do that! Maybe he's regressing, and I should do something to stop it." Such a critical reaction may show in raised eyebrows, squinted eyes, or clinched teeth and will be quickly perceived by the child as disapproval. The child's reaction, then, is likely to be feelings of guilt for engaging in "baby" play. If the therapist readily responds to some play activities by the child and not so readily to others, the child takes note of that as disapproval of the play that is not readily responded to.

These are subtle but significant forces in the play therapy relationship, and they have a major impact on the degree of acceptance experienced by the child. Warm caring and acceptance are basically an attitude of receptiveness toward the experiential world of the child and facilitate in the child an awareness that the therapist can be trusted.

Sensitive Understanding. The typical approach in most adult-child interactions is characterized by an attitude of evaluation of children based on what is known about them. Seldom do adults strive to understand the internal frame of reference of children, their subjective world. Children are not free to explore, to test boundaries, to share frightening parts of their lives, or to change until they experience a relationship in which their subjective experiential world is understood and accepted. Sensitive understanding of children occurs to the extent the therapist is able to put aside his or her own experiences and expectations and appreciate the personhood of children, their activities, their experiences, their feelings, their thoughts. According to Rogers (1961), this kind of empathy is the ability to see the world of another by assuming the internal frame of reference of that person: "To sense the client's private world as if it were your own but without ever losing the 'as if' quality—this is empathy, and it seems essential to therapy" (p. 284).

Attempting to sensitively understand children from their viewpoint may be one of the most difficult and also potentially most critical factors of the therapeutic relationship, for as children feel understood by the play therapist, they are encouraged to share more of themselves. Such understanding seems to have a magnetic quality for children. As they feel understood, they feel safe enough to venture forth further in the relationship and their perception of their world is changed. This process of coming forth and familiar objects taking on new meaning is graphically described in the delightful story of *The Little Prince* (de Saint Exupery, 1943). The fox in the story tries to convince the little prince to tame him (to establish a relationship with him). He tells the little prince his life is monotonous and boring, that he hunts chickens and men hunt him. There is no change in expectation or the routine. He described the chickens as all being just alike, and all the men are just alike. Then the fox said, "But if you tame me, it will be as if the sun came to shine on my life. I shall know the sound of a step that will be different from all the others. Other steps send me hurrying back underneath the ground. Yours will call me, like music, out of my burrow. And then look: you see the grain-fields down yonder? I do not eat bread. Wheat is of no use to me. The wheat fields have nothing to say to me. And that is sad. But you have hair that is the color of gold. Think how wonderful that will be when you have tamed me! The grain, which is also golden, will bring me back the thought of you. And I shall love to listen to the wind in the wheat . . . " (p. 83). The similarity between this description and the impact an understanding and accepting relationship in play therapy can have in changing perception is striking.

Being empathic with a child often is regarded as a passive process of sitting in a chair in a playroom and allowing the child to do whatever comes to mind with little or no reaction or response from the play therapist. Nothing could be further from the truth. Sensitive understanding that is accurate requires the therapist to maintain a high level of emotional interaction with the child. The therapist has a sense of personal identification (as if) with the child rather than a mere reflection of feelings now and then as the child plays. This process of being fully with the child and sensitively and accurately understanding the child requires a commitment of self to the relationship with the child. Being fully committed to the relationship with the child results in one of the most active experiences in which a therapist can be engaged, necessitating great effort of heart and mind. This is not some objective observational activity to be entered into lightly. Mental and emotional effort is required to accurately sense and enter into the child's private world with understanding. Children "know" when they have been "touched" in this way.

Sensitive understanding means the play therapist is in full emotional contact with the perceptual experiential world of reality of the child. No questioning or evaluation is made of the child's verbal or acted out description of feelings or experiences in relation to this personal world of experiencing. The therapist tries hard to be fully in tune with all that the child is experiencing and expressing at the moment. The therapist does not try to think ahead of the child's experience or to analyze the content in some way to derive meaning. The attitude of the therapist is to sense as deeply as possible the experiencing of the child at that moment and to accept as fully as is possible the emerging intuitive empathic response within self as being sufficient for the moment. Thus, the relationship with the child is a continual prizing of the uniqueness of the child and an empathic experiencing of the moment-by-moment living out of the child's world at a pace of unfolding determined by the inner direction of the emerging child.

The therapist does not try to send painful experiences of the child away by unnecessary reassurance such as reassuring a frightened child that "everything will be okay" or attempting

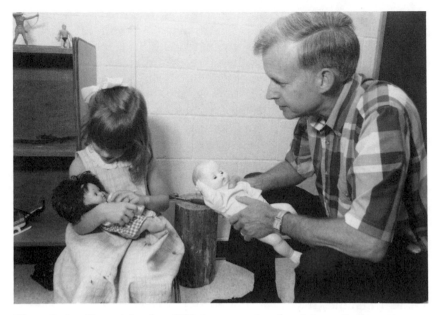

The relationship with the child is a continual prizing of the uniqueness of the child and an empathic experiencing of the moment-by-moment living out of the child's world at a pace of unfolding determined by the inner direction of the emerging child.

to comfort a child with "but your mother really does love you." To do so would be to reject what the child is feeling at the moment. Such responses give a clear message to the child that it is not permissible to experience pain. Whatever the child feels is considered by the therapist to be a legitimate feeling. If Bobby feels sad over the loss of a favorite crayon, the therapist experiences that sadness, perhaps not to the extent that the child feels it, but nevertheless an experiencing occurs of the sadness "as if." Even though the therapist may never have been physically abused by an alcoholic father, the terror and anger felt by Kevin are experienced within the intuitive experiencing of the therapist "as if." The therapist must be careful not to allow his/her life experiences to encroach upon and "color" such feelings and experiences. The experiencing of this kind of giving of self by the therapist is a releasing, rewarding, and recuperative act for the child. Few, if any, other places in a child's life is this emotional part of the child so completely identified with and accepted as being worthwhile.

The Therapeutic Relationship

Attempting to describe the almost imperceptible but nevertheless fully present subtle nuances characteristic of a shared relationship with the person of a child is a bit like trying to pick up a small bubble of mercury with your fingers. The very nature of the mercury is such that it defies being picked up. How does one adequately describe the shared experience, the exuberance of a child who struggles to express the unbelievable emotional release experienced in the safety of being fully accepted as a person of worth? Are words which will adequately describe the emotion experienced in such moments? If so, they are unknown to me, for words always seem to be such an inadequate means for attempting to convey the essence of such a shared moment with a child. Perhaps we should look to children who live out such experiences in the playroom for descriptions of the meaning of the relationship. Five-year-old Philip stood in the middle of the playroom flinging his arms up and down and excitedly repeated, "Who would have thought there was such a place like this in the whole world!" Indeed, this relationship is for most children like no other they have experienced. Here the adult allows the child to be, just that, to be! The child is accepted for whom and what he/she is at that time.

This kind of relating, of truly experiencing being with a child with the permission of the child to know the child's inner world, is not learned by training or by sharpening our intellect. It is a learning open only to the heart. The importance of responding out of one's heart in a relationship with a child is vividly described by the Tin Woodman in his conversation with the Scarecrow in the *Wizard of Oz* (Baum, 1956, pp. 55-56):

> "I don't know enough," replied the Scarecrow cheerfully.
> "My head is stuffed with straw, you know, and that is
> why I am going to Oz to ask him for some brains."
>
> "O, I see," said the Tin Woodman. "But, after all, brains
> are not the best things in the world."

"Have you any?" inquired the Scarecrow.

"No, my head is quite empty," answered the Woodman, "but once I had brains, and a heart also; so having tried them both, I should much rather have a heart."

Respect for the person of the child and a prizing of the child's world are not activities of the mind. They are genuinely felt and experienced in the inner person of the therapist and are sensed and felt by the child, who deeply appreciates and values the therapist for such unconditional acceptance. This relationship with the child in the playroom, then, is a mutually shared relationship of acceptance and appreciation in which each person is regarded as an individual.

I have sometimes experienced a fantasy that the developing relationship with a child in play therapy is like going into a completely dark room in which someone has placed a beautiful and very valuable vase on a stand. I enter the pitch black room knowing the vase is in there somewhere and wanting to make contact with the vase so that I can discover what it is like and appreciate it's beauty. Under such conditions I would not stride right into the darkness of the room and begin to grope for the location of the vase. Neither would I swing my arms rapidly to try to make contact lest I unexpectedly and unintentionally strike the stand or the prized vase causing it to vibrate from my blow and topple to the floor. Such behavior would be unthinkable. Instead, I enter the darkness of the room with caution and first stand there to begin to adjust to these new surroundings, trying to sense the dimensions of the room. I would focus all of my energy on being sensitively aware of the possible existence of nearby objects. Having adjusted to the initial darkness of the room and guided by great caution, I proceed to gently explore what is available to me in the room. My movements are slow. I begin to get acquainted with what I experience in the room, to see as clearly as I can in my mind that which I experience and sense with my total being. Everything about me is straining to sense the presence of the vase. After a few moments of not being successful in my efforts to locate the vase, I would not change my approach and move ahead quickly or try a new procedure and start crawling around on the floor. Quite the contrary, I know the vase is here somewhere; so I proceed with great patience to gently feel for the vase. I would not try to rush the discovery. Instead, I persevere with persistent patience in my effort to make contact with the vase. Finally one of my gentle hand movements touches something; I am very still, knowing it is here! I experience a flood of relief, joy, anticipation and wonder at what the vase will be like. Then I begin ever so gently to touch the vase as I allow my hands to explore it's shape, it's beauty and to picture that beauty in my mind. In like manner I want to experience and "touch" the emotionally vulnerable child.

If I am to be helpful to the child, I must make contact with the person of the child at all levels of experiencing in our shared time together. I would like to gently touch the child's emotional world and also to hear as fully as I can the child's expressed thoughts and descriptions. I would like the total response of my person to convey to the child the depth of my yearning to know and understand, to the extent to which I am fully capable, his/her experiential inner world of feelings and thoughts as known, experienced, felt, expressed, and lived out at the moment. Just as I want to hear, the child has a longing to share what may be perceived by the child as a frightening part of his/her life, or a part of the child's life which the child's fears may be rejected by me or others. So the child ventures forth in this relationship in ways which may seem to lack focus or direction as the child experiences this inner conflict of wanting to be heard and fearing evaluation and criticism. At such times a tentative and perhaps almost imperceptible sharing occurs of this vulnerable part of self in what may be an obscure or oblique manner which could easily go unnoticed because the message is so inconspicuous or veiled.

In many such relationships, the child is perhaps at that moment only vaguely aware at some deeper level of this underlying part of self or experience which he/she would like to share, perhaps not even at a conscious level in the immediacy of our experiencing relationship. At other times, one can sense at an immediate conscious level a deep longing on the part of the child to have this vulnerable part of self heard and accepted. The essence of what is occurring is as if the child is crying out "Does anyone hear me?" At these moments in our sharing together a developing relationship, I would like by my attitude, words, feelings, tone of voice, facial, and bodily expression, by the total person I am, to communicate my hearing, understanding, and acceptance of this deeper message in a way that will help the child to feel safe, accepted and appreciated. Sometimes, to me, by my response in such moments, I am very gently opening a door the child has come to stand in front of in our journey together and by that gesture, I am saying to the child, "I'm really not sure either what is on the other side of the door. I understand what is there may be frightening to you or something you had rather not face, but I am willing to walk through that door *with* you. I am not willing to lead you through the door nor will I push you or follow you through the door. I will be fully present beside you and we will discover *together* what is there. I trust you in this process to be able to face and cope with whatever we find there." This kind of relationship is described by Rogers (1952, p. 70) as ". . . the process by which the structure of the self is relaxed in the safety of the relationship with the therapist, and previously denied experiences are perceived and then integrated into an altered self."

The beginning of this movement toward a different self is facilitated when the warmth, interest, caring, understanding, genuineness, and empathy experienced by the therapist are perceived and felt by the child. In this climate of facilitative psychological attitudes (Rogers, 1980), the child comes to rely on his/her own vast resources for self-directed behavior and for altering his/her self-concept and basic attitude. Thus the power to change resides within the child and is not a result of direction, advice, or information the therapist might have to offer. As expressed by Rogers (1961, p. 33), "If I can provide a certain type of relationship, the other person will discover within himself the capacity to use that relationship for growth and change, and personal development will occur." The relationship then can be described as therapeutic and a function of basic key attitudes of the child-centered play therapist who is willing to know the child and to be known in the process of the developing relationship.

Child-centered play therapy is an immediate and present experience for children in which the therapeutic process emerges from a shared living relationship developed on the basis of the therapist's consistently conveyed confidence in children's ability to be of help to themselves thus freeing children to risk using their own strengths. Experiencing this acceptance of themselves, children begin to value themselves and come to perceive and accept themselves as unique and separate. As children gradually experience being themselves, they are free to experience living in the present and to make creative, responsible use of their individuality. The therapist can do nothing to make this happen. The therapist contributes to and facilitates the process by being as fully as possible the person he/she is at that moment.

Since the motivation for learning and change spring from an intrinsic self-actualizing tendency in the child, the therapist has no need to motivate the child, to supply energy, or to direct the child's behavior toward some predetermined goal. In the child-centered approach, the child selects the theme, content, and process of the play. The child chooses which toys to play with and sets the pace. The therapist does not make decisions for the child, no matter how insignificant the decision may seem to be. Thus, the child is encouraged to accept responsibility for self and in the process discovers his/her own strengths.

The nature of the interaction between the therapist and child in the child-centered approach is clarified by Axline (1969) in her eight basic principles which serve as a guide for therapeutic contact with the child. These principles in revised and extended form are the following eight:

1. The therapist is genuinely interested in the child and develops a warm, caring relationship.

2. The therapist experiences unqualified acceptance of the child and does not wish that the child were different in some way.

3. The therapist creates a feeling of safety and permissiveness in the relationship so the child feels free to explore and express self completely.

4. The therapist is always sensitive to the child's feelings and gently reflects those feelings in such a manner that the child develops self-understanding.

5. The therapist believes deeply in the child's capacity to act responsibly, unwaveringly respects the child's ability to solve personal problems, and allows the child to do so.

6. The therapist trusts the child's inner direction, allows the child to lead in all areas of the relationship and resists any urge to direct the child's play or conversation.

7. The therapist appreciates the gradual nature of the therapeutic process and does not attempt to hurry the process.

8. The therapist establishes only those therapeutic limits which help the child accept personal and appropriate relationship responsibility.

In this approach, the child and not the problem is the point of focus. When we focus on the problem we lose sight of the child. Diagnosis is not necessary because this is not a prescriptive approach. The therapist does not vary the approach to meet demands based on a specific referral problem. The relationship that develops and the creative forces this relationship releases in the child *generate* the process of change and growth for the child. It is not preparation for change. Whatever develops in the child was already there. The therapist does not create anything. The therapist only helps to release what already exists in the child. In this process, the child is responsible for self and is quite capable of exercising that responsibility through self-direction resulting in more positive behavior.

In child-centered play therapy, the relationship, not the utilization of toys or interpretation of behavior, is the key to growth. Therefore, the relationship is always focused on the present, living experience:

person	rather than	problem
present	rather than	past
feelings	rather than	thoughts or acts
understanding	rather than	explaining
accepting	rather than	correcting
child's direction	rather than	therapist's instruction
child's wisdom	rather than	therapist's knowledge

The relationship provides the consistent acceptance of the child which is necessary for the development of enough inner freedom and security by the child to express self in self-enhancing ways.

Objectives

When we speak of objectives in the child-centered play therapy approach, the emphasis is on broadly defined therapeutic objectives rather than individualized prescriptive goals for the child. When specific objectives are set for the individual child, the therapist will almost assuredly drift into the trap of subtly or directly pushing the child to work on the objective related to the identified problem and will thus restrict the child's opportunity for self-direction. Does this then mean the therapist is not interested in the "problem" parents or teachers have identified? Not at all, for such information about the child is a part of the child's total life and can, but not necessarily so, help the therapist to better understand what the child is communicating in the playroom. An important caution to note is that knowing such pretherapy information about the child, may bias the play therapist's perceptual view of the child and result in the therapist not "seeing" other parts of the child. Although this is a realistic concern, it is largely unavoidable in that the therapist will often need to interview parents or teachers prior to working with the child because the setting precludes the availability of another staff member to conduct the interview. This potential problem can largely be overcome if the therapist has a high degree of self-understanding, is aware of the potential perceptual bias, and is committed to the process of allowing the child to be fully the person he/she is at the moment with the therapist.

The general objectives of child-centered play therapy are consistent with the child's inner self-directed striving toward self-actualization. An overriding premise is to provide the child with a positive growth experience in the presence of an understanding supportive adult so the child will be able to discover internal strengths. Since child-centered play therapy focuses on the person of the child rather than the child's problem, the emphasis is on facilitating the child's efforts to become more adequate, as a person, in coping with current and future problems which may impact the child's life. To that end, the objectives of child-centered play therapy are to help the child

1. develop a more positive self-concept,

2. assume greater self-responsibility,

3. become more self-directing,

4. become more self-accepting,

5. become more self-reliant,

6. engage in self-determined decision making,

7. experience a feeling of control,

8. become sensitive to the process of coping,

9. develop an internal source of evaluation, and

10. become more trusting of self.

These objectives of child-centered play therapy provide a general framework for understanding the characteristics and the process of the approach. Since specific objectives are not set for the child, the therapist is free to facilitate the development of these person focused objectives. This does not preclude the child from working on specific problems the child feels a need to express and this often happens. In this child-centered relationship, the therapist believes in and trusts the child's capacity to set his/her own goals. Children in play therapy, though, seldom establish specific goals for themselves, at least not verbally and perhaps not consciously. A four-year-old does not voluntarily say, "I need to stop hitting my two-year-old brother," or a five-year-old state, "My goal is to like myself better," or a six-year-old say, "I'm here to work on the anger and rage I feel toward my father who sexually abused me." Although such problems may not be stated as goals by children, such problems will often be acted out through their play, and in the process of the relationship children *will* work on the problem in their own way.

In this view, no attempt is made to control a child, to have the child be a certain way, or to reach a conclusion the therapist has decided is important. The therapist is not *the* authority who decides what is best for the child, what the child should think, or how the child should feel. If this were to be the case, the child would be deprived of the opportunity to discover his/her own strengths. In this approach, children need not be aware that they have a problem for play therapy to be beneficial.

What Children Learn in Play Therapy

Since the majority of children who are referred for play therapy are involved in some sort of school experience, a pertinent topic to examine is that of learning. Most teachers spend their day involved in the process of helping children learn and so teachers naturally may want to know just what children learn in play therapy, especially if the child has to miss part of the instructional time in order to attend play therapy sessions. Actually, for children play therapy is a unique learning experience under the most favorable growth promoting conditions possible and, as such, is viewed from a developmental perspective with objectives consistent with those of the school: to assist children in learning about themselves and their world.

Play therapy assists the development of children by helping them learn to know and accept themselves. Play therapy also assists in accomplishing the broader school objective of learning about the world by helping children to get ready to profit from the learning experiences provided by teachers. Children who are anxious or worried, have poor self-concepts, are experiencing a divorce in the home environment, or have poor peer relationships cannot achieve maximum learning from even the most masterful teacher. Play therapy, therefore, is an adjunct to the learning environment, an experience that helps children maximize opportunities to learn in the classroom.

Risk taking, self-exploration, and self-discovery are not likely to occur in the presence of threat or the absence of safety. The potential learning experiences available in play therapy are directly related to the degree to which the therapist is successful in creating a climate of safety within which children feel fully accepted and safe enough to risk being and expressing the innermost totality of their emotional being. This is not a conscious decision on the part of children but rather the result of a permissive climate void of criticism, suggestions, praise, disapproval, or efforts to change them. Children are accepted just as they are; therefore, there is no need to please the adult in this relationship. As one child expressed it, "In here you can just be your own little 'ol self.'" Since there is no threat to self, self-exploration and self-discovery occur naturally. This is not meant to imply that self-expression occurs with reckless abandon as might be the case in the early stage of the therapeutic process. In response to the feeling of permissiveness established in the playroom, the safety to be fully one's self, and the careful use of therapeutic limits, which will be discussed later, *children learn self-control and responsible freedom of expression.*

Most of what is learned in the play therapy relationship is not a cognitive learning but a developing experiential, intuitive learning about self that occurs over the course of the therapeutic experience. The play therapist maintains and communicates a constant regard and respect for children regardless of their behavior, whether playing passively, acting out aggression, or being whiny and dependently insisting on help with even the simplest of tasks. Children sense the therapist's respect, feel respected, and, since an absence of evaluation and an ever present acceptance exists, they internalize the respect; thus **children learn to respect themselves.** Once children have respect for themselves, they learn to respect others.

Through the process of playing out their feelings in the presence of an adult who understands and accepts even the intensity of the feelings, **children learn their feelings are acceptable.** Children also learn to be more open in expressing their feelings. Once those feelings have been openly expressed and accepted they lose their intensity and can more easily be appropriately controlled. As **children learn to responsibly control their feelings,** they are no longer controlled by those feelings. This, then, is a freeing process for children to experience in that they are then free to go beyond those feelings.

In the natural process of development, children strive toward independence and self-reliance but are often thwarted in their efforts by adults who, although well intentioned, take charge by doing things *for* children and thus deprive children of opportunities to experience what it feels like to be responsible for self. In the play therapy relationship, the therapist believes in children's ability to be resourceful and so resists doing anything that would deprive children of the opportunity to discover their own strength. As the therapist allows children to struggle to do things for themselves, **children learn to assume responsibility for self** and discover what that responsibility feels like.

When children are allowed to figure things out for themselves, to derive their own solutions to problems, to complete their own tasks, their own creative resources are released and developed. With increasing frequency, then, children will tackle their own problems and experience the satisfaction of doing things all by themselves. Through this process, **children learn to be creative and resourceful in confronting problems** which formerly were overwhelming. Although children may initially resist the opportunity to solve their own problems, the creative tendency of the self will come forth in response to practiced patience by the therapist.

Learning self-control and self-direction is not possible if no opportunities are available to experience being in control. Although this principle seems almost to be too simplistically obvious, the absence of such opportunities in children's lives is overwhelmingly conspicuous when one takes the time to observe carefully children's interactions with significant adults. Unlike most other adults in children's lives, the play therapist does not make decisions for children or try to control them by either direct or subtle means. Limits on children's behavior in the playroom are verbalized in such a way that children are allowed to control their own behavior. Since control is not externally applied, **children learn self-control and self-direction** because they are allowed to make their own decisions.

As children experience being accepted just as they are with no conditional expectations from the therapist, they gradually, and in sometimes imperceptible ways, begin to accept themselves as being worthwhile. This is both a direct and an indirect process of communication and learning about self. The therapist does not overtly tell children they are accepted because that would have little or no positive impact on the relationship or the way children feel about themselves. Acceptance is an attitudinal message communicated through the total behavior of the therapist by all that the therapist is and does in and through interactions with the children. Acceptance is first felt by children and then becomes known to them. As they experience being accepted nonjudgementally for who they are, just as they are, with no desire that they be different, **children gradually learn, at a feeling level, to accept themselves.** This increased self-acceptance is a major contributing factor to the development of a positive self-concept.

Life is partially composed of a never ending series of choices. However, how can children learn the feeling of making a choice if they are not allowed to experience the process of making choices, the indecision, the struggle, wanting to avoid, feeling incapable, the anxiety, and the apprehension that one's choice will be unacceptable to others? Therefore, the therapist avoids making even simple choices for children, such as which color to use in a drawing, knowing that **children learn to make choices and to be responsible for their choices** by being allowed to experience the process of making choices.

REFERENCES

Axline, V. (1969). *Play therapy*. New York: Ballentine.

Baum, L. (1956). *The wizard of oz*. New York: Rand McNally.

Boy, A., & Pine, G. (1982). *Client-centered counseling: A renewal*. Boston: Allyn and Bacon.

de Saint Exupery, A. (1943). *The little prince*. New York: Harcourt, Brace.

Meador, B., & Rogers, C. (1989). Person-centered therapy. In R. Corsini & D. Wedding (4th Ed.), *Current psychotherapies*. Itasca, IL: F.E. Peacock.

Moustakas, C. (1981). *Rhythms, rituals and relationships*. Detroit: Harlow Press.

Patterson, C. (1974). *Relationship counseling and psychotherapy*. New York: Harper & Row.

Rogers, C. (1951). *Client-centered therapy: It's current practice, implications, and theory*. Boston: Houghton Mifflin.

Rogers, C. (1952). Client-centered psychotherapy. *Scientific American, 187*, 70.

Rogers, C. (1961). *On becoming a person*. Boston: Houghton Mifflin.

Rogers, C. (1977). *Carl Rogers on personal power: Inner strength and its revolutionary impact*. New York: Delacorte.

Rogers, C. (1980). *A way of being*. Boston: Houghton Mifflin.

Rogers, C. (1986). Client-centered therapy. In J.L. Kutash & A. Wolf (Eds.), *Psychotherapist's casebook* (pp. 197-208). San Francisco: Jossey-Bass.

CHAPTER 6

THE PLAY THERAPIST

Man is perfectly human only when he plays.

F. Schiller

The play therapist is a unique adult in children's lives, unique because the therapist responds out of his/her own humanness to the person of the child while controlling any desire to direct, probe, or teach and instead provides responses that are freeing to the child's natural urge toward self direction. That children are aware of this uniqueness may be seen in this excerpt from a play therapy session.

Chris: What color should I paint this frog?

Therapist: In here you can decide what color you want the frog to be.

Chris: I don't know. Would black be o.k.? Are some frogs black? My teacher said frogs are green.

Therapist: You would like to paint your frog black but, you're not sure that would be o.k.

Chris: Yeah, you're supposed to tell me what color to use.

Therapist: You would like for me to make the decision for you.

Chris: Yeah, everybody else does.

Therapist: Everybody else would just decide for you so you
           think I should too, but in here you can decide
           the color you want your frog to be.

Chris: It's going to be blue! The world's first blue frog!
           You're funny!

Therapist: I seem different to you because I don't tell you
           what to do.

Chris: Yeah! . . . like a blue frog.

Creating Differences

Chris is right, of course. Therapists who utilize play therapy
are "funny" people. They are not "funny" as in creating humor,
but "funny" as in creating a new and different kind of adult
relationship for the child to experience. The creation of this
relationship is contributed to by the presence of play media
materials which provide unique opportunities for communication
and relationship development which are not possible in verbally
bound experiences with children. The playroom is not necessarily
unique, for most children will have already played with many
of the materials available. The playroom does, however, make
it possible for the therapist to create those differences which
make the therapist truly unique—"funny" in the child's thinking.
This adult, the play therapist, exhibits characteristics which
children rarely experience with adults.

The characteristics of acceptance of the child, respect
for the child's uniqueness, and sensitivity to the child's feelings
identify the play therapist as a unique kind of adult. The
therapist sees the child as an individual with thoughts, feelings,
beliefs, ideas, desires, fantasies, and opinions worthy of respect.
Many adults never see the child. They are too busy to notice
the child. They have too many "important" things to do, that
must be done now, and after all, it is important that things
be done in a hurry. Consequently, the child is not really
seen. In such circumstances, the adult is only vaguely aware
of the child's presence. For most children who come to the

playroom, receiving an adult's complete and undivided attention for forty-five minutes, is a truly unique experience. The adult notices everything the child does and is genuinely interested in the child's feelings and play activities. Unlike most other adults, the therapist has a block of time which is devoted exclusively to the child.

The play therapist is *intentional* about creating an atmosphere. Therapists must be aware of what they do and why they do it. This makes therapists unique because they are not stumbling through a relationship with a child, but rather are being careful about their own words and actions. The therapist is working hard at creating an atmosphere conducive to the building of a relationship with the child. A difference is created because the time together is child-centered, and the child is allowed to be separate from the therapist. The child is viewed as a capable and unique individual. A difference is created because the therapist has great respect for the child.

Being There

When a child first views the play therapist, no observable significant differences exist between the therapist and other adults. This adult may be taller or shorter than most adults, or he/she may have a memorable face, but no physical differences exist that can signal to the child that this person will be special. The differences between an effective play therapist and other adults, therefore, must come from within as the self of the therapist is made fully present and available to the child.

Several qualities make the effective play therapist a different kind of adult to the child and one of the most significant is the art of being there by being fully present. Moustakas and Schalock (1955) concluded from their observations of the totality of the play therapist's behavior that the primary emphasis was on being there, that is, interacting with the child by observing, listening, and making statements of recognition. In many children's relationships with adults, being there, rarely exists. Children are observed through the din of the television set or listened to from behind the evening paper and are recognized primarily when they do something wrong.

One of the most graphic illustrations of not being there is presented in the film "The Day That Sang and Cried" (1970). The movie begins with a child who wakes up on a summer morning, rolls out of bed, and heads for the kitchen for breakfast. The house is eerily quiet, and after the boy gets out the milk and pours his cereal from the box, he reaches to the middle of the table and flips on a tape recorder which plays the following message:

> Good morning, John. Did you sleep well? Be sure and take out the garbage this morning. Your Dad left for New York today—he'll be back in two days. I'll be home a little late tonight because I have to go do some shopping after work. Oh—your Dad says that you need . . .

The effective play therapist is not a cassette tape. Instead of prepackaged life, the play therapist is an adult who intently observes, empathetically listens, and encouragingly recognizes not only the child's play but also the child's wants, needs, and feelings. The play therapist knows that being present with the child requires much more than a physical presence; that being there is truly an art form that makes the play therapy experience unique for the child.

The uniqueness of the play therapist is heightened by listening actively not only to what the child verbalizes but also to the messages conveyed through the child's activity. The therapist understands that the toys and materials children select and how they play has meaning as a part of their total effort to communicate. The child receives the therapist's complete attention. Unlike many other adults who are too busy and too involved with satisfying their own needs, the therapist is unhurried, is committed to understanding the child's needs, and really does want to hear the child. In fact for the duration of the time they have together, to hear and understand are primary objectives of the therapist.

Personality Characteristics

The following discussion may very well sound like a description of an unattainable perfect person. However, that is not the intent in attempting to describe personality characteristics which are conducive to helping children grow and develop in ways that are personally rewarding to them. The attainment of these characteristics is not nearly as important as the continual self-motivating never-ending process of striving to attain and incorporate these dimensions into one's life and relationships with children. The play therapist's intentionality in this striving is the dynamic therapeutic facilitative quality in the process, not the attainment of describable dimensions. Intentionality defies description but never-the-less exists in the inner recesses of the therapist's attitudes and motivations, and determines the extent to which the following characteristics are identifiable in the therapist's behavior.

The effective play therapist is objective enough to allow the child to be a separate person and is flexible in accepting and adapting to the unexpected with an attitude of willingness to be receptive to the new. This is based on an uncompromising resistance to imposing conforming behavior on children. The therapist has a genuine appreciation for the world of children and their experiences. This appreciation is characterized by a sensitive understanding of, interest in, caring for, and liking of children.

RULE OF THUMB:

How the therapist feels about the child is more important than what the therapist knows about the child.

The therapist has no need to evaluate and/or judge children or what they produce or do not produce. This unwillingness to judge or evaluate stems from the therapist's experiential understanding of just how rewarding an experience can be when one is not being judged or evaluated.

The therapist should be open-minded rather than close-minded. Openness and sensitivity to the child's world are basic prerequisites for play therapists. Children are considered and related to primarily on the basis of their own merit, who they are rather than who they have been described to be. There is an absence of any need to distort meanings because the therapist is relatively free of threat and anxiety, and is, therefore, open to receiving children as they are or will become. The therapist is able to turn loose of his/her world of reality and to experience the child's world of reality. This open-minded dimension allows the therapist to receive fully and with accuracy the meanings communicated by children verbally, nonverbally, and in their play.

Effective play therapists have a high tolerance for ambiguity which enables them to enter into the child's world of experiencing as a follower, allowing the child to initiate activity, topic, direction, and content with encouragement from the therapist who continually centers responsibility on the child. Since the child is always in a process of becoming, the play therapist should project a future-mindedness in relating to the child by not restricting the child through attitude or verbal response pertaining to the past. The therapist is always trying to "catch up" to where the child is and so has no need to find out about yesterday, or last week, or last month, or what happened a year ago unless the child's leading goes in that direction. Then, the therapist is quite willing to follow. The therapist does not refer to the previous session because the child is no longer at that point. Assuming once a week sessions, the child has had a whole week to grow, develop, and change since the therapist last saw the child. Therefore, the therapist will need to "catch up" to where the child is this week. This future-mindedness does not project or lead the child into the future, but is an attitude of receptivity to the child being in a continuous process of becoming.

The effective play therapist acts and/or responds out of personal courage by admitting mistakes, by being vulnerable at times, and admitting inaccuracies in personal perceptions. Personal courage is needed to take risks and to act on intuitive feelings in response to the child's creative expressions of self at the moment. Allowing one's self to be vulnerable enough to be impacted or touched emotionally by the child's experiences and feelings requires personal courage and an openness to risk sharing self in a very personal way that is nondefensive. Personal courage based on inner confidence may be required when a child is testing the limits of the relationship such as threatening to throw a block of wood at the therapist or shooting the therapist with a dart gun. Therapists who have low tolerance for risk-taking behavior may respond inappropriately in such situations by being punitive or threatening. Such situations also call for a high degree of patience. This personality variable is described at length in a later section of this chapter.

Since the dimensions of being real, warmth and caring, acceptance, and sensitive understanding have been discussed in the previous chapter, they are only mentioned here to let the reader know the writer recognizes their worth as personality dimensions in the therapeutic process. These dimensions can be further described as being loving and compassionate.

Helen Keller (1954) described in her autobiography the significance a loving, compassionate person can have in facilitating a life changing process.

> Once I knew the depth where no hope was and darkness lay on the face of all things. Then love came and set my soul free. Once I fretted and beat myself against the wall that shut me in. My life was without a past or future, and death a consummation devoutly to be wished. But a little word from the fingers of another fell into my hands that clutched at emptiness, and my heart leaped up with the rapture of living. I do not know the meaning of the darkness, but I have learned the overcoming of it. (p. 57)

The effective play therapist is personally secure and thus recognizes and accepts personal limitations without any sense of threat to his/her feelings of adequacy. Some play therapists feel they must be helpful to all children. Out of their own fear of being perceived as inadequate, they continue to work with children far beyond their ability to be helpful, or they accept child clients whose emotional difficulties exceed the limits of the therapist's training. Knowing when to make a referral is an absolute must for the play therapist.

Children have fun. They enjoy playing and discovering. They laugh right out loud when something is funny to them.

The play therapist should possess a sense of humor and be able to appreciate the humor in what the child experiences as being humorous. However, for the therapist to laugh at a child is never appropriate.

Therapist Self-Understanding

General agreement exists among authorities that, regardless of the age group worked with, all therapists need self-understanding and insight into their own motivations, needs, blind spots, biases, personal conflicts, and areas of emotional difficulty as well as personal strengths. Therapists should not assume they can keep their own values and needs compartmentalized and separate from their relationships with children. The therapist is a real person, not a robot. Therefore, personal needs and values are a part of the person and thus become a part of the relationship. The question, then, is not whether or not the therapist's personality will enter into the relationship, but rather to what extent. A responsibility of the therapist is to be involved in a process of self-exploration which will promote self-understanding, thus minimizing the potential impact of the therapist's motivations and needs. This process of knowing self can be facilitated through personal therapy and either individual or group therapy is highly recommended to learn about self. Another source of self-exploration would be supervisory or consultive relationships which allow the therapist, out of personal willingness, to explore his/her motivations and needs. Since self-understanding is a process and not an event, being involved in such a process throughout their professional career can be helpful to therapists. Exploring the following questions might enhance the process of self-understanding:

What needs of mine are being met in play therapy?

How strong is my need to be needed?

Do I like this child?

Do I want to be with this child?

What impact do my attitudes and feelings have on this child?

How does this child perceive me?

A therapist who is unaware of personal biases, values, emotional needs, fears, personal stressors, anxieties, and expectations of self and others probably will not be effectively sensitive to such dimensions in children. The therapist does not leave personality needs outside when entering the playroom with a child. Consequently, these needs become a part of the relationship and the developing therapeutic process. If the therapist is not fully aware of a need to be liked, a fear of rejection, guilt feelings related to limit setting, or a need to be admired, or successful, these needs will emerge in subtle manipulative ways that control and restrict the exploration and expression of the child.

The most significant resource the therapist brings to the play therapy relationship is the dimension of self. Skills and techniques are useful tools, but therapists' use of their own personality is their greatest asset. As important as training and skills are in becoming a play therapist, they simply are not enough. The therapist must be the kind of person who appreciates the perceptual-experiential world of children, a person who delights in being with children and experiences their world as exciting. Although training and the use of therapeutic procedures are important, the therapist's ability to be human is of prime importance. The person of the therapist is more important than anything the therapist knows how to do. The therapist must be the kind of person with whom children feel safe, safe enough to explore, safe enough to risk being themselves; the kind of person children experience as being trustworthy and caring. With such a person, children will find satisfying encouragement for self-growth.

Therapist Self-Acceptance

The child-centered play therapy approach is a function of the therapist's attitude toward self and the child. This attitude is characterized by an acceptance of self and the child and a deep and abiding belief in the capacity of the child to be responsible for self in the process of exercising self-direction resulting in more positive behaviors. This attitude of commitment to the child respects the child's right to make choices and recognizes the capacity of children to make choices that are both maturely satisfying to them and ultimately acceptable to society. A significant objective, therefore, of the therapist is to help the child to feel safe enough to change or not to change, for only when the child feels free not to change is genuine change possible. The objective of the therapist is to create a climate in which the child feels free to be fully who the child is at the moment in the shared experience of learning about self and each other. Out of a deep respect for the child the therapist gives full, complete, and undivided attention to the child.

Giving of self in this way means the therapist is keenly sensitive to personal experiences and feelings which may be identified with the child and is careful to sort out or distinguish those feelings that are emotional reattachments to previous experiences. The therapist is careful to avoid projecting emotional reactions or needs onto the child. Thus, the play therapist must be engaged in a continual process of self-awareness and self-acceptance. Being in the process of self-discovery can be as rewarding to the therapist as to the child and is necessary for self-acceptance. Play therapists often begin this process of self-acceptance as a result of experiencing such acceptance in training programs. The impact can be seen in this self-evaluation by a graduate student.

> Play therapy is very rewarding to me because I am helping a child to accept himself. A great deal of the reward in play therapy comes from being able to keep my personal needs out of the child's way. I believe when a person is able to keep her needs in check that she is not only recognizing her own feelings, but accepting those feelings and, therefore, accepting herself. I began the process of accepting myself during this class. I was able to act responsibly and keep my needs out of the play sessions. Of course, the process of accepting one's self is continuous throughout life, but oh, what a beginning I have been able to make. Now, I want to begin generalizing my self-trust to the other areas of my life! Thank you for accepting me.

Another student wrote, "The feedback in my supervision sessions gave me permission to be more myself, to go with my intuitive responses. That's important. I needed that. As I relaxed more and really got into the experience, I thoroughly enjoyed it!"

The play therapist has faith in the nature of children, believes that a universal characteristic of children is the urge to unfold, and respects that unfolding as characterized in the uniqueness of each child. The inner dynamics of this urge may have been suppressed or thwarted, but can be revitalized under the proper conditions. The therapist's belief in growth and change does not come from a static, intellectual decision position but is determined largely by an experiential process of being aware of his/her own continuous developmental unfolding of discovery about self in relationships and life experiences. This self-understanding and accompanying self-acceptance enables the therapist to wait expectantly for the emerging self within the child. No impatience is felt toward the current projected self of the child because there is a willingness to accept personal imperfection and to forgive self for not being perfect. The therapist accepts his/her own humanness. Therefore, no need exists to have the child be perfect.

RULE OF THUMB:

You cannot accept another person's weakness until you are able to accept your own.

The freeing aspect of self-understanding and self-acceptance is described by a beginning play therapist as

> The more I understand myself and admit to being imperfect, the more I can let go of self-consciousness and the need to fulfill a role expectation of being a therapist. This preconceived image has deprived me of the freedom and spontaneity through which my best strengths may be developed. I no longer feel in the playroom that I am performing a stressful chore, but constructing a personally creative encounter with Michael. I am discovering that when I am uptight it is difficult to approach another, and that with increased relaxation I can see myself in action, to note the false moves or the extra steps I have unconsciously incorporated into my behavior.

The attitude of the play therapist sets the tone of the play therapy session and quickly permeates the entire experience.

Play therapy is not a role; it is a way of being. The therapist who attempts to use a "method" or set of techniques will appear to be stilted and artificial and will ultimately be dissatisfied and unsuccessful. The inner person of the child is much more likely to emerge in growth enhancing ways to the extent that the therapist is able to give up a role of authority and leadership in the play therapy experience. Such positions serve to create dependency expectations on the part of the child. The therapist's goal is to project a personal self as fully as possible. This in turn facilitates the movement of the child toward becoming the self the child is in the developing relationship. Children are very sensitive to all the subtleties of the person of the therapist, and are, therefore, much more impacted by the person of the therapist than by a technique the therapist may use. Effective therapists appreciate their own uniqueness and are, therefore, able to accept the uniqueness of others.

Role of the Play Therapist

The therapist has no need to direct or lead the child to a particular topic or activity. The therapist allows the child to lead the way and is content to follow. What is important is not the therapist's wisdom, but the wisdom of the child; not the therapist's direction, but the child's direction; not the therapist's solution, but the child's creativity. Therefore, the child is accepted for all that he/she is in order to free the child to be unique.

The play therapist is not a supervisor, teacher, peer, baby sitter, or parent-substitute. Dibs summed up his view of the therapist by saying, "You're not a mother. You're not a teacher, you're not a member of mother's bridge club. What are you? It does not really matter. You are the lady of the wonderful playroom" (Axline, 1964, p.204). The therapist does not solve problems for the child, explain behavior, interpret motivation or question intent, all of which would deprive the child of opportunities for self-discovery. Does this then mean that the therapist is passive? Absolutely not! The therapist assumes an active role. Must the therapist do things for or to children before the therapist can be described as being active? Does being active require the therapist to exhibit a high level of physical activity? Being active does not have to be an observable quality. The therapist is emotionally active requiring sensitivity, an appreciation of what the child is doing and saying, and an attitude of receptive responsiveness. This emotional investment is characterized by an interactive quality that is both felt by the child and therapist and overtly experienced in the interactive verbal expressions of the therapist. The therapist maintains an active role in the process of play therapy, not in the sense of directing or managing the experience, but by being directly involved and genuinely interested in all of the child's feelings, actions, and decisions.

Can the therapist's efforts, teach children about themselves? Can the wisdom of the therapist that comes from years of graduate study, reading, and experiencing children be imparted to child clients? Gibran's (1923) *Prophet* addressed this issue and said, "No man can reveal to you aught but that which already lies asleep in the dawning of your own knowledge . . . For the wisdom of one man lends not its wings to another man . . ." (p. 32). The play therapist is not a person who tries to make things happen, for that is not an option within the possibilities that exist in reality. To *make* happen or create *for* others the inner wisdom necessary for living life simply is not possible. Whatever is important or necessary for children's growth already exists in children. The therapist's role or responsibility is not to reshape children's lives or make them change in some predetermined way. The living of life is never a static occurrence, it is a process of relentless learning and renewal. Pasternak was reacting to this process when he said:

> When I hear people speak of reshaping life it makes me lose my self control and I fall into despair. Reshaping life! People who can say that have never understood a thing about life—they have never felt it's breath, it's heartbeat, however much they may have seen or done. They look on it as a lump of raw material that needs to be processed by them, to be ennobled by their touch. But life is never a material, a substance to be molded . . . Life is constantly renewing and remaking and changing and transfiguring itself . . . (Salisbury, 1958, p. 22)

Supervised Practice Facilitates Self-Insight

Graduate classwork, discussions, reading, workshops, role playing, and observing experienced play therapists are necessary and significant prerequisites in learning to be a play therapist. However, the most important learnings are those derived from experiences, and the possibilities for learning about self, children, and play therapy from supervised play therapy experiences are limitless. Not until children are experienced can they be known. Not until the therapist experiences the struggle to relate to a child can the play therapy relationship be understood. Not until the therapist experiences being with a child can apprehensions be discarded. Not until the therapist attempts to apply training can developed skill be appreciated. The following self-evaluations from play therapists in training give a glimpse into the impact and insight derived from supervised play therapy experiences.

Play Therapist: Margaret

Through experiencing children in play therapy, I have come to understand the living nature of the therapeutic relationship. I more fully understand and feel the dynamic experience of encountering a child, finding in Jeffrey what I can never discover in textbooks—myself *in action* with the child. I needed to move beyond intellectual descriptions and classification, beyond the abstract view of helping, and to encounter my own inner experience. It is not easy to be in intense relations with a child. In some ways my education has allowed me to retreat behind logical thinking and rational analysis. I very much needed the chance to recover the sense of freshness and presence that is the sign of a living human relationship.

Play Therapist: Keith

One of the most clear discoveries I have had in my play therapy sessions has been a realization that I am too impatient. I have not learned to wait, and this compounds the experience of stress. Perhaps this is why it is difficult for me to see things from any perspective but my own. I have learned that I need to respond to the child instead of trying to make a good response. When Justin refused to leave the playroom, I was able to stand patiently by the door and experience how effective acceptance of feelings and permissiveness can be when he walked out the door under his own steam after only a couple of minutes.

Play Therapist: Kathleen

My apprehensions about the setting were centered on the effects certain toys would have on children. Would the guns make the aggressive child violent? Would this child turn aggression on me? Would the manipulative child try to use certain toys to get me to do things for him? Matt dispelled many of my apprehensions concerning the setting. He did use the guns and knife in an aggressive way, but his aggression was used to get near me rather than to hurt me. He also tried to get me to solve problems for him with the toys, and it was exciting to see his reaction when he was able to handle situations himself.

Play Therapist: Douglas

This second session brought with it the realization of one of my worst apprehensions—the child who continually asks questions. It was obvious from the types of questions Eric asked that he had a poor self-concept. It seemed to be difficult for him to rely on his own judgment, or to decide for himself how to use his time in the playroom. For me, it was difficult to answer his questions simply and then give the lead back to Eric. He sought my approval on almost every new activity he took on. Some of my responses were facilitative, others were not. I learned that this inconsistency can facilitate more questions which in turn, increases my anxiety and my inappropriate responses. I think it is extremely important to remember that the child learns something from what I say. It is important to communicate that I have faith in the child's own judgment so that he can learn to rely on his own judgments. The responsibility to change or not to change is in the child's hands. What a boost for the child's self-confidence, self-respect, and self-esteem.

Play Therapist: Allan

I think my major concern was to not overinterpret what I thought the child was feeling, but to relate to the activity and expression of the child. I realize that my concern seemed to limit me in that I experienced myself as "canned" and unnatural. I learned that I have to be me, and that it is appropriate to relate to what the child appears to be feeling. I must relate from my gut feeling and trust my judgment.

Play Therapist: Ching

During my play therapy sessions, I found that initially the child felt strange with me because of my differences in nationality and speech pattern and also because I was too quiet and not responsive enough. The initial difference set an unfamiliar stage for the child and then my reserved or quiet behavior added to the unfamiliarity. I learned that I must increase my rate of response to help put the child at ease.

Play Therapist: Carol

My greatest apprehension was that I would not be able to respond to the child in a therapeutic manner. I was afraid that I would look at the child's behavior as a teacher, making assessments and trying to control rather than respond. I was surprised at how easy it was for me to adopt the proper mind-set. I found that I was able to devote my whole attention to the child in much the same way that I would attend to an adult client.

I found that I felt comfortable in the playroom, and, for the most part, I was at ease with the child. What I had the greatest problem with was in being spontaneous in my responses. I often hesitated, trying to come up with the right response, and by the time I was ready, the child had moved on to something else, and my response would have been distracting rather than facilitating. I also found it difficult to reflect the feelings of the child. This is a problem that I continue to have. Openly expressing and acknowledging feelings does not come naturally to me, but I am working on developing this skill.

The Inner Struggle of a Beginning Play Therapist

A counselor, who had earlier attempted to use play therapy but had no previous training, described in a paper for my class the confusion felt when he did not understand the process, the resulting disappointment, and the inner struggle to know what play therapy really is.

Play Therapy—What's That, Really?

As an untrained play therapist, I often found myself struggling to find some direction or meaning in the time I spent with children. Though I had read most of the usual books, I remained unenlightened as to what I was supposed to be doing. I persevered, however, spending time with my child clients in alternately directive and nondirective ways. It did not seem to matter much to the children what I did. Incredibly, some improved, but more, understandably, did not. Gratefully, few got worse.

I grew increasingly disillusioned with my ability to have an impact upon children. I needed some direct, immediate feedback, which children rarely provide. Working with adults I felt I was able to make an impact by listening, paying careful attention to dramatic, feeling-laden words. In retrospect, these words were simply much more interesting to me than the child's activities of socking a punching bag, or perhaps preparing a meal in the kitchen of a doll house.

It seemed to me that the task of providing a therapeutic experience for children was the difficult responsibility of communicating understanding to them. I tended to make much more out of an expression or word than what the child intended, i.e., by "reading into" her play beyond her meaning. I was impatient, unwilling to accept the child in her relatively simplistic, literal state. It was as if I demanded the dramatic. I did not understand the child as she was or, accept or her as she was.

What is play therapy, then, really? Certainly it is not what I thought it was. Children are not what I thought they were. It seems I needed to learn what is not before I could see what is. Children, as well as adults, require the communication of empathy, respect, genuineness, and concreteness. Both play and "talking" therapy are alike in this respect. Being helpful to children means being accepting toward them. Children rarely find the therapist's own "technical" understanding of them, however accurate, to be useful. Acceptance of feeling is almost always therapeutically useful to them. The communication of this acceptance is a skill not easily acquired. However, without it, a therapist's knowledge is of little value to anyone but himself.

Play therapy is interacting with a child on her own terms, providing the opportunity for the free expression of herself with the simultaneous acceptance of this feeling by an adult. I now find interest in those child activities which previously seemed dull. I have learned patience, no longer expecting the child to unfold immediately and dramatically, bursting forth with startling insight. Removing my expectations increases my acceptance of children. I find gratification in the changes which children can bring about from within themselves, sometimes beyond, and notably without, my own understanding.

In assuming responsibility as a play therapist, I formerly assumed responsibility for the child. It was very difficult for me to allow the child to be responsible. I set, often without thought, many more limits on the child's play than I do now, because I could only accept the child within my own limits. My "range" of acceptance was comparatively narrow. Very often it must have seemed to the child that he could gain acceptance of himself on my terms only. Under this condition, play therapy was really just play, providing little opportunity for an important new experience. If a child can experience herself as responsible for herself, then I believe she will gain more inner control and develop potential more than she ever has before. This then is play therapy, really.

Play Therapy Requires Special Training

Based on what we know of the frightening increase of child abuse, childhood emotional disorders, childhood cancer patients, children with AIDS, two and three-year-old children confined in psychiatric hospitals, children suffering from stress, and children experiencing the disintegration of their family through divorce, an urgent need exists for professionals to provide play therapy experiences. However, as the student of play therapy knows so well, little has been written about play therapy since the 1950s and only a few university graduate programs offer extensive training in play therapy. Despite the lack of training opportunities, the number of mental health professionals utilizing play therapy is rapidly increasing. It would probably be a safe guess that the majority of professionals currently practicing play therapy have had little or no training in play therapy in the form of courses and supervised practicums devoted exclusively to play therapy.

This issue of training is indeed a perplexing one. What constitutes adequate training in play therapy? Do we wait until professionals are adequately trained in play therapy before we encourage them to utilize this approach in meeting the increasing needs of children? For those of us in the position of training play therapists, what is our obligation to children? Should professionals with only a few hours of training obtained from conferences and workshops engage in play therapy? If they do not, how will children's needs be met? If they do, will children be harmed? These are not easy questions to answer. At the risk of being misunderstood, I would propose that the vulnerability of children should be protected, and at the least, therapists who lack supervised training in play therapy should proceed with great caution. Therapists who had witnessed an hour demonstration of hypnosis would not be encouraged to implement hypnotic procedures in their practice. However, a common practice is for therapists to engage in "play therapy" with only a few hours of workshop experience to their credit. Practicum supervisors have even been known to assign child clients for play therapy with masters degree level supervisees who had no previous experience with children in any setting, had no training in play therapy, and had never even viewed a play therapy session. These experiences are often, at best, little more than babysitting. Such attitudes show little respect for children. Play therapy is much more than gathering a few toys together and sitting in a room or office watching a child play. Special skills are needed and a way of communicating and interacting that is not common with adult clients. Even the most experienced and highly effective therapists with adults will often have great difficulty transferring their therapeutic skills to play therapy sessions with small children.

Play therapy is a special area of training requiring attitudes and skills not typically found in most adolescent or adult training programs in the helping profession field. Seldom, if ever, are therapists with adults confronted with a reluctant client who cries, falls on the floor and refuses to go into the therapist's office, or a client who says nothing for the entire session, or a client who is significantly developmentally below the therapist's level of abstract reasoning ability, or a client who tries to throw things at the therapist, or a client who repeatedly acts out the same fantasy scenes.

Recommended Training Program

Commitment to children demands that the therapist make every effort possible to insure that children receive quality help from competent play therapists. The field of play therapy is experiencing a growing and enthusiastic interest as a viable approach for meeting children's needs, and since children cannot speak for themselves on this matter, professionals in the field must try to insure that individuals who practice play therapy do indeed possess specialized knowledge and skills that render them effective in play therapy to serve the best interests of children. With this commitment in mind, the following tentative guidelines are suggested for training play therapists. A basic premise is that the professional standards required for utilizing play therapy in counseling with children should be no less than those required for working with adults in a counseling relationship.

> master's degree in an area of the helping professions such as counseling, psychology, social work, or related area;

> content areas of study in child development, theories of counseling and psychotherapy, clinical counseling skills, and group counseling;

content area of study in play therapy equivalent to 45 clock hours of instruction;

personal counseling, either as a member of a counseling group, individual counseling, or other pertinent experience which provides opportunities to examine self over an extended period of time;

observation and case analysis of children from the normal population as well as maladjusted children;

observation of experienced play therapists with opportunity to discuss and critique the sessions; and

supervised experience in play therapy by a professional who has experience in play therapy.

In my Introduction to Play Therapy course, which is a one-semester, three-hour graduate credit course, students are involved in the following sequence of laboratory experiences in addition to lectures, discussions, reading and writing papers related to various aspects of play therapy:

observe play therapy sessions of master's and doctoral practicum students in our Center for Play Therapy;

observe and critique video tapes of my play therapy sessions;

observe at least one of my current play therapy sessions or a special demonstration for the class to observe;

role play, with me playing the part of the child, to improve their responding skills and to become comfortable with the unexpected things children may do in the playroom;

role play in pairs in the playrooms, taking turns being the child to gain insight into children's feelings and their perception of the experience;

conduct play sessions with volunteer adjusted children in an undisturbed room in a nursery school, day care center, church Sunday School classroom, or room in their home. Students bring a box of appropriate toys, audio tape the sessions, and write a critique of the experience focusing on what they learned about the child, play therapy, and themselves; and

participate in supervised sessions with volunteer adjusted children in the Center playrooms. Sessions are supervised by doctoral students and play therapists in private practice. Students write a critique of the experience.

In addition to this introductory course, students may take an advanced play therapy course, group play therapy, or filial therapy. Students recieve supervision in a one semester on-campus supervised practicum in the Center for Play Therapy. Following successful completion of the practicum, the graduate students are placed in an off-campus field based practicum in an agency or clinic where they can continue their supervised play therapy experience.

These guidelines for training are made with full recognition that until more university programs offer training in play therapy, some of these requirements will need to be fulfilled in nontraditional academic ways such as intensive training workshops. These workshops could be offered in a format of 45 hour sequencing that builds on previous workshop training. The typical one and two-day general overview introductory workshop will not suffice. The crucial factor is supervised experience, and although no substitute exists for that, a variety of ways are available so that the play therapist can receive supervision other than through a traditional, organized campus practicum. A qualified play therapist could be contracted for individual supervision, or with several staff members in an agency on a regular basis, or arrangements could be made for a university play therapy program to provide a condensed, short-term, 45-hour, supervised practicum in play therapy. One of the most dynamic experiences I have ever had was supervising eight private-practice professionals in a one-week, eight-hours-per-day, individual and group play therapy practicum, assisted by four of my advanced doctoral students. These suggestions are intended as minimum procedures and should not be taken as recommended standard procedures.

REFERENCES

Axline, V. (1964). *Dibs: In search of self.* New York: Ballantine.

Gibran, K. (1923). *Prophet.* New York; Alfred Knopf.

Keller, H. (1954). *The story of my life.* New York: Grossett & Dunlap.

Moustakas, C.E., & Schalock, H.D. (1955, June). An analysis of therapist-child interaction in play therapy. *Child Development.* 143-157.

Salisbury, F. (1958). *Human development and learning.* New York: McGraw.

The day that sang and cried. (1970). Lawrence, Kansas: Centron Educational Films.

CHAPTER 7

THE PLAYROOM
AND MATERIALS

The atmosphere in the playroom is of critical importance because that is what impacts the child first. The playroom should have an atmosphere of its own which conveys warmth and a clear message "This is a place for children." Creating an environment friendly to children requires planning, effort, and a sensitive understanding of how it feels to be a child. Children are more likely to feel comfortable in places where a sense of openness exists that says to the child, "You are free to use what is here. Be yourself. Explore." The feeling in the playroom should be like putting on a well-worn warm sweater. The look of the toys and materials should say, "Use me." It is very difficult to accomplish this kind of feeling in a new room with all new toys. The feeling in such rooms is often cold. Great effort and creativity are required to transform a new playroom into a comfortable place that invites the child's interaction. The Center for Play Therapy on the University of North Texas campus has two new play therapy rooms, and after a year of use, we are still struggling to create a "try me on, let's spend some time together" feeling in the rooms. An older, well worn room is preferred.

Playroom Location

Since children are sometimes quite noisy, the playroom should be located in an area of the agency, school, or suite of offices least likely to distract or disturb other clients and staff members. If parents or other children hear what is going on in the playroom, the child may feel that his/her privacy has been violated and the relationship will suffer. Likewise, the parents may unnecessarily question the child about what they heard, thus threatening the child. Although some writers have recommended the playroom be soundproof, that seems to be unrealistic and largely unattainable. When a child yells, throws the blocks, or pounds with the hammer, the noise will be heard outside the playroom. Acoustical tile on the ceiling will reduce the noise level considerably. Do not put acoustical tile on the walls because the texture invites children to pick, poke, and pull pieces off. Also, there is absolutely no way paint can be washed off or removed from the porous material. Complete isolation of the playroom is probably an unrealistic goal, although I once worked for several years in a private counseling agency that had a small house located on the back of the property which we converted into a children's place with two play therapy rooms. It was a wonderful experience, and the children quickly identified with the "little house."

Playroom Size

A room approximately twelve feet by fifteen feet seems to meet the purposes of play therapy best. Although I have worked in playrooms with smaller dimensions, an area of 150 to 200 square feet feels almost ideal because the child is never too far away. A long narrow room or a larger room would defeat this purpose. In larger rooms, the therapist may "chase" the child around the room in an effort to be close and in the process deprive the child of the opportunity to take the lead in approaching the therapist on the child's terms.

A room of the size recommended here provides ample space for group play therapy with two or three children but no more because the typical high activity level causes too many conflicts resulting from physical encroachments on other children's activities, or on the child who wants to play alone for a few minutes, or on the child who wants to sit contemplatively. Enough space must be available for children to have their own activity space if they desire without continually bumping into each other or disrupting each other's play. Yes, children do need to learn to play together. However, the play therapy setting can be a very intense emotional experience for children and some need the opportunity to pull aside, to be alone, to regroup psychologically, and they they are not able to ask for such space nor are other children likely to recognize the need in the midst of their own self-motivated period of high activity. The combination of not enough space and too many children, is potentially anti-therapeutic and damaging to children. For larger play therapy groups of three to five children, a playroom of approximately 300 square feet is desirable.

Playroom Characteristics

The room should provide privacy from view with no windows on inside walls or in the door. A window on an outside wall will probably not present a problem but should have curtains that can be drawn or mini-blinds of some kind. No windows to contend with is the best plan.

Vinyl tile squares is the preferred floor covering because of durability, ease of cleaning, and damaged squares can be easily and inexpensively replaced. For that reason, solid sheet vinyl is not cost effective. Carpet of any kind should be avoided. It is difficult to keep clean, almost impossible to sweep sand out of it, and spilled paint makes a real mess to clean. In playrooms and play areas where carpet cannot be replaced. a large piece of sheet vinyl can be placed under the easel. However, this procedure may convey to children that they should be careful and clean. Carpet also can present the same message.

The walls of the playroom should be painted with washable enamel. As with the other parts of the room, ease of cleaning is a major consideration. Vibrant, dark, and somber colors should be avoided. An off-white color is preferable because it contributes to a bright, cheerful atmosphere.

If funds permit, a special addition is the inclusion of a one-way mirror and wiring for sound for supervision and training purposes. Play therapy sessions can be filmed through the one-way mirror thus avoiding distracting the child with the presence of the video camera in the playroom. Having a camera in the playroom usually results in children "hamming it up" for the camera, and the therapist's anxiety level will be accelerated if an expensive camera has to be protected. Parents should not be allowed to watch play therapy sessions. However, a highly desirable procedure is for parents to watch demonstration sessions with their children when parent training, as in filial therapy, is employed. For parent training, the one-way mirror can be the most valuable tool available. The opportunity for parents to see the therapist demonstrate what has been discussed in the training, and then having the opportunity to have their own session with their child supervised is invaluable. All play therapists should be engaged in a process of never ending self-critique and viewing one's own video taped session is by far the best possible means of self supervision and supervision by other professionals.

A sink with cold running water is recommended. Hot water is potentially dangerous and is not needed. Disconnect or turn off the hot water valve underneath the sink and screw the cold water valve about half closed so the child can turn the water on full force without it splashing all over the place. The sink also is less likely to overflow with less water coming out of the faucet. This kind of planning ahead allows the therapist to be more permissive and eliminates the need for so many limits.

A chalkboard with a tray across the bottom should be mounted to the wall approximately twenty-one inches from the floor to best accommodate the wide variability in children's height. An eraser and white and colored chalk should be available. Break the new chalk in pieces so the children will not feel they have to be careful.

The typical playroom will probably need shelves on two walls to provide enough space for the toys and materials to be displayed without being crowded or piled on top of each other. Self-contained, boxed shelves sturdy enough to be climbed on and permanently fastened to the wall are ideal. The top shelf should be no higher than thirty-eight inches so small children will be able to reach the toys without assistance or having to climb on top of something.

Sturdy shelves make a great place to hide when feeling small and vulnerable.

If you have the opportunity to design a playroom for a new building or remodeled space, a very small bathroom with just enough space for a commode and designed for the door to open into the playroom will eliminate the problems associated with the child having to leave the playroom to go to the bathroom. The therapist's dilemma of how many times to allow a trip to the bathroom and whether or not the request is based on genuine need will be eliminated. Children also will use the bathroom as an extension of the playroom to act out bathroom scenes, as a place to hide or retreat from the therapist, and to find out what it is like to completely shut out and ignore an adult.

Sturdy, wood or hard surface child size furniture should be selected for the playroom. A table and three chairs, one adult size, will be needed. A storage cabinet with counter top, for painting, clay play, finger painting, etc. is highly recommended. This could be a part of the sink area.

Other Settings for Play Therapy

Although desirable, a fully equipped playroom is not essential for children to express themselves. What is important is that children be provided with an opportunity to choose the mode of communication which is most natural for them. For some children, this may be a combination of the two modes available—play and verbalization. An immediate therapeutic dividend resulting from being allowed to choose is that children can set their own directions and assume responsibility for doing so.

Many therapists in private practice and agencies are quite effective in conducting play therapy sessions in one end of their office when the space is large enough. In elementary schools where the counselor typically serves more than one school and has a tiny "cubby hole" for an office or shares an office with other staff members, play therapy sessions can be held in the corner of an unused regular classroom, a workroom, the nurse's office, or the corner of the cafeteria after the cooks have left for the day. One innovative elementary school counselor utilizes space in the bookroom after textbooks have been removed and distributed at the start of the school term. She displays the toys and materials on several of the empty bookshelves and the children play in the floor space and on the shelves. She reports significant results in this setting. Another counselor obtained permission from a church adjoining the school grounds to use one of their Sunday School classrooms. Other counselors have reported satisfactory results using the stage of the auditorium or cafetorium. These areas are often unused and a portion of the stage or off-stage area can be made more private by closing the stage curtains.

In settings such as the cafeteria or classroom, a physical approximation of the boundaries for the session can be indicated by using chairs or tables to indicate the designated play area. The child should not be allowed to roam all over the entire room. The development of a therapeutic relationship would be almost impossible under such conditions. In these settings the therapist must be ready to set more stringent limits. Wherever play therapy sessions are held, every effort must be made to protect the confidentiality of the sessions. When complete privacy and confidentiality are not possible, children should be informed that they may be heard and/or seen by others.

In these modified settings, the therapist can keep a selection of toys and materials stored in a box or tote bag under the desk, in a corner, or in a closet, and the play materials can be arranged on the corner of the desk, on a chair seat, and on the floor just before each play therapy session. A bookcase with a curtain across the front or a cabinet with doors makes an excellent place to house play materials. Open display of play materials prior to each session helps children feel more comfortable, invites participation, and conveys permissiveness in a setting that seems to say, "This is just for you."

Rationale for Selecting Toys and Materials

Thirty years ago Ginott (1961) pointed out that the literature contained very few guidelines for selecting the proper toys and materials for use in play therapy. That condition is still true today. Therefore, the intent in this chapter is to present some tentative guidelines for the therapist to use in selecting toys and materials which will serve as a medium for children to express feelings, explore relationships, and understand self.

Some general guidelines to consider are that the toys should be durable and should communicate a message of "Be yourself in playing" rather than a message of "Be careful." Toys and materials should provide children with variety in choice of medium of expression. The toys should not be complex and should be age-appropriately manageable so children will not be frustrated in their efforts to express themselves. No toy should require the child to seek the therapist's help to manipulate. Many children in need of play therapy are already prone to be dependent and such behavior should not be reinforced. Children should be able to play with the toy by themselves. Many games do not fit this criteria and by their very nature necessitate the direct involvement of the therapist often in a competitive role. The therapist is then forced into a position of either usually defeating the child or being dishonest and allowing the child to win. Children are usually sensitive to the later position and thus do not feel the satisfaction that is so important to the development of positive self-esteem. Noncompetitive games can be quite facilitative with older children.

Selecting toys and play media materials should be a deliberate choice based on a sound rationale and should always take into account the basic rationale for using play therapy with children in the first place, that being a recognition of children's developmental level which is expressed naturally through their play and activity. As has already been pointed out, toys are children's words and play is their language. Therefore, toys and materials (words) should be selected which facilitate children's expression by providing a wide range of play activity (language). Since children can express their feelings and reactions more fully through their play, the toys and materials selected for play therapy are a significant therapeutic variable. The following questions can serve as important evaluative criteria for selecting toys and materials. Do the toys and materials

1. facilitate a wide range of creative expression?

2. facilitate a wide range of emotional expression?

3. engage children's interests?

4. facilitate expressive and exploratory play?

5. allow exploration and expression without verbalization?

6. allow success without prescribed structure?

7. allow for noncommittal play?

8. have sturdy construction for active use?

Because toys and materials are part of the communicative process for children, careful attention must be given to the selection of appropriate items. The rule is selection rather than accumulation. Play areas and playrooms containing an assortment of randomly acquired toys and materials often resemble a junk room and doom the play therapy process to failure.

RULE OF THUMB:

Toys and materials should be selected, not collected.

Toys and materials should be carefully selected for (1) the contribution they make to the accomplishment of the objectives of play therapy, and (2) the extent to which they are consistent with the rationale for play therapy. All play materials do not automatically encourage the expression of children's needs, feelings, and experiences. Toys and materials are used by the child in the act of play to communicate a personal world to the counselor. Therefore, toys and materials should be selected which facilitate the seven essentials in play therapy: establishment of a positive relationship with the child, expression of a wide range of feelings, exploration of real life experiences, reality testing of limits, development of a positive self-image, development of self-understanding, and opportunity to develop self-control.

Establishment of a Positive Relationship with the Child. The relationship between therapist and child is based on the ability of the therapist to understand the child's communications and to create an environment which allows the child to communicate freely. Selecting toys that promote clear understanding for the therapist and allow the child to play out themes of real life, aggression, and creative expression help to establish clear communication. Therefore, providing a family of dolls that represent all members of the child's family will give the child opportunity to create scenes that the therapist can understand more readily than if the same scene were played out with less identifiable objects.

The importance to the therapeutic relationship of understanding the meaning of children's communication and how appropriately selected toys can make it easier for the therapist to understand the meaning of children's play is underscored in some excellent examples by Ginott (1961).

> Children usually play out family themes by using dolls that represent mother, father, and siblings. In the absence of such dolls, a child may symbolically play out family themes by using big and little wooden blocks. But the exact meaning of the message may escape the therapist. Banging two blocks together may represent spanking or intercourse, or it may merely be a test of the therapist's tolerance for noise. Inserting a pencil into a pencil-sharpener may represent intercourse, but it may also mean that the pencil needs sharpening. However, when a father doll is put on top of a mother doll, the therapist has less room for misinterpretation. For the child, pencil and doll may be equally useful as a means of expression, but to the therapist they are not. The presence of a doll family enables the child to assist the therapist in understanding him. (p. 54)

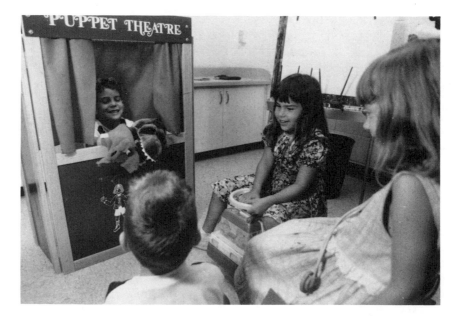

Puppets provide a safe way to express feelings without being threatened since the characters of the puppets are the ones expressing the feelings.

Expression of a Wide Range of Feelings. The expression of a wide range of feelings can be promoted when toys, such as puppets, are available which lend themselves to the expression of those feelings. Choosing toys which are easily used in the expression of feelings will facilitate the expression of those feelings when the need arises within the child. If the need arises and the means to express a particular feeling is not available, the child is stymied in that area. Puppets provide a safe way to express feelings without being threatened since the characters of the puppets are the ones expressing the feelings.

Exploration of Real Life Experiences. The expression of real life experiences is an essential ingredient in any therapy whether for the child or adult because real life experiences are what lead to the need for therapy. Selecting toys, such as a medical kit, which the child can use to develop a feeling of control of self in life situations, promotes inner balance in the child. When the child is able to express real life experiences in play and have those experiences understood and accepted by the therapist, then those real life experiences are trimmed to a manageable size.

Reality Testing of Limits. Children will act out aggression, so toys, such as a dart gun, give the child an opportunity to test the limits of what is permissible and what is not. In the process of play therapy, the child can learn where to draw the line between the two. Testing of limits enables the child to find out where the boundaries are in the relationship with the therapist. The testing of limits is also a reality experience in what could otherwise be fantasy. Pent-up feelings can be expressed with great vigor as limits are tested.

Development of a Positive Self-image. Many children in need of play therapy have a poor self-image, so providing toys and materials such as tinker toys, which can be mastered and manipulated easily are necessary for building up a feeling of "In here I can do things for myself. I can be successful." These feelings are then generalized to the rest of the child's life. Complicated and mechanical toys make mastery difficult and may reinforce an already existing poor self-concept.

Development of Self-understanding. Self-understanding grows out of the interaction with the play therapist which provides a permissive relationship in which the child feels safe enough to be, to express feelings. Many of these feelings are often negative. As the child expresses these feelings and experiences the therapist's acceptance and reflection of those feelings, the child comes first to introject the therapist's acceptance and then seems to understand self better. A variety of toys and materials, such as the bop bag and dolls, facilitate the expression of a wide range of feelings and thus contribute to self-understanding.

Opportunity to Develop Self-control. The development of self-control grows out of the interaction between the child's responsibility to make decisions, to choose without adult interference or guidance, and the child's redirection of unacceptable behaviors into controlled acceptable avenues. Sand is an excellent medium for expressing feelings and provides ample opportunity for limit setting and the development of self-control.

Categories of Toys

Although in this chapter a great deal of emphasis is placed on the selection of appropriate toys and materials, the intent is not to imply that toys and materials are considered to be of primary importance in establishing a therapeutic relationship with the child. Nothing can take the place of the emotional climate that develops as a result of the therapist's attitude, use of his/her own personality, and the spontaneous interaction between the therapist and child. Toys and materials can, however, determine or structure the kind and degree of expression by the child and the interaction with the therapist, and therefore, must receive careful attention as to their selection. Some toys and materials, by the very nature of their construction and design, are prone to elicit certain kinds of behaviors more than others and to some extent structure the behavior of the child. The bop bag is a good example. As it stands there in the middle of the floor, everything about it seems to say, "Hit me" and so children are more likely to push, shove, or hit the bop bag than to pretend it is a sick friend and nurse it back to health. This initial structuring based on the qualities of the toy is more likely to occur in the early stages of therapy when the child does not feel safe enough to be creative.

Suggestions offered in this chapter are intended to provide the play therapist with some broad guidelines for selecting a variety of structured and unstructured toys and materials which seem to facilitate children's exploration and expression. Appropriate toys and materials for play therapy can be grouped into three broad categories.

1. Real-life Toys. A doll family, doll house, puppets, and nondescript figures (Gumby) can represent family members in the child's life and thus provide for the direct expression of feelings. Anger, fear, sibling rivalry, crises, and family conflicts can be directly expressed as the child acts out scenes with the human figures. A car, truck, boat, and cash register are especially important for the resistive, anxious, shy, or withdrawn child because they can be played with in noncommittal ways without revealing any feelings. When children are ready, they will choose play media that will help them express their feelings more fully and openly. When the therapist is ready, or when the therapist wants certain feelings expressed is not important. A child should never be pressured to discuss topics or express feelings. When the child feels safe, experiences being accepted, and knows the therapist can be trusted, feelings will be expressed spontaneously.

The cash register provides for a quick feeling of control as the child manipulates the keys and calls out numbers. The car or truck gives an excuse for moving about and exploring the room. This is also a safe way to approach the therapist, "to find out what the therapist feels like" when the child gets physically close. There are subtle reasons why children do many of the things they do in the playroom, and the therapist should be sensitive to these possible motivations. The presence of a chalkboard conveys permissiveness to many children who come to the playroom from classrooms where the rule is "Don't mess with the chalkboard!" An atmosphere of permissiveness is crucial if the therapist is to make contact with the inner person of the child rather than external safe behaviors the child perceives are expected by typical adults.

2. Acting-out Aggressive-release Toys. Children in play therapy often have intense pent-up emotions for which they do not have verbal labels to describe or express. Structured toys and materials such as the bop bag, toy soldiers, alligator puppet, guns, and rubber knife can be used by children to express anger, hostility, and frustration. Aggressive children seem to experience the permission to release aggressive feelings in the accepting environment of the playroom as satisfying and are able to move on to more self-enhancing positive feelings. Shooting, burying, biting, hitting, and stabbing are acceptable in the playroom because they are expressed symbolically. The intensity with which angry/aggressive feelings are expressed in the playroom can sometimes be unsettling to the beginning play therapist. In such situations the therapist must be aware of a personal need to protect self from his/her own awkward, unsettled feelings and must refrain from moving quickly to interfere with the child's expression. However, at times setting a limit on some of the child's behavior may be necessary, if, for example, the child begins to throw sand all over the room. Driving nails into a soft wood log or pounding on a pegboard releases feelings and at the same time facilitates the focusing of attention and energy in a manner that increases concentration.

Ginott (1961) suggested including animal toys that depict wild animals because some children in the early stages of play therapy find it difficult to express aggressive feelings even against human figure dolls. These children for example will not shoot a father doll but will shoot a lion. Some children will express their hostility through the alligator puppet by biting, chewing and crunching. Clay is an example of a material that fits into two categories, creative and aggressive. It can be pounded, smashed, rolled out with great vigor, and torn apart with intensity. Clay also can be used by the child to create figures for play.

3. Toys for Creative Expression and Emotional Release. Sand and water are probably the most used unstructured play media by children but the least likely materials to be found in play therapy settings, even though Ginott (1961) described water as the most effective therapeutic substance of all playroom materials. The absence of sand and water in play therapy settings is most likely the result of therapist's

Sand lacks structure and can be whatever the child wants it to be, the surface of the moon, quicksand, the beach, something to clean with, the possibilities are limitless.

low tolerance for messiness and a need to keep things neat and clean. Reluctance may also stem from a legitimate concern about having to clean up. However, this does not seem to be a valid reason since appropriate limit setting will likely keep most of the sand and water confined to receptacles. Even in nonplayroom limited space settings, a dishpan with an inch of sand and a bucket with a couple of inches of water would serve the purpose quite well. Sand and water lack structure and can be whatever the child wants them to be, the surface of the moon, quicksand, the beach, something to clean with, the possibilities are limitless. There is no right or wrong way to play with sand and water. Therefore, the child is assured of success. This is especially helpful for shy or withdrawn children.

Blocks can be houses, they can be thrown, they can be stacked and kicked down, allowing the child to explore what

Easel paints afford the child an opportunity to be creative, to be messy, to pretend bathroom scenes and smear, to express feelings.

being constructive and destructive feels like. As with water and sand, the child can experience a feeling of satisfaction because there is no correct way to play with blocks. Easel paints afford the child an opportunity to be creative, to be messy, to pretend bathroom scenes and smear, to express feelings.

Tote Bag Playroom

Until children reach a developmental level of expressive competence with verbal communication that allows them to express and explore fully the person they are and their inner world of emotions, toys and materials should be carefully selected to facilitate this process. My experience has been that children can communicate a wide range of messages and feelings with a limited number of toys and materials. A second consideration, then, in selecting toys and materials for use in a modified play therapy setting is their size and portability. The following toys and materials are considered to be the minimal requirements for conducting a play therapy session and are recommended because they can encourage a wide range of expressions and can easily be transported in a tote bag or stored out of the way in a corner or in a closet:

crayons (8-count box),
newsprint,
blunt scissors,
nursing bottle (plastic),
rubber knife,
doll,
clay or Play-Doh,
dart gun,
handcuffs,
toy soldiers (20-count size is sufficient),
two play dishes and cups (plastic or tin),
spoons (avoid forks because of sharp points),
small airplane,
small car,
Lone Ranger type mask,
Nerf ball (a rubber ball bounces too much),
bendable Gumby (nondescript figure),
Popsicle sticks,
pipe cleaners,
cotton rope,
telephone,
aggressive hand puppet (alligator, wolf, or dragon),
bendable doll family,
dollhouse furniture (at least bedroom, kitchen, and bathroom),
a small cardboard box with rooms marked on the bottom (cut door in one side and window in another; doubles as storage container for toys),
transparent tape,
costume jewelry.

If storage space is available, an inflatable vinyl punching come-back toy would be a special asset. A dishpan size plastic container with an inch of sand in the bottom also would be useful in a more permanent setting. Rice could be used in place of the sand if clean up is a problem.

Recommended Toys and Materials for the Playroom

The following toys and materials have been found to be useful in facilitating children's expressions in the Center for Play Therapy playrooms at the University of North Texas. This list is the result of twenty-five years of experimentation resulting in discarding items and adding others and keeping those items which a wide range of children consistently utilized in a variety of ways to express themselves.

doll furniture (study wood)
bendable doll family
Gumby (bendable nondescript figure)
dolls
doll bed, clothes, etc.
pacifier
nursing bottle (plastic)
purse and jewelry
chalkboard, chalk
colored chalk, eraser
refrigerator (wood)
stove (wood)
dishes (plastic or tin)
pans, silverware
pitcher
dishpan
plastic food
empty fruit and vegetable cans, etc.
egg cartons
sponge, towel
broom, dust pan
soap, brush, comb
crayons, pencils, paper
transparent tape, paste
toy watch
building blocks (different shapes and sizes
paints, easel, newsprint, brushes
Play-Doh or clay
Lone Ranger type mask
pipe cleaners
tongue depressors, Popsicle sticks

ATV (multiwheel type vehicle for riding, scooting around on)
truck, car, airplane, tractor, boat
bus (Fisher Price type)
pounding bench and hammer
xylophone
cymbals
drum
toy soldiers and army equipment
fireman's hat, other hats
pine log, hammer, nails
sandbox, large spoon, funnel, sieve, pail
zoo animals, farm animals
rubber snake, alligator
Bobo (bop bag)
suction throwing darts
target board
rubber knife
handcuffs
dart gun
toy machine gun
balls (large and small)
telephone (two)
blunt scissors
construction paper (several colors)
medical kit
play money and cash register
rags or old towels
hand puppets (doctor, nurse, policeman, mother, father, sister, brother, baby, alligator, wolf)
Tinker toys
rope
tissues

Many of these toys and materials can be obtained inexpensively from garage sales or donations from parents whose children have outgrown the toys. Community agency therapists could present their play therapy program to civic groups, outlining their needs for materials and ask for financial support. Elementary school counselors could do the same with their PTA organization and request sponsorship of the play therapy program with an annual donation for specific materials. A list of the above items could be posted in the agency or teacher's lounge asking for donations of the items their children have outgrown. This should only be done after the counselor has explained the play therapy program in a teacher's meeting. Avoid a random request for toys because many items will be "collected" that are not appropriate for play therapy.

Special Considerations

Although the successful completion of puzzles can facilitate the development of frustration tolerance and a sense of adequacy, they are not recommended because at least one puzzle piece will invariably get lost. Experiences in the playroom should not perpetuate negative experiences in children's lives. Children who suffer from feelings of inadequacy and have difficulty completing tasks should be able to experience success and the resulting feeling of satisfaction.

A special note is necessary about the log, hammer, and nails. The log should be about twelve inches tall and must be soft wood. The hammer should be a regular size hammer. Children do not find a child size hammer to be satisfying. Two sizes of nails should be provided, short large head roofing nails and longer finishing nails. The short nails will not bend and children can select their own level of difficulty.

Remove broken toys. Whatever is in the playroom should be intact, complete, and should work. Many children referred for play therapy come from confusing and frustrating environments. What is in the playroom should not add to that confusion or frustration by being incomplete or broken.

Tempera paints should be kept fresh. Nothing inhibits or frustrates a child more than the discovery of cups of dried, caked paints. Paints also sour and develop a terrible odor and will need to be replaced periodically. When mixing tempera paints, squirt a few drops of liquid detergent into each cup of paint to help retard the growth of the odor producing bacteria. The detergent also makes removal of the paint from clothes easier. The use of small disposable coffee cups inserted into the paint containers also makes the job of cleaning and changing paints an easier task. Place only an inch or so of paint in each cup as a precaution against paints being spilled and to make the job of clean up easier if paints are spilled. Children do not need full cups of paint. That's only asking for trouble.

A sturdy, small plastic swimming pool can make an excellent sandbox. The sand should be heavily sprinkled with water periodically to keep the dust down.

Children need a place to escape or hide from the therapist. Arrange the playroom so that some item such as the stove sits out into the room. Children can then play on the other side of the stove out of the view of the therapist when they feel the need to do so. Such separation or rejection of the therapist is significant in the development of freedom in the relationship.

The playroom should not be used as a place for babysitting. Other staff members who do not work with children often have a tendency to view the playroom as just that, a place for their parent clients' children to play while the parent is in a counseling session. This rule also applies to children who are in play therapy. The play therapy relationship is a special emotional relationship that takes place in the special playroom. Allowing a child to play unattended in the playroom while the parent is being seen by the play therapist interferes with the development of the relationship.

The playroom should be cleaned up and toys put back in their proper place after each session. Since toys are the child's words, the child should not have to go searching for the toys needed for expression. The playroom should present an image of order and consistency. A part of that consistency is that toys are always in their designated place. The baby bottle is not sometimes on one side of the playroom and at other times on the opposite side of the room. Items should always be somewhere on their designated shelf. This does not mean the playroom must be neat and clean, only orderly. Children feel more secure when they always know where things are. That helps to make the room and the relationship predictable. When several staff members use the same playroom, an advisable procedure is to schedule a once-a-month cleaning time when everyone who uses the room meets in the room and gives it a general cleaning and putting into order. If this is not done, the room can get to be a real mess in a hurry, and a playroom that looks and feels like a junk room is not therapeutic.

Suggested Titles for the Play Therapy Program in Schools

In view of the emotional reaction to the term "therapy" by some teachers, principals and parents, the elementary school counselor may want to consider a title for the program other than play therapy program. Play therapy programs in schools could be referred to as counseling with toys, emotional growth through play, developmental growth through play, or a similar title. The elementary school counselor will be the best judge of the potential reaction to the term play therapy in the local setting. Such an important program for children should not be prevented from functioning simply because someone objects to the term. The elementary school counselor is encouraged to take a creative approach to developing a title which best describes the spontaneous and expressive use children make of toys and materials provided for their use in communicating their world to the counselor. When using play therapy, elementary school counselors are encouraged to emphasize that they are employing an approach which assists them in their efforts to effectively assist children in their developmental growth. The ultimate objective is to help children to get ready to profit fully from what teachers have to offer.

Implementing A Play Therapy Program in Schools

Careful planning is essential in developing and implementing a play therapy program in a school. Don't assume that the supervisor of counseling, the principal, or teachers understand what play therapy is or what you hope to accomplish. The task of the elementary school counselor is to be a good salesperson for the program.

The elementary school counselor should review the literature on play therapy, develop a rationale for counseling with toys, and detail in outline format how such a program works including how it is done, what can be accomplished, the materials needed, and areas in the school that could be utilized. A plan should be developed for obtaining the necessary materials. Meet first with the supervisor of counseling to obtain support for presenting the program to the principal(s). Present the program to the principal, and ask for time at a teacher in-service meeting to acquaint teachers with the play therapy program. Then follow up the in-service meeting with written information.

REFERENCES

Ginott, H. (1961). *Group psychotherapy with children: The theory and practice of play therapy.* New York: McGraw-Hill.

CHAPTER **8**

THE PARENT'S PART IN THE PROCESS

Counseling with children requires consideration of certain dimensions and aspects of the relationship not encountered in counseling with adults. Children are usually dependent on a significant adult, usually the parent, in their life to make arrangements for scheduling play therapy. Therefore, any effort by the therapist to be helpful to children must begin with consideration for the parameters of the relationship to be established with the parent. Will the parent be involved in therapy? What are the complexities involved in informing parents of children's behavior in the playroom? Maintaining sensitivity to the complexity of the changing parental role in our society is a major challenge requiring awareness and sensitivity to high divorce rates, increasing numbers of single parents, changing parental roles, increasing levels of stress in families, and greater personal isolation. Such factors critically impact the parent's level of involvement and directional intensity. Although parents today are generally more sophisticated about counseling, the therapist cannot assume they know anything about play therapy. Parents also need assistance in informing their children about play therapy and how to help in the separation process for the first session.

Background Information

Interviews with parents and teachers can provide useful information to help the therapist better understand what is going on in the child's life outside the playroom experience and can provide cues to understanding the meaning of children's play. Such information can result in the therapist being more sensitive and empathic with the child and then is helpful in facilitating the process of the developing relationship. However, "outside information" also can stimulate the therapist's latent tendency to be interpretative with the child in a way the therapist would never be without outside information. Consider the following case of four-year-old Paula, who learned along with her therapist, of her mother's pregnancy four weeks prior to the occurrence of the following events in the playroom.

> For two consecutive sessions, Paula busily arranged all the chairs in a tight cluster, bound them together with string, and covered the entire construction with paper. She left a small opening and crawled in and out with some nervous giggling. Armed with his knowledge of the pregnancy, the therapist "understood" the play as a symbolic acting out of fantasies about pregnancy and birth. After making some observations to Paula about her manifest behavior, her pleasure and her "worried" giggle, he considers the best way for interpreting to her his "certain" interpretation of its latent meaning. However, since the second of these sessions is about to end, he decides to wait to deliver his interpretation until next week. In the intervening week, he meets with Paula's parents in a regularly scheduled interview. They tell him that three weeks earlier, the family had gone camping. They were very pleased that Paula was able to manage this experience without significant fears and say, "That's something she couldn't have done a few months ago." They did note that she was a bit anxious about sleeping in a tent with them and her older brother, but she was easily reassured. (Cooper & Wanerman, 1977, p. 185)

Clearly the play behavior is related to the more recent camping trip and the tent episode. What therapist, knowing about the mother's pregnancy and not knowing about the camping trip, would be able to refrain from "reading into" the child's playroom behavior anxiety about the mother's pregnancy?

Information received by the therapist does not result in a change in approach by the child-centered play therapist. This is not a prescriptive approach which varies with the presenting problem. No attempt is made to match a certain technique with a specific problem. The therapist's belief in the child is unwavering regardless of the specific problem. Thus the therapist is consistent across sessions and with different children. The therapist at all times interacts with the child rather than focusing on a problem. Therefore, background information is not essential to the child-centered therapist but may be secondarily helpful in formulating an overall picture as a basis for assessing growth or change or may be used as a basis for offering parenting suggestions.

An ideal procedure would be for another therapist to interview and counsel with the parent(s), thereby removing the play therapist from the potential bind of having to disregard background information in order to remain perceptually open to the child. This also would alleviate the problem of interference with the therapist-child relationship when the child knows the therapist is talking with the parent(s). Because most play therapists do not work in a setting where another therapist is available to work with the parent(s), if counseling with parents is necessary, they can be scheduled for a separate time when the child is not with them. However, many parents' work schedules prohibit their making two trips to the therapist's office. When this is the case, the therapy hour may have to be split between the child and the parent(s) for periodic parental sessions. This procedure is not recommended as a standard course of action, but may be the only course of action if the therapist considers working with the parent(s) to be essential. If the therapy hour is split between the parent(s) and the child, the parent(s) should be seen first. This helps to diminish the tendency of children to feel the therapist is "telling on them" as happens when the child is seen first. Children should always be informed of meetings with parents so they will not be surprised to find out such a meeting has taken place.

Must Parents Also Be In Therapy?

Without a doubt parents play a vital and significant role in the lives of their children and, therefore, should be included in some kind of therapeutic procedure whenever possible. Whether parents need therapy or training in better parenting skills is a question for the play therapist to determine. In most cases, an advisable procedure is to move in the direction of providing parenting skills training if working with the parents is considered to be necessary. In therapy parents may gain new insights, improve their self concepts, experience less anxiety, etc. and still go home and subject their children to less than helpful parenting practices. Many parents simply do not know how to be helpful to their children's emotional adjustment and cannot be expected to know because they have had no appropriate training anywhere in their lifetime. However, when parents feel better about themselves, are less anxious, etc., they are more likely to respond in positive self-enhancing ways to their children. The point being made here is that parent training is the preferred but not the exclusive approach.

A frequently asked question is "Can play therapy be effective if the parents do not receive therapy?" While involving parents in therapy or parent training is always recommended if possible and positive results may be achieved in less time if they are, children in play therapy can and do change in significantly positive ways without their parents being involved in therapy or parent training. Children are not completely at the mercy of their environment. If they were, how would we account for those children who have grown up in absolutely terrible home environments, yet go on to be quite well adjusted and successful adults. Although this is possible, it is not typical, but it does point to the individual's capacity to grow and to overcome. Play therapy can be effective without parents receiving therapy or parent training. Further evidence of this can be seen in elementary school counseling programs.

To expect an elementary school counselor to work with the parents of every child seen in a counseling relationship is inconceivable. In most elementary schools, counselors report significant changes in children's behavior even though they have only limited contact with a minimum number of parents. And what of residential institutions for children where parents are not available? Can therapy with children in these settings be effective? Is help to be withheld because parents are not there? Or is help to be withheld until a newly placed child forms a relationship with a significant adult staff member in the institution so the significant adult can be worked with?

The answer to such questions is obvious. Experiences in schools and residential institutions have demonstrated children's capability to cope, adjust, change, and grow even though parents did not receive counseling. Most research studies that have demonstrated the effectiveness of various approaches to therapy with children have not included parents in therapeutic procedures.

To insist that children not be seen in therapy until their parents can be worked with, is to deny the growth potential and coping ability of children and the ability of parents to alter their own behavior in relation to the child's change in behavior. When a child changes behavior as a result of the play therapy experience, parents unconsciously perceive the change, be it ever so slight, and in turn respond to the child in a slightly altered way thus encouraging the change in the child. Said another way, the child goes home and is a little different; so the parents respond a little differently. Some obviously gross exceptions do exist to this premise, as in the case of severely emotionally disturbed parents or parents who habitually abuse drugs, but generally this premise is true.

How this process of change works can be seen in the following case. Three-year-old Sarah's father described her as, "We don't dare leave her alone for one minute or something will be destroyed. She messes everything up, colors on the walls. She just can't be trusted" In play therapy, as Sarah experienced the therapist's consistent acceptance of her, her persistent demands, her "baby" behavior (sucking on the nursing bottle, etc.), and her need to be messy, she became less demanding and much more agreeable. Some of her messy behavior resulted in therapeutic limit setting thus allowing her to learn to control her terrible mess in the bathroom at bathtime which was father's task to clean up. As Sarah began to demonstrate greater self-control, father became more accepting of her, relaxed with her, and began to play with her spontaneously. They began to have fun together, and Sarah felt accepted.

Sarah no longer tried to pinch or hurt the five-month-old baby brother, began to play by herself more, and in mother's words "She doesn't follow me around whining all the time." Mother also relaxed with Sarah, became more trusting of her, responded more readily to her need for nurturing, and was able to say "I have my loveable little girl back." Neither parent was worked with in therapy nor were they told anything about what Sarah did in the playroom. As is demonstrated in this case, children not only can change but do, without concomitant parent therapy.

The Parent Interview

Admitting that they or their child needs help is a very sensitive and difficult area for most parents. The tendency is to put off asking for help as long as possible, hoping "things will get better." And so in many cases, when the parent finally contacts the therapist, the area of concern is usually long standing or has escalated in intensity to the point of frightening or frustrating the parent. The therapist should be especially sensitive to the struggle the parent has undergone to reach the point of asking for help and should relate to that struggle with understanding rather than rushing to focus on the presenting problem. The parent may feel guilty, frustrated, inadequate, or angry and these feelings will need to be related to first.

In the majority of parental referral cases, the mother is the one who takes the initiative to arrange for an appointment and to bring the child for therapy. Therefore, the mother's own emotional adjustment and level of frustration tolerance may be the determining factor in whether or not a child in need of therapy is referred. A study by Shepherd, Oppenheim, and Mitchell (1966) of 50 children referred to a child guidance clinic and a group of 50 children matched for age and symptom who had not been referred for therapy found that the mothers who had been seen in the clinic were depressed, upset by stress, anxious, perplexed by their children's problems, and worried about what to do. Mothers in the matched group tended to be casual about their children's behaviors and viewed their children's problems as temporary, requiring patience and time to overcome. They seemed to have more self-confidence.

The findings of this study and others highlight the need for the therapist to be sensitive and responsive to the emotional dynamics underlying the parent's reactions. The skillful therapist will, with the help of the parent, weave an intricate tapestry of interaction going in and out of focusing on the presenting problem and the parent's feelings as the therapist follows the parent's movement back and forth between these issues in the initial interview. If the session were to be dissected, some parts would be just like a therapy session, other parts would clearly portray typical intake interview material, and other parts would reveal a parental guidance function with the offering of suggestions for the parent to consider. For example, in a case involving difficulty in getting a child to bed at night, upon learning that the parent did not read to the child, the therapist suggested the parent read a short story to the child just before tucking her into bed. The therapist must be very cautious in making such suggestions before the parent, child, and the relationship are more fully understood. This process of smoothly responding to all levels of the parent's concerns is illustrated in the following initial interview just prior to seeing the child for a preliminary diagnostic session in the playroom to determine the need for play therapy.

Parent: I have 5 kids put into one.

Therapist: That must keep you very busy.

Parent: Yes, I work a full-time job and keep a house and him. As far as school, he does pretty good as long as he's on his medication. Now, if he's not on his medication, that kid, there's no controlling him.

Therapist: What kind of medication is he taking?

Parent: He's on Ritalin.

Therapist: Did you give him medication this morning?

Parent: Uh huh. He gets two before he goes to school in the afternoon and another one after school. He seems to get a streak of energy right at night time when the medication has worn off. That kid's got energy.

Therapist: Sounds like that's a busy time, a hard time for you, when he gets that streak of energy.

Parent: Yes. It's night time and that's when I'm tired and I want to relax. It's hard trying to work a full-time job and take care of him and the house and with all his energy. He's had that energy since day one.

Therapist: Working full-time and taking care of Anthony is just about all you can keep up with, and he has been overly active ever since he was a tiny baby.

Parent: Yes. Nobody would agree with me. I said he was hyper and had a lot of energy but no one would agree with me. I was home almost two years with him. When we put him in daycare and started having trouble, that was when people finally started listening to me and said, "This kid has something wrong." He's very artistic. He can be good when he wants to be, but the majority of the time he's not.

Therapist: But you know that he can control his behavior when he decides to, is that what you're saying?

Parent: Sometimes.

Therapist: You're not very sure he really can.

Parent: Not very often. And you really got to get after him and I mean you got to get hard on him.

Therapist: What does that mean, you have to be hard on him?

Parent: You have to keep after him constantly, I mean stay on him. You know, you tell him to do something, and he won't do it.

Therapist: You have to follow him around and see that he does it?

Parent: More or less, and there's times that he's gotten paddlings for not doing what he's told, and he's got a very smart mouth.

Therapist: So he talks back to you.

Parent: Yes. He tries.

Therapist: How often would you say that you paddle Anthony?

Parent: It's hard to say because I try to avoid it. Like I was saying, when he breaks the camel's back.

Therapist: The last resort.

Parent: Yes, it's not something that happens every day, and I try to avoid it unless he just gets to the point where I can't take anymore of it.

Therapist: Uh huh.

Parent: Then—you see, now I don't even have to use it. Sometimes all I have to do is threaten to use it.

Therapist: And then he stops the behavior.

Parent: He starts doing what he's told.

Therapist: So it sounds like he can control himself, but then at other times he's so active that he doesn't think about controlling himself.

Parent: Right. That's about it. He's got too much energy— if we could drain the energy out of him I think everything would be all right. (laughs) But there's no way to do that except with the medication which slows him down.

Therapist: How long has he been on the medication?

Parent: About 2 years now.

Therapist: When was the last time the pediatrician adjusted his medication?

Parent: It was about maybe a month ago. We alter the dosage depending on what he goes through. The doctor more or less goes by what I feel. If I see that he's doing good then we bring the dosage down. We brought it down for a while because he seemed to be doing better. Then once he started school again, he started getting up again so we increased it.

Therapist: You said a minute ago that the medication seems to wear off by night time. What are bedtimes like for Anthony?

Parent: Horrible!

Therapist: What does that mean, horrible?

Parent: Well, it's not really that bad going to bed, he usually falls asleep on the couch with me. I'll be sitting on the couch relaxing, and he'll fall asleep. But it's usually 10 o'clock before he falls asleep. Now, he's waking me up between 4 and 5 o'clock every morning, and I'm not up at 4 o'clock in the morning! (laughs)

Therapist: That's really early for you. You're not functioning very well.

Parent: Very early! And he wants to lay in bed with me and I won't have it. There's not enough room, and I want to sleep comfortably with the little bit of sleep I do get. I finally put him back in bed or on the couch, and he'll sleep for awhile. Sometimes he'll argue with me, sometimes he won't. But he doesn't need a lot of sleep. We also have a problem with bed-wetting. I can't get him to quit. And, it's getting to be a pain. I mean he's six-years-old. It's got to quit. Now his doctor said she could give him medication, but I didn't want to push another medication on him. I think that one is enough.

Therapist: You're really frustrated with the bedwetting. Has there ever been a period when he did not wet his bed at night?

Parent: Yes. We've gone through periods off and on, going back a few years, where he would get up in the middle of the night, go to the bathroom, and go back to bed without ever disturbing me. He did that for awhile. But it's been going on for quite awhile now. I would guess 6 months, a year.

Therapist: That must seem like a long time.

Parent: Yes, it's been a long time.

Therapist: So he wets his bed every night or almost every night.

Parent: Almost every night.

Therapist: There are some nights when he doesn't.

Parent: Yes. But the majority of the time he's wetting his bed at night. I think it's laziness. He doesn't want to get up out of bed and go to the bathroom is what I think it is.

Therapist: So you've decided he could stop if he wanted to.

Parent: Yes if he would. If he could get his mind when he's sleeping, to get him up, yes.

Therapist: Have you ever tried a routine of waking him up and taking him to the bathroom?

Parent: No. (laughs). I don't get enough sleep as it is to think about that. He wakes me up so early.

Therapist: This is a hard time for you, not enough rest. How about Dad, does he ever get up with him?

Parent: Daddy goes to bed, he puts his head down, and he doesn't know anything until the next morning. A bomb could go off under the bed, and he wouldn't know it.

Therapist: Nothing bothers him. It's all up to you then.

Parent: Not in the least. The only time he gets his sleep disturbed is when one of us is very sick. I mean we've got to be deathly sick is the only time he would hear anything. Anthony comes jumping in the bed at 3, 4, 5 o'clock in the morning, and Daddy doesn't know anything. So as far as that goes, that wouldn't work.

Therapist: So you don't think you could depend on Dad for any help.

Parent: No. Not when he comes to bed late.

Therapist: Sounds like from some of the things that you've said, that you're primarily responsible for taking care of Anthony and trying to help him change his behavior.

Parent: Pretty much, the majority. Until a month ago, Anthony spent two months home with Daddy because Dad was out of work, and I couldn't pay for a babysitter as long as he was out of work; so he did take care of Anthony at that time. And things seemed to be pretty good. I mean he still was overactive. They got along and were pretty good at it, hardly any problems in school or anything, but now we're back to babysitters. Now, I can't keep him in a daycare. I've gone through four or five different daycares and none of them can handle him because of his activeness. Right now, he's at a home sitter which seems to be working pretty good. And it's a one on one.

Therapist: So things are a lot better at home and school when Anthony has lots of close attention.

Parent: He needs one on one attention is what I've been told by the majority of the people. He needs one on one. I've threatened him to quit working and stay with him 24 hours a day because of trying to keep him someplace, and he doesn't like the idea. He doesn't want Mommy to quit working, because then there's no more toys, there's no more extras.

Therapist: Sounds like you're so exasperated you are willing to try almost anything to get him to control himself.

Parent: Yes, but to get him to control himself totally, he doesn't understand that. I don't know if it's that he doesn't want to or he can't.

Therapist: I really hear the confusion there for you. There's a part of you that thinks, "Well, maybe if he really worked hard at it he could control himself." But there's another part of you that kind of knows it's not something he really can control sometimes.

Parent: I don't know.

Therapist: Just not sure about that.

Parent: No. What I'd like and what happens are two different things. I mean I've been putting up with it for so long. My major problem, though, is I'm afraid about what will happen when he's finished kindergarten. We've got the medication to control him pretty much now, but what's going to happen when he goes to school all day? And he's very big for his age. And that's another problem I'm afraid of—I mean he is tall.

Therapist: So you've looking ahead to first grade and knowing that if this is still going on, he is going to have some real problems.

Parent: And I'm going to have the problems.

Therapist: And you're also going to have problems with him. I hear your frustration. There are times when you just get so frustrated, almost too much for you to take care of.

Parent: Yes, and other people don't see it, what I go through and there have been a couple of times over the last six months that I thought I was going to have a nervous breakdown trying to control everything. At one point I thought I almost did. Something has just got to be done, and if it's not done soon, it's not going to be a question of Anthony surviving, it's going to be Mommy surviving.

Therapist: The pressure has really been hard on you. You've been working hard a long time to keep everything together, and now you're just almost at the breaking point sometimes.

Parent: Yes, I am and it's got to change that's all there is to it. But I'm the one who has been pushing this, and I'm the one who needs it, and I just feel that—at one time I had a hard time even getting my husband to go to this stuff. It's hard to get him—I mean my husband is a lot older. My husband is 58 years old and he's set in his ways. And that's another thing that I'm fighting against, is that he's set.

Therapist: It's hard for you to get him involved, and you feel you need some help. It's almost overwhelming to you trying to take care of everything by yourself.

Parent: Yes. I mean he's been getting more involved lately than he had ever before because I've been doing a lot of screaming and yelling because I'm at the point of no return and I can't handle it.

Therapist: So you're finally getting your message across to him that you really need some help, but even that you have had to work so hard at. You just feel so desperate.

Parent: Yes, that's pretty much the way it is and I've just got to have some help.

(The session ended with an explanation of play therapy.)

Obtain Permission From Legal Guardian

Permission must be obtained from the child's legal guardian prior to scheduling for play therapy. The therapist would be well advised not to assume that the parent who arranges for the child to be in play therapy has custody of the child. The adult in your office discussing the child may indeed be the child's mother, but may be divorced and the father has full custody. The recommendation is that the therapist have a form for parents to sign giving permission for the named child to be in play therapy and verifying that the parent is the legal guardian. A separate form may be needed for granting permission for release of information and to make audio and video recordings of the sessions.

Always obtain parental permission before discussing a child's case with school personnel, an agency, etc. This point cannot be overemphasized. Never release information or discuss a child with teachers or other significant individuals in the child's life, other than legal guardians, without obtaining permission from the legal guardian. This rule would not apply in many elementary schools where the counselor is viewed as a part of the educational team and discussions with teachers are recommended.

Confidentiality

Very young children typically are not concerned about the issue of confidentiality, and yet need to be informed that this is a safe, confidential, time. Older children are more perceptive and socially aware, and thus are more likely to wonder who the therapist might tell and what the therapist might tell, since they have heard parents tell specifics of their behavior to friends and relatives. Caution must be exercised in how the child is informed, lest the child feel this is a secretive time and feel guilty about keeping it from parents. This is an especially sensitive area when dealing with sexually abused children who have been emotionally seduced or frightened into secrecy. It should be sufficient to say to most children "In this special time, what you say or do is private. I will not tell your parents or teacher or anyone. If you want them to know what you do here, you can tell them. That will be fine. You can decide."

Children's art work should not be displayed on the playroom wall or in the hallway, because this would be a violation of their privacy. A transcript of a counseling session with an adult would not be hung on the wall or displayed in the hallway. Children's art work is their way of communicating and should not be shown to teachers or parents unless the child decides to do so. Displaying art work also can influence and structure the activities of other children who enter the playroom, see the art work on the wall, and assume that is what they are supposed to do. Also, children invariably feel in competition with displayed art work.

A general guideline when working with children in play therapy is never to reveal the specifics of what a child has said or done in the playroom unless permitted to do so by a professional code of ethics. A child's exact comments and specific play behavior are for the therapist's eyes and ears only and professional colleagues who are in a consultive role. What then can be shared with parents? The therapist must use discretion in trying to assess just how parents will react or use such information. Generally, when the issue of confidentiality is involved, the best procedure is to err on the side of caution. The therapist's impressions of the child and the behavior must be conveyed to the parent without violating the strict rules of confidentiality. Showing understanding in the face of the parent's desire to know some confidential information can help to avoid the parent feeling "put off" and resentful or angry. Conveying only general information to parents without them feeling "put off" requires great skill by the therapist.

Confidentiality is a difficult issue when working with children. The parents are, after all, legally responsible for the child, and they may genuinely want to know how they can be helpful to the child. They also pay the bills for therapy and may feel they have a right to know what they are paying for and what is going on in the sessions. Where does the parent's right to know end and the child's right to privacy begin? This is a difficult question to answer, and the decision is always dependent on the parent's ability to use the information appropriately, the content of the information, the emotional vulnerability of the child, and the physical safety of parties involved.

Children must always be protected from potential physical harm from themselves and others, as in the case of threatened suicide or a threat to run away. Parents must be informed, and the therapist will need to be well versed in taking parents through precautionary steps to help insure children's safety when suicide is a possibility. As a part of the procedure, parents will need to be cautioned to hide medications, weapons, kitchen agents for clogged drains, caustic cleaners, etcetera.

Psychiatric Referral

In cases such as potential suicide, a psychiatric evaluation may be needed. If residential care is deemed to be necessary, the therapist may need to be reminded that many psychiatric facilities are not equipped to adequately care for young children. The therapist will want to visit facilities and ask important questions of the staff. What kind of training and experience do they have in working with children? What degrees and licensure or certification do the staff members hold? What procedures are used with children below the developmental age of ten? Do the staff members seem to really care about and understand children? Are they warm persons? Is there a play therapy room? If so, ask to see it. You cannot assume a highly qualified staff exists in all areas just because the program is a part of a psychiatric facility. This is information the therapist will need in order to assist in referrals. The general public tends to react to the term "psychiatric" with awe and to assume that everyone employed in such a setting is trained at the highest levels possible. As one parent said,

"Well, I think everyone there is just about like a psychiatrist." Some naive therapists may even think that. Play therapists have a professional and ethical obligation to be informed and competent.

Explaining Play Therapy to Parents

Helping parents understand what play therapy is may be one of the most important things the play therapist does because, in most cases, the cooperation of the parent is essential in bringing the child to the sessions. Parents immediately think of fun and games when they hear the term play therapy and wonder why they are asked to bring their child to play when the child already plays at home. If parents do not understand how play therapy works, they cannot be expected to trust the process or to have faith in the therapist, and, if they do not, their negative attitude may affect the child's feelings about the sessions. Comments like "It's costing a lot of money for you to just go in there to play. And besides, you're still wetting the bed" are sure to make the child feel guilty and undermine the therapeutic relationship. The following explanation could be given, modified to allow the therapist's own uniqueness and approach to be communicated.

I know you are concerned about Lisa. She seems to be having a difficult time coping (at home, at school, with the divorce, with other children, etc.). In the process of growing up, most children experience difficulty adjusting at some time. Some children may need more help than others in some areas and less help in certain areas. Children have a hard time sitting in a big chair, like the one you are sitting in, and talking about what bothers them. They just don't know the words to describe what they are feeling inside or what they are thinking, so sometimes they act out or show how they feel.

In play therapy we provide toys, and I will show you the playroom in a few minutes, for children to use to say with the toys what they have difficulty saying with words. When children can communicate or play out how they feel to someone who understands, they feel better because the feelings have been released. You have probably experienced the same thing when you were bothered or worried about something and told someone who really cared about you and understood, then you felt better and could handle the problem better. Well, play therapy is like that for children.

They can use the dolls, puppets, paints, or other toys to say what they think or how they feel. Therefore, how children play or what they do in the playroom is very important, just like what you say here is very important. In play therapy, children learn how to express their thoughts and feelings in constructive ways, to control their behavior, to make decisions, and to accept responsibility.

After the play therapy sessions, if you were to ask Lisa what she did, she would probably say she just played in the same way that if someone asked you what you did here today, you would probably say we just talked. But what we have talked about is very important. Also, children are sometimes unaware at the moment that something important has happened. Sometimes it is easier for children to explore feelings, especially their fears or anger, with someone who can be objective and accepting than it is with parents or teachers. Therefore, it is best that you refrain from quizzing Lisa about what she did, what happened, or if she had fun.

The time in the playroom is a special private time for children. They should not feel they have to give a report to anyone, even parents. Play therapy sessions with children are confidential, just like counseling sessions with adults. I want to respect Lisa just as much as I respect you as an adult. Therefore, I will be happy to share with you my general impressions and to offer suggestions, but I am not free to tell you the specifics of what Lisa says or does in the playroom. If you came to see me for counseling and shared something you were concerned about, I would not later tell your spouse or your employer. Our time together would be confidential. When Lisa and I come out of the playroom, it would be best if you didn't ask "How did things go?" or "Did you have fun?" Just say "Hi. We can go home now."

Sometimes Lisa may take a painting or drawing home with her. If you praise the painting, she may feel she should make other paintings for you. It would be best just to make comments about what you see in the painting. "You used lots of colors. There's some blue, and green, and a lot of brown all the way across the bottom of the picture." Since paints can sometimes be messy and the playroom floor may have sand spilled on it, I suggest you let Lisa wear some old play clothes you won't mind getting soiled. Please do not reprimand Lisa or be surprised if she has paint smeared on her. The paint is washable. Some children really enjoy the freedom to be messy with paints.

I am sure you are wondering what to tell Lisa about coming to see me. You may tell her she will be coming to be with Mr. Landreth in his special playroom every week where there are lots of toys for you to play with. If Lisa wants to know why she is going to the playroom, you can tell her something general like, "Things don't seem to be going very well for you at home (or other general statement related to the identified problem) and sometimes it helps to have a special time just for yourself to share with a special person."

As a part of the initial interview, a tour of the playroom or opening cabinet doors in your office to reveal play materials will help the parent to better understand what you have been trying to explain about play therapy. Don't rush this part of the process. Be sure to encourage the parent to ask questions. This is a good time to explain further the purpose of play.

Preparing Parents For Separation

Parents often feel awkward and embarrassed if their child is reluctant to go to the playroom and may make some very inappropriate statements in an effort to get their child to leave the waiting room with the therapist. A parent who says "If you don't go with the nice man to his playroom, he will think you are ugly" has doomed the beginning of the relationship to a difficult start. A reluctant child is just expressing self in the only way the child knows how at that moment—no more and no less. Being reluctant and saying "I don't want to go to the playroom" doesn't mean the child is ugly or bad or anything negative. It just means the child doesn't want to leave mother or doesn't want to go the playroom or some other reason the adults don't understand at the moment. When parents know what to expect on their first visit with their children to the playroom and have been told how to respond, the process of separation is usually less difficult for parent and child and a relief to the therapist. With preparation, parents are better able to help their children assume more independence. The therapist may find the following explanation helpful to parents.

When children come here for the first time, they are sometimes reluctant to go with me to the playroom because this is a strange place to them and they have never seen me before. Most children, though are quite ready to go see the playroom. When I come into the waiting room and introduce myself to Robert, I will say "We can go to the playroom now." It would be helpful if you would say "Fine. I'll wait here, and I'll be here when you're finished in the playroom, Robert." (Parents should not say "Bye bye" because that may result in the child feeling he is going to be gone a really long time or perhaps even forever! Always remember how things may seem to the child.) If Robert is reluctant to go to the playroom with me, I may ask you to walk down the hall to the playroom with us. When we get to the door of the playroom I will let you know if I think you need to go into the playroom with us. If I should ask you to go into the playroom, just go right in, sit down and watch. If Robert wants to show you toys or interact with you, just respond as you might at home.

Parents should be forewarned that they may hear their child yelling or banging with the hammer, and that such noises are not unusual because children play hard in the playroom. Or they may hear their child crying because they want to leave the playroom. This behavior is also acceptable. Loud noises and crying do not mean anything is wrong.

Often parents want to tell the therapist something about their child just as soon as the therapist enters the waiting room. The therapist should remind parents that he/she wants to give their child full attention in the waiting room. Therefore, the best procedure would be for parents to hold their comments until a scheduled meeting time.

If doubts or concerns exist about the child's physical functioning, advise parents to consult the pediatrician. This is always an appropriate suggestion when problems such as bedwetting or enuresis are discussed.

REFERENCES

Cooper, S. & Wanerman, L. (1977). *Children in treatment: A primer for beginning psychotherapists.* New York: Brunner/Mazel.

Shepherd, M., Oppenheim, A., & Mitchell, S. (1966). Childhood behavior disorders and the child-guidance clinic. *Journal of Child Psychology and Psychiatry, 7,* 39-52.

CHAPTER **9**

BEGINNING THE RELATIONSHIP: THE CHILD'S HOUR

"Who would have thought there was a place like this in the whole world."

a child in play therapy

Just what is that, really, the child's hour? It is one of those rare times, one of those rare relationships where the child directs self, a time when the child determines how time will be used. No effort is made to direct the child's play. This is a special time belonging to the child to do with in accordance with the child's wishes, to make of as he/she chooses. The child can be just as slow as he/she wants, inch along, and no one says "Hurry up." The child can be grumpy, act grumpy, look grumpy, and no one says "Be happy." The child can do nothing, accomplish nothing, and no one says "Get busy. Do something." The child can be loud, noisy, bang things together and no one says "Be quiet." The child can be silly, giggle, laugh right out loud, and no one says "Act your age." The child can be small, tiny, suck on the bottle, and no one says "You're too big for that." The child can use the glue, scissors, paste, make a space ship, and no one says "You're too little to do that." This is an extraordinary, singularly uncommon time, place, and relationship when the child can be, experience, and express all he/she is at the moment and be accepted fully. That makes this the child's hour.

The therapist recognizes that growth is a slow process, not to be pushed, prodded, and hurried along. This is a time when the child can relax, a place where growth takes place naturally without being forced, a special relationship. Standing in the middle of the playroom, five-year-old Rafael summed up his feeling about the uniqueness of the hour by saying "I wish I could come live here." His statement catches the essence of this special time, place, and relationship for the child.

Objectives of the Relationship

The child-centered play therapist does not attempt to establish objectives for the child to accomplish but is concerned about objectives as they relate to facilitating the development of a therapeutic relationship with the child. The following objectives express that purpose.

1. To Establish an Atmosphere of Safety for the Child. The play therapist cannot make a child feel safe. The child discovers that in the developing relationship. The child cannot feel safe in a relationship that contains no limits. A feeling of safety also is promoted by the consistency of the therapist.

2. To Understand and Accept the Child's World. Acceptance of the child's world is conveyed by being eagerly and genuinely interested in whatever the child chooses to do in the playroom. Acceptance also means being patient with the pace of the child's exploration. Understanding is accomplished by relinquishing adult reality and seeing things from the child's perspective.

3. To Encourage the Expression of the Child's Emotional World. Although the play materials are important, they are secondary to the expression of feelings by the child which they facilitate. In play therapy, there is an absence of evaluation of feelings. Whatever the child feels is accepted without judgment.

4. To Establish a Feeling of Permissiveness. This is not a totally permissive relationship. An important aspect, however, of play therapy is that the child feel or sense the freedom available in this setting. Allowing the child to make choices, creates a feeling of permissiveness.

5. To Facilitate Decision Making by the Child. This is accomplished largely by refraining from being an answer source for the child. The opportunity to choose what toy to play with, how to play with it, what color to use, or how something will turn out creates decision-making opportunities which, in turn, promote self-responsibility.

6. To Provide the Child with an Opportunity to Assume Responsibility and to Develop a Feeling of Control. Actually being in control of one's environment may not always be possible. The significant variable, though, is that children feel in control. Children are responsible for what they do for themselves in the playroom. When the play therapist does for children what they can do for themselves, children are deprived of the opportunity to experience what self-responsibility feels like. *Feeling in control* is a powerful variable and helps children develop positive self-esteem. A survey of 2800 children from inner-city schools showed that the best predictor of academic achievement was the child's sense of control over the environment (Segal & Yahraes, 1979).

Making Contact with the Child

Since the child probably has not made a self-referral to play therapy, the implied assumption is that significant adults in the child's life think the child needs to be changed. Therefore, the child comes to the first play therapy session with the expectation that the therapist also wants him/her to change. Consequently, when viewed from the child's frame of reference, one can understand that the child initially may be resistive, angry, or withdrawn, feeling the need to protect or defend self. Whatever the feeling, that is the existence of the child at that moment, and the child has brought to the relationship what is being experienced. The therapist does not view these initial reactions and feelings as extraneous and something to get past to the "real reason the child is here." That is the child, and whatever the child is feeling is accepted as a declaration of the person of the child at that moment under those conditions.

The process of making emotional contact with the child begins when I first come into the child's presence. I experience a challenge of "What will we, the child and I, be able to create here? What is the person of this child like? What does this child want? How does this child feel right now? How does this child perceive me? What does this child need from me?" Uppermost in my mind at such times is the thought "I don't want to be like most other adults in my interactions with this child." Actually, it is more than a thought, for I experience a genuine desire to be different. I do not want to crowd the child physically, to come into the child's presence too quickly or to get too close. This child has never seen me before. "I wonder what I look like to this child? What does he/she see in my face? What does this child hear in my tone of voice? Does the liking, the warmth I feel for children show in my face? Does my tone of voice reveal kindness? I would like somehow to be smaller at this moment in order to enter more fully into this child's world. Does my body posture say that to the child? Does the child know that I think he/she is important, the most important person in this room, more important to me than even his/her mother? Do my eyes show that? Is my caring about how the child feels inside being communicated? Do my words convey that caring?" In most experiences and relationships, especially those that are new, children are always wondering:

Am I safe?	(I don't know you. Will I be safe with you? Is this a safe place? What is going to happen to me here? What are you going to do to me?)
Can I cope?	(What if I can't do what you ask me to do? What if I don't know the answers to your questions? What do I do if you don't tell me what you want? What if I make the wrong choice?)
Will I be accepted?	(Will you like me? Will you like what I do? What can I do to make sure you like me?)

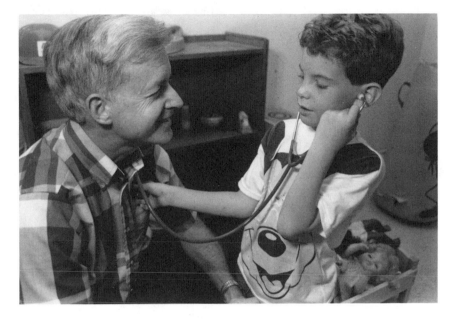

Children often use toys as a way to make contact with the therapist in the building of the relationship.

RULE OF THUMB:

Be sensitive to the child's world.

The building of a relationship begins with what the child sees and perceives in the therapist and is dependent on the therapist's sensitivity to the child's experiencing at the moment. Making contact with the child means responding with gentleness, kindness, and softness to the child's communication of self. Through the process of accepting the child's attitudes, feelings, and thoughts, the therapist enters the child's world. Once contact with the child has been made in this way, a trusting relationship can begin to develop. According to Moustakas (1981), making contact with a child ". . . can happen only when therapy is approached with a passion, with a courage to pursue in depth, with a determination to stay on the path with the child, no matter what" (p. 11).

Being sensitive also means being aware that in most other places where children are taken for a required purpose someone does something to them, doctor, dentist, testing for school placement, etcetera. That children expect the play therapist also to do something to them is understandable. How does the setting look to children? Is it an inviting looking place or austere, like going to a hospital? Are the hallways sterile looking? Is there any color anywhere? Are the pictures on the walls ones children appreciate? Are they hung at the children's eye level? Does the image of the waiting room say this is a place for children? Therapists should look at themselves and the surroundings through children's eyes.

The Initial Encounter In the Waiting Room

Building the relationship begins with the initial interactions between the therapist and child in the waiting room. The therapist enters the waiting room with eager anticipation of the exciting possibilities this new relationship may bring and is usually met by a concerned parent who is prepared to inform the therapist about concerns related to the child's behavior. The parent has what he/she considers to be important information about the child that the therapist should know and may have rehearsed the points so the therapist will know exactly the nature of the problem. The therapist greets the parent who immediately begins to bring the therapist up-to-date. This is not an appropriate time for the therapist to practice active listening or to be patient and hear the parent out. While the therapist stands there talking to the parent, the obvious message is that the therapist considers the parent more important than the child. That is not a recommended way to begin a significant relationship with the child. The child probably already feels insignificant and like a nonperson because this scene has been experienced many times—the parent talking about the child in the third person as though the child was not present.

Perhaps the therapist should ponder what it would feel like to be an appendage, just stuck on, no real useful purpose, jerked here and there at the whim of giants. Surely that is how some children feel, unimportant and unnoticed, unless, of course, they cause one of those giants a problem. Then they get plenty of attention. Well . . . even negative attention is better than no attention. Certainly the therapist does not want to perpetuate such a perception of self for the child. Therefore, the therapist will politely inform the parent that now is not a good time to discuss those issues because they are important and time is needed to explore them, and a time will be arranged later for that purpose. The therapist then should immediately crouch down and greet the child. The therapist will find it helpful to enter the waiting room, give the parent a short warm greeting, immediately crouch down, make eye contact, give a warm smile, and make an introduction to the child without giving the parent a chance to initiate conversation. The child is the most important person in the whole building at that moment. The therapist is there to build a relationship with this important little person, and to communicate the child's importance. Therefore, the therapist will not stand in the child's presence and discuss the child.

Following the short introduction to the child, the therapist can say "We can go to the playroom now. Your mother will wait here so she will be here when we come back from the playroom." The therapist should then stand up, giving a visual cue to support the verbal statement. The therapist should not say "Would you like to go to the playroom?" because that just asks for trouble from a skeptical or resistive child. Also, a choice is implied when one is not intended. If the child does indeed wish he/she did not have to go into the playroom, that is best dealt with inside the playroom where the child is fully free to express desires with materials selected for that purpose. Outside the playroom, the presence of parents or other observers may interfere with or stimulate reactions in the child that otherwise might not originate. Questions or choices that need not be dealt with should not be presented to the child. Stating that the parent will wait in the waiting room and will be there when the child comes back from the playroom reassures the child. The therapist must always remember that the child is going off with a perfect stranger, to an unknown place, and for what could be a "forever" time in the child's perception.

If the child is still reluctant, the therapist can say, "Mom, you may go down the hall with us to the playroom so Robert will know you know where the playroom is." Robert can participate in this decision by the giving of a choice to decide if he wants to walk beside Mom or hold her hand. This almost always results in the child moving toward the playroom because he is not about to stay in the waiting room by himself while mother walks away down the hall with the therapist. Usually the child will go right into the playroom without the parent. If the child doesn't, the therapist can ask the parent to accompany the child into the playroom. Once inside the parent can be asked to just sit down and watch. As the session progresses and the child relaxes, the therapist can indicate to the parent an appropriate time to leave the playroom. The parent should leave the room with no comment.

Whether or not to allow the parent into the playroom is at the discretion of the therapist. The therapist does need to anticipate that once in the playroom it may be even more difficult for the child to separate because the child has already experienced reluctant behavior getting the parent to stay. Generally, the longer the parent stays in the playroom, the more difficult the separation is for both parent and child. The therapist should recognize that the issue of separation may be more difficult for the parent than it is for the child and consequently the child, sensing that, reacts to the parent's feelings. If that is the case, the issue of separation may as well be dealt with at the door of the playroom. Another factor to be considered is the therapist's feelings. The therapist may be much more comfortable allowing the parent into the playroom than having to deal with a reluctant child. However, as long as the parent is in the playroom, the definite possibility exists that the child will not feel safe enough to explore some areas of importance.

Whether or not to go for therapy is much too weighty an issue for a four-year-old to decide.

RULE OF THUMB:

Grant responsibility commensurate with the child's ability to respond responsibly.

Parents would not allow a child, whose tonsils were so swollen that the child could not swallow, to decide whether or not to take medication because a four-year-old is not mature enough to handle that kind of responsibility. Nor would a parent allow an eight-year-old who had a broken leg to choose whether or not to be taken to the hospital. Likewise, the decision of whether or not to go for therapy is too much responsibility to grant a child. A suicidal ten-year-old would not be allowed to make a choice about receiving therapy. However, once inside the playroom, the child is free to decide whether or not to participate in the experience, to take advantage of the opportunity to change. Children can be provided with opportunities for change, but they cannot be made to change. That is for the child to decide.

The child could be allowed to choose which day to go, or whether to go to the playroom or an office, but eventually there must come a time when a decision has to be made. A child's emotional well being is no less important than physical or educational well being. This is a time for the courage of conviction tempered by great patience. The decision to be made is the parent's and the child's. Some writers recommend the therapist may have to carry the reluctant child to the playroom. I do not feel comfortable in that position. As an absolute last resort, the parent may decide to carry the child to the playroom, but physical struggles always should be avoided if possible. Although I have never had to use this approach, I have been involved in some experiences which required twenty to thirty minutes of hard work to help the child get ready to go to the playroom.

Structuring the Relationship in the Playroom

The structuring of the relationship begins with introducing the child to the playroom experience as the therapist and child enter the playroom. Verbal communication should be kept to a minimum at this point. This is not the time to try to convince the child of what a wonderful time will be had. The value of the therapeutic experience cannot be explained verbally to a child who has lived with fears of criticism, condemnation, or rejection throughout life. The value of the relationship can only be known and felt as it is being experienced. Attempting to explain too much about the relationship may unintentionally set limits on the relationship that will inhibit the child's exploration and expression. The mystery of the playroom cannot be removed with words. That can only happen as the child risks exploring.

Words should be chosen carefully to communicate to the child freedom, self-direction, and the parameters of the relationship. The therapist might say something like "Melissa, this is our playroom, and this is a place where you can play with the toys in a lot of the ways you would like to." Actually, this statement is somewhat directing and structuring because the implied expectation is that the child will play, when in fact the child is just as free not to play. However, expressing to a child that they are free not to play is difficult without getting caught up in a lengthy explanation. The statement is freeing in that it conveys to the child responsibility for direction. Boundaries on freedom are conveyed by the words *"in a lot of the ways"* which in effect communicates limits on behavior. This is a key phrase. The words *"any way you want"* are avoided because this is not a place of complete freedom. Inexperienced therapists often introduce a child to the playroom with "This is our playroom, and this is a place where you can play with the toys *any way* you wish" only to have to withdraw their absolute approval as they are about to be shot with the dart gun or as the child throws the airplane at the observation mirror. The therapist is encouraged to give considerable thought to the initial structuring phrase used.

Since this is the child's time, the therapist should now sit down, further communicating to the child willingness to allow the child to lead. Remaining standing may result in the therapist towering over the child and conveys that the therapist is in charge or is about to do something else, so the child waits expectantly. Also, the tendency while standing is to follow the child around the room, making the child feel overly self-conscious with the therapist watching over his/her shoulder. The child should be allowed to separate from the therapist and to maintain the physical distance which feels comfortable. There is a reason why Karla sits playing with farm animals across the room with her back to the therapist, and that reason should be respected. The child will approach the therapist when she feels comfortable in doing so or when she needs to do so. The therapist is being very child-centered when this dimension of the relationship is respected. Such behaviors communicate subtle but powerful messages about the relationship.

The child can be followed around the room without doing so physically, although that also might be appropriate at times. The therapist can be quite active without leaving the chair by shifting body posture forward on the edge of the chair as the child moves away or by leaning forward, arms folded across legs, to be closer to the child's activity in the dollhouse, for example, which may be four or five feet from the therapist's chair. This brings the therapist's head down to a lower level and seems to project the therapist into the child's play, conveying interest and involvement, as well as projecting the therapist's presence. Sustained involvement also is conveyed by moving the whole body to swing around from one side of the chair to the other as the child moves around the room.

RULE OF THUMB:

The therapist's toes should follow his/her nose.

In supervising play therapists, I often have observed therapists turning their head ninety degrees to track children with their eyes while the rest of their body remained motionless and projected away from the child, communicating only minimal involvement with the child. When the therapist's whole body swings around and the toes are pointed toward the child, the child feels the therapist's presence.

The therapist also can follow the child around the room by thinking about the child and by being totally absorbed in the child and the child's activity, trying to feel the child's intensity, sensing the child's involvement, wondering at the child's creativity, puzzling over the possible meaning in the child's play, feeling the atmosphere of the moment, and communicating this feeling of "being with" in facial expression, tone of voice, and general attitude. The therapist can be involved in and a part of the child's activity without physically following the child around the room. No amount of routinely following a child around the room will ever communicate the kind of involvement that is projected through an attitude of genuine caring, unwavering interest, and heartfelt desire to know the child's internal frame of reference.

After the child and therapist have begun to know and trust each other, the therapist may feel comfortable moving his/her chair to a different vantage point in the room to be able to observe the child's play. Since this is meeting the therapist's need and not the child's, a helpful procedure is to inform the child of what is about to take place so the child will not be startled or the child's activity disrupted. This could be accomplished by saying "Carlos, I'm going to move my chair (as the therapist now begins to move the chair) right over here by the sandbox so I will be able to see your play." To say "so I can see what you are doing" sounds like a parent checking on a child and does not convey the therapist's intent. Again, these are subtle differences, but the impact on the relationship is significant.

Some therapists try to rush rapport building by unnecessarily reassuring the child that everything is okay, and in the process, run rough-shod over the child's feelings. Seven-year-old Clarice sits in a chair whining "You don't have any good stuff. I don't wanna stay here." The therapist says, "Clarice, honey, other children really have a lot of fun here. See the dolls over there. Maybe you would like to play with them for a little while." The therapist now feels better because a suggestion has been offered, but the child feels worse because feelings have been ignored. An accepting therapist does not push the child to play or talk. That is for the child to decide. Permissiveness implies the child can choose to play or not to play. Pushing the child to play or talk ignores the child's feelings and deprives the child of decision making. In like manner, the accepting therapist does not ask probing questions to "get the child started." The child is allowed to lead the conversation as well as the play.

The accepting therapist recognizes each feeling as being valid and so accepts each feeling. No attempt is made to convince the child that no good reason exists for feeling the way he/she does. Some therapists, unaware of their own needs, reject a child's feelings in the process of trying to unnecessarily reassure the child or make the child feel "better." Andy enacted an elaborate scene in the dollhouse involving a child playing alone in a room and the mother doll coming into the room and stabbing the child doll repeatedly. Considerable fear was acted out as the child doll tried to escape. In a following scene, the mother doll came into the child doll's bedroom, carried the sleeping child doll outside the dollhouse, and threw the child doll into the lake (sandbox). During this enactment, Andy verbalized his fear that "Mother will get me. She's going to do something real mean to me." Having known the mother quite well from previous relationships, the therapist responded, "Andy, now you know your mother loves you, and she would never ever do anything to hurt you." Although the therapist may have substantial evidence on which to base this conclusion, the therapist can never be completely sure of another person's behavior. We cannot speak for other people. We simply do not know what may take place in another person's home. In her need to reassure the child, the therapist ignored Andy's feelings and, so the child did not feel understood. The therapist felt better, but at what expense?

Responding to the Reluctant Anxious Child

The child is free to direct the interaction in the way the child chooses. However, what if the child is anxious, stands in the middle of the playroom, and says nothing? Then what? The therapist would make a therapeutic mistake to assume nothing is happening to which one can respond just because the child is nonverbal and nonplaying. Children are at all times communicating something about themselves. Therefore, something is always present to be responded to by the therapist. Four-year-old Angela entered the playroom for her first session and said nothing. She obviously was very anxious and unsure of what to do or of what was expected in the playroom. The therapist already had made an introductory statement about the playroom.

Angela:	(stands right in front of therapist, twisting hands, looking at therapist, and then looks at toys on shelf)
Therapist:	I see you're looking at the toys over there. (pause)
Angela:	(looks at observation mirror, sees herself and grins)
Therapist:	And you saw yourself in the mirror there. (pause) I guess sometimes, maybe. . .it's just hard to decide what to do first (pause, Angela glances at the toys again) but this is a place where you can play with any of the toys you want to play with.
Angela:	(begins to pick at a frayed piece of fingernail on one of her fingers)
Therapist:	Hmmmm . . . you've got something right . . . there, (pause, points to Angela's fingernail) right there on your finger. (pause) Hmmmm, looks like you are trying to pick something off your fingernail.
Angela:	This thread. I picked the other one off. . .
Therapist:	Oh, you have already picked one off.
Angela:	At school.
Therapist:	At school you did it. Uhmmm, so now you're doing this one.

The therapist's responsiveness to Angela's nonverbal cues helped her to relax, and the therapist's verbalized attentiveness resulted in Angela verbally joining in the interaction. Even without a verbalized response everything would have been fine because Angela was already communicating with her eyes, face, and hands. When a child is nonverbal because the child feels anxious or awkward in the playroom is no time for the therapist to be nonverbal. That only increases the child's feeling of being on the spot and not knowing what to do. This point was experienced by a beginning play therapist: "I learned that I can inhibit a child by my silence, my facial expression, and my size, and that I can free a child in purposive ways having to do with acceptance, permissiveness, and feelings. I must be careful how I use myself. Children can be more easily injured by me than I by them."

The Child's View of the Play Therapy Relationship

My mom says I'm going to have fun. Yeah, I've heard that line before! She's telling me that I'll be in a room with lots of toys and things six-year-olds like to do. She says I'll be spending time with some lady they call the counselor. But who is this lady who wants to spend time playing with me? What is she like? Will I like her? Will she like me? What's she going to do to me? Maybe I'll never go back home again. I don't even know what she looks like. Oh, no, I hear footsteps . . . could it be . . . Gulp . . . .

This lady must be the person they call the counselor. She is warm and friendly and she says "Hello" to my mom and introduces herself to me. She smiles a lot. That makes me feel more comfortable now so I say "Hi." She bends down close to me, says "Hi" and notices my Spider-man shirt and my new tennis shoes with red stripes. She says they look like racing shoes. They sure are! Oh, I like her better now! Maybe she'll be OK after all.

Well, here we go down the hall. She's also noticing that I'm a little afraid. She says this must seem strange because I haven't seen her or her special playroom before and sometimes that's a little scary to children. Guess she's kinda saying that it's OK to be afraid. It's funny to hear that coming from an adult! She must be an understanding person, and she seems to care about me. Maybe she was afraid once in her life, too.

She takes me to what she calls her special playroom. Boy, it is different! There are toys in here! She tells me we'll be together in the playroom for forty-five minutes. Hmmm, that's strange. No one has ever told me how long we would be together or how long I would have to play. She says this is a place where I can play with the toys in a lot of ways I would like to. Wow, can she really mean that? Yeah, she seems to care about me and she seems to like me, even though she hardly knows me. That's strange! I wonder if she treats every kid like that. Maybe I had better wait and see what she wants me to do. Other adults always tell me what to do. I'm going to be kinda quiet for a few minutes. She notices me looking at the paints and says sometimes it's hard to decide just what to do first, but that this is a place where I really can decide for myself. This whole thing sure is different. I pick up the paintbrush and splash red all over the paper . . . feels good.

I think I'll paint a purple apple tree. Wonder if that will be OK? Maybe I should just make it red and green, but I hate green—reminds me of asparagus. Yuk! I'll ask her what color I should use. She says that's something I can decide. Boy, everybody else would have told me just what colors to use. Seems like I make most of the decisions in here. Well, here goes the purple paint. She says it looks like I've decided to use lots of purple. Yep, I sure have! It's kinda hard to get this thing to look just right. Hmmm, that's a funny looking apple tree, but I like it because it's big. Wonder if she thinks it looks OK. I'll just ask if she likes it. She says it looks like I worked hard to get it just the way I want it. Yep, that's right. It's just like I wanted it to be—all purple. This lady let's me please myself.

This is a funny place. I bet it would be fun to paint her nose purple! A lady with a purple nose. Now, that will be something! Boy, I'll just paint this whole blob of purple on her. I bet that will get her out of the chair. She'll probably run clear around the room! Hmmm, she doesn't look scared. She doesn't even yell at me to stop. She just says she knows I would like to put paint on her, but she's not for painting. She says I can paint on the paper or I can pretend the Bobo is her and paint on the Bobo. She's so calm about everything. It's no fun to put paint on her if she's not scared. Anyway, that sounds like a super idea to paint the Bobo. I hadn't thought of that.

I'm starting to play with some other toys now. Funny, this person they call the counselor seems to really be noticing what I'm doing. I like what I'm doing. Wonder if she thinks it's important. She's paying attention to me. Most adults don't do that. She's smart and catches on to what I'm doing. She even comments on what things I enjoy playing with the most. Yeah, she knows that the clay is my favorite. She's really interested in me and in what I'm doing.

Gosh, I like it here already. I think I'll try a few more things, like playing in the sandbox. I'd like for her to play in the sandbox with me, but she says she'll just watch me play in the sandbox. I like the way she's so straightforward about it. Most adults would just say, I'll play with you in a few minutes" and then they'd forget all about it. Anyway, I think I'm only going to stay in here for a few minutes. I start to leave. She says we have fifteen more minutes together in the playroom and then I can leave. She seems to believe I'll just do what needs to be done. That feels good.

Let's see—what'll I do next? It's fun getting to decide what I want to do next. At home, I hardly ever get to do what I want to do. The sitter always says what we're going to do at such-and-such time, or my brothers are always pushing me to do something I don't want to do, or my parents make me try something that I'm not ready to try. Not this lady— she's not pushy at all; she waits for me to make the move that I want to make. And she doesn't criticize me for being slow like all the kids at school do. She likes me because I'm me. Or at least, I think she does!

I think I'll play ball with this person they call the counselor. It's fun because we can talk and catch the ball at the same time. Gosh, she's so interested in whatever I do. And she's got a lot of what grown-ups call self-discipline. When I throw the ball away from her so she will miss it, she just lets the ball go, and she stays where she is. She says that if I want the ball, I can go and get it. It would be a lot easier for her to get the ball because she's closer. But she knows that I'm trying to trick her. I like the way she doesn't let me get away with that. My Mom would have finally picked up the ball—IF I had asked her enough times. But then, too, my Mom would end up screaming. This lady just never gets upset about anything.

I'm really enjoying spending time with this person they call the counselor. She believes I can do things without her help. When I asked her to take the top off the paste jar because I was afraid I couldn't get it off, she said that was something I could try. I did, and you know what? It came off! I wish I knew I could do things outside this room. Then I could hit home runs at the ball game instead of always striking out and embarrassing my Dad. Hmmm, maybe I can do some things like she believes I can. This lady is lots of fun. This is a fun place to be. It feels good to do things all by myself . . . just the way I decide.

I think I'll try to paint a picture of a police car. Boy, it's looking neat . . . all bright blue! Drat! The red paint for the light on top is running right down the side of my car! That really makes me mad. She says I look angry about that. Well, I am! But how did she know? Nobody else ever recognized my feelings. Does that mean it's OK to get mad about some things? Must be OK. She doesn't seem to mind my being mad.

Wonder what she will think if I pretend this big throwing dart is a rocket ship. Guess I could ask her what it's for. She says in here it can be anything I want it to be. Imagine that! An adult who lets it be what I want it to be. Wow, now I can zoom around the room and pretend I'm going to the moon where no one can boss me . . . kinda like in here where I'm the boss of me.

I wish it wasn't time to leave now. There are so many things I wanted to tell her, but didn't get a chance to say. It's funny how sometimes it's so hard to tell my parents just little things. But I feel like I could say anything to her. She tells me to come back next week—that she looks forward to spending some time with me again. She sounds like she really means it. I feel so good right now because she's the first person who has ever treated me like a real person, not just a kid. She respects me - that's what it is. And she knows that I can do great things. Or at least, that's the way I feel now!!!

Questioning Techniques of Children

A common practice of children is to ask the therapist a multitude of questions which may be their way of making contact with the therapist and beginning to build the relationship. However, the therapist should consider that children already know the answer to many of the questions they ask.

Examined from this perspective, responding to children's questions becomes a matter of trying to understand the motivation behind the question rather than attempting to provide an answer. Providing answers to questions can inhibit children's use of items by binding children to the therapist's world of reality. When five-year-old Hershel holds up the handcuffs and asks, "What are these?" and the therapist answers, "Handcuffs," they can no longer be the special new kind of space ship he was thinking about. The therapist could facilitate the coming forth of Hershel's creativity and imagination by responding, *"That can be whatever you want it to be."* Hershel is then free to proceed with what he already had in mind but had not verbalized. When Judy asks, "Who broke this doll?" she very well may be wondering what happens to children who break toys in the playroom. A sensitive therapist would respond, *"Sometimes accidents happen in here."* Judy then knows this is not a place of punishment, or a place where you must be careful. This is an adult who understands that accidents do happen. She then feels more free to express herself more spontaneously and completely.

RULE OF THUMB:

Don't answer questions that haven't been asked.

Answers to obvious questions can result in lengthy question and answer routines which increase the children's dependency. When children ask questions in play therapy, the therapist would do well to consider what the underlying meanings are before responding to what seems to be the objective of their questions. Trying to anticipate what children are saying in their questions rather than attempting to answer the questions, is usually much more facilitative of expression and exploration. What the therapist senses at the moment would determine the kind of response to be made. The following questions and possible meanings underneath the obvious questions are provided for consideration in stimulating awareness of what children may be communicating.

1. Do other children come here?

   David might be

   a. wanting reassurance he is special,
   b. establishing a sense of belonging in the playroom—
      "my place," a sense of possessiveness,
   c. curious about the playroom because of its
      uniqueness,
   d. wanting to feel secure in knowing the room is his
      for this time,
   e. wanting to know if other children play with the
      toys,
   f. wanting to know if there are going to be other
      children with him in the room,
   g. wanting to know if he can bring a friend, and/
      or
   h. noticing something is different about the room this
      week.

2. Do you know what I'm going to do next?

   Laura might be

   a. indicating that she has something definite in mind
      that she plans to do,
   b. wanting to include the play therapist in her plans,
      and/or
   c. finishing a project or changing the theme of play—
      a way of closure on one aspect of play.

3. Can I come back tomorrow?—or—When can I come
   again?

   Dwight might be

   a. involved in a project that is important to him and
      wanting to finish it,
   b. enjoying what he has been doing—wanting the
      opportunity to do it again,
   c. saying—"This is an important place to me."

d. seeking reassurance of his time—that he does have a time in the playroom that belongs to him,
e. unsure about trusting his world to be consistent and not disappointing him in this situation as it has in others, and/or
f. saying—"I really like to come here," "It is important to me that I can come again."

4. Does anybody play with this?

    Rachel might be

    a. saying—"Is it okay for me to play with this?"
    b. unsure of the permissiveness of the playroom, seeking permission or reassurance of that permissiveness,
    c. unsure of what the toy is or what she wants to do with the toy,
    d. trying to decide what she wants to do, and/or
    e. wanting to make contact with the therapist.

5. Do you know what this is?

    Mike might be

    a. proud of something he has made,
    b. wanting to make contact with the therapist,
    c. ready to use the toy for a specific purpose—has plans for the use of the toy, and/or
    d. asking for information.

6. What is this?

    Valerie might be

    a. unfamiliar with the toy or play material and unsure of how it could be used,
    b. trying to decide what she would like to do with the toy,
    c. unsure of the permissiveness of the playroom— saying—"Is it okay for me to play with this?"— Testing the permissiveness of the playroom,
    d. wanting to make contact with the therapist,

e. seeking direction or approval from the therapist
f. wanting to use the item for something other than the apparent use,
g. trying to establish a superficial relationship with the play therapist while she checks out the room and the play therapist, and/or
h. trying to put things back on a "safe" level—often the play therapist will have touched on a sensitive issue or feeling.

7. Do you like children?—or—Do you have any kids?

Kevin might be

a. establishing rapport with the play therapist,
b. trying to find out more about the play therapist,
c. affirming that he does indeed feel liked and accepted by the play therapist (this question usually seems to be followed by the statement—"I like coming here."),
d. showing possessiveness toward the play therapist,
e. trying to take the focus off himself,
f. trying to make "polite" conversation, and/or
g. leading up to "whose side are you on" type questions.

8. What time is it?—or How much time is left?

Theresa might be

a. enjoying herself and not wanting to leave,
b. wanting the feeling of certainty that there is time left,
c. wanting to feel in control that she knows,
d. anxious to go, and/or
e. planning a project and wanting to be sure it can be finished.

9. Why do you talk like that?

Robert might be

a. unaccustomed to talking with adults,

b. having a surprise reaction to the verbal attention,
c. annoyed by too much reflection of words, and/or
d. saying he notices the difference in the play therapist's reflective-type responses.

10. Will you fix this or do this for me?

Cheryl might be

a. dependent and lacking confidence in her ability to do things,
b. trying to make contact with the play therapist, and/or
c. testing the freedom of the experience together.

11. What would happen if I did this?

Kent might be

a. testing the limits of his environment,
b. expressing curiosity, and/or
c. wanting attention.

12. Do I have to clean this up?

Wendy might be

a. becoming acquainted with the playroom and learning to feel secure there,
b. wanting to be messy,
c. wondering where the boundaries are, and/or
d. trying to find out if this place is different.

13. Do children ever play together in here?

Kirk might be

a. feeling lonely,
b. feeling insecure,
c. trying to avoid building a relationship with the play therapist, and/or
d. wanting to bring a friend.

14. Will you tell my Mommy?

Serena might be

a. afraid of being punished for doing something,
b. getting ready to break a limit, and/or
c. wanting to confirm the confidentiality of the relationship.

15. Did you get any new toys?

Jeff might be

a. having difficulty making decisions about what to do,
b. bored and saying he would like new materials, and/or
c. indicating he is getting ready to terminate.

16. How does this work?

Sarah might be

a. actually wanting to know,
b. trying to manipulate the play therapist,
c. expressing dependence—getting the play therapist to show her so she doesn't have to figure it out by herself, and/or
d. wanting to establish some contact with the play therapist.

17. When will I come back?

Jason might be

a. wanting reassurance that he will get to come back,
b. wanting to know when he will come again,
c. having anxiety about coming and wanting to know if he has to come back, and/or
d. feeling his behavior has been so bad the therapist won't let him come back.

18. What should I do?

Nicole might be

a. wanting to shift responsibility to the play therapist,
b. wanting to know what she is allowed to do,
c. seeking permission to play, and/or
d. wanting to please the play therapist.

19. Who broke this?

Greg might be

a. curious about who broke the item,
b. wondering what happens when someone breaks something, and/or
c. upset about the toy being broken.

20. Where did you get this?

Monica might be

a. curious about where it came from,
b. wanting to make contact with the therapist, and/or
c. wanting time to check out the room and the therapist.

21. Can I take this home?

Chuck might be

a. wanting permission to take the item,
b. wanting to know what will happen to him if he takes it,
c. wanting to extend the experience and/or relationship,
d. feeling possessive of the playroom,
e. trying to take the focus off himself,
f. trying to make "polite" conversation, and/or
g. leading up to "whose side are you on" type questions.

22. How do you play with this?

Anita might be

a. wanting the play therapist to interact with her,
b. afraid she will do something wrong, and/or
c. feeling insecure or dependent.

Explaining the Observation Mirror and Recording

Trying to explain video taping through a one-way mirror to young children can be a confusing task and in many cases does not seem to be necessary. Young children have difficulty comprehending being able to see through a mirror when all their experiences have been with mirrors at home that can not be seen through. Some young children think there is a room and people inside the mirror and that can be a very strange experience. Although taking young children into the observation room for a look through the mirror into the playroom does not seem to help them comprehend, they should be shown the observation room if they express an interest in seeing "the other room and those people." The process can be explained, however, to older children, and they should be reassured that parents, teachers, etc. will not be watching. If an audio recording is made, children probably will notice the recorder in the playroom and may want to listen to the tape. The last few minutes of the session seem to be the best time for this. If video taping is used and children express curiosity about what is on the tape or want to see themselves, their request should be honored. Typically children do not request to listen to or view recordings. However, those who do may react with awkwardness and embarrassment to some of their negative behavior. They also may be genuinely amused at themselves and some of their antics in the playroom. Viewing their own behavior can result in new insights as well as facilitation of the expression of additional feelings. Seeing himself drip paint on the floor while painting at the easel, Jeremy remarked, "I thought you were going to get on to me for splattering that paint." (Viewing of self on video is an area in need of research.)

Taking Notes During the Session

This is really an individual matter. In my initial experiences with play therapy, I took notes but found that to be distracting to me and the child. I would look down at my note writing and look back up to discover the child was in a different place, and I had missed some of the child's play behavior. Therefore, I had missed some of the child's communication since the child's play is his/her language. I also noticed that I only took notes on certain happenings, not everything the child did, only those things I felt were important. The child also noticed that, and I became aware of the child doing more of some of the things which I made an effort to record. I was influencing and structuring the child's play although that was not my intention. Knowing that something is being written down may be threatening to some children and, consequently may restrict the child's play.

On one occasion, while I was writing notes during a session with six-year-old Matthew, he came over and wanted to see my notes; so I handed them to him (there should be no secrets in the playroom). Matthew took my tablet over to the easel, promptly painted the whole page with black paint, and handed the tablet back to me. I experienced that as a very powerful message about his reaction to my writing down what he did! That was the last time I ever took notes during a session. Sometimes I learn quickly! I am able to give the child my attention more fully when I am not concerned about recording what the child is doing. Other therapists may have a perfected note-taking system which allows them to take notes during the session with minimal distraction. Notes on the session can be recorded immediately following the session and are important for the therapist's understanding of the development of themes in the child's play and to determine progress. One innovative play therapist I know in private practice clips a voice-activated cassette recorder to his belt while he straightens the playroom after each session and talks his notes into the tape recorder.

Play Therapists' Reactions To Their First Session

Kathy: It had all begun before I had a chance to realize that it had. There I was sitting in that chair reserved for that person they call a counselor who has a playroom, the one I'd heard about, read about, and was supposed to be about this very moment. Diverse thoughts flooded my mind, and although I wasn't counting, I could have sworn several butterflies had found their way to my stomach. I don't recall being nervous as much as I remember being eager for the experience and for whatever it might bring. It was a strange, but special feeling. I had experienced some apprehension but for that brief thirty minutes that passed like seconds all that was, strangely enough, the furthest thing from my thoughts.

Bill: I thought I was ready. I thought everything would come naturally, but I honestly had to struggle with the process. I wanted to direct the child's actions, to tell him what to play with, to literally "move him on." I wanted to explain what things were and "lead" the way, to do things for him, e.g., fix, put together, open, close, etc. I had to experience my frustration and leave him to struggle with his own frustration so we could both grow. I think this session was actually more therapeutic for me than it was for Brian. I learned so much about me and my needs, especially my need to help, to lead, to direct, to make things easier for children. Most importantly, I learned to hold me down in order to give children a chance to grow.

Marilyn: Before my first play therapy session I felt myself becoming nervous and uptight. My mind seemed to go blank as I tried to remember the "right" things to say. It was one of the best things that could have happened. As I walked hand-in-hand to the playroom with Karen, I felt myself relaxing and enjoying the child at my side. As we entered the playroom, I no longer felt that my mind was blank and in place of that feeling, I felt open, receptive, and ready to experience with her the marvelous relationship that was beginning.

Stephen: My first experience in the playroom was an exhilarating experience. I was able to drop the role of authority and healer and to accept the child and let her take the lead. I did not feel that I had to persuade or teach her. I could watch her and try to understand her world. I was able to concentrate on her, not my technique. I know now that I was feeling as much freedom as the child.

Basic Dimensions of the Relationship

The development of the relationship with a child, which we refer to as play therapy, is facilitated by the therapist's subtle use of self in responding to the child's communication of self in the process of play and is dependent on the therapist's sensitivity to, and understanding of, the dynamics of the child's world, as well as the child's emotional expression communicated in the relationship. Only when the child begins to feel safe with the therapist will he/she begin to express and explore the emotionally meaningful and sometimes frightening experiences which have been experienced. The therapist must wait for this development. It cannot be rushed or made to happen. This is the child's time, and the child's readiness or lack of readiness to play, talk, or explore must be respected.

When the child experiences the freedom and permissiveness of directing his/her own play in the context of an empathic and caring relationship, the child develops self-discipline and perseverance that comes from the sustained effort required to carry through or complete a self-selected activity or project. The process of independently choosing an activity, directing the action,and relying on self for the outcome enhances self and develops self-reliance.

Eric can build his own walls of safety and remove them when he feels safe enough to do so.

The therapist's responsibility in the relationship can be summed up in the following four messages which the child-centered therapist works hard to communicate to the child at all times and with the totality of the therapist as a person:

I'm here. (Nothing will distract me. I will be fully present physically, mentally, and emotionally.)

I hear you. (I will listen fully with my ears and eyes to everything about the child, what is expressed and what is not expressed. I want to hear the child completely.)

I understand. (I want the child to know I understand what he/she is communicating, feeling, experiencing, and playing and so will work hard to communicate that understanding to the child.)

I care. (I really do care about this little person and want the child to know that. If I am successful in communicating fully the first three messages, the child will know I care.)

REFERENCES

Moustakas, C. (1981). *Rhythms, rituals and relationships.* Detroit: Harlow Press.

Segal, J., & Yahraes, H. (1979). *A child's journey: Forces that shape the lives of our young.* New York: McGraw-Hill.

CHAPTER **10**

CHARACTERISTICS OF FACILITATIVE RESPONSES

The natural response of many adults to children is to question, command, or provide answers and is the consequence of an attitude that children only need to be told what to do to "straighten them out." Responding to children in a way that communicates sensitivity, understanding, and acceptance and conveys freedom and responsibility is for many adults like learning a foreign language and requires a drastic shift in attitude and a restructuring of words used in responses. A beginning play therapist expressed the change this way, "I know *how* to respond. I just don't know *how* to put it into words." From this new perspective children are viewed as being capable, creative, resilient, and responsible. An objective of the adult-child relationship, then, is to respond to children in ways that release or facilitate the development of these existing capacities. The therapist genuinely believes children are capable of figuring things out for themselves, trusts their decisions as being appropriate for them within the boundaries of their developmental capabilities, and communicates this attitude through responses to children.

Sensitive Understanding: Being With

Rachel was a small first grader who always walked the few blocks home from school. Her mother constantly reminded her that she was to come directly home immediately after school was over for the day. This was drummed into Rachel repeatedly, and her mother's concern was understandable when Rachel was a few minutes late getting home one day. Rachel's mother walked to the sidewalk and looked down the street, no sign of Rachel. She paced the driveway for ten minutes, and still no sign of Rachel. After fifteen minutes, Mother became almost frantic. Twenty minutes had passed when Rachel finally came into view. Mother was relieved, but then became quite angry. She yelled at Rachel in a loud voice, grabbed her by the arm, and ushered her into the house. After several minutes of being angry, Mother finally asked Rachel for an explanation. Rachel told her mother that on the way home she had passed by Sally's house and found Sally outside in the yard crying because she had lost her doll. "Oh," Rachel's mother replied, "and you stopped to find Sally's doll for her?" "No, Mommy," Rachel said, "I stopped to help Sally cry."

The typical approach in adult-child interactions is characterized by an attitude of evaluation of the child based on what is known about the child and previous circumstances. Seldom do adults strive to understand the immediate internal frame of reference of the child, the child's subjective world, to genuinely be with the child. Sensitive understanding of the child occurs to the extent the therapist is able to put aside personal experiences and expectations and appreciate the personhood of the child, as well as the child's activities, experiences, feelings, and thoughts. Children are not free to explore, to test boundaries, to share frightening parts of their lives, or to change until they experience a relationship in which their subjective experiential world is understood and accepted.

As with the other therapeutic dimensions, the attitude of the therapist is critical in making contact with children in such a way that they feel understood and accepted for who they are. This depth dimension understanding means remaining free of a stylized role and participating deeply and meaningfully in the work of understanding the child. This means putting aside the tendency to evaluate and judge and to see from the viewpoint of the child. When understanding and acceptance are lacking, little, if any, effective therapeutic work is going on in the relationship.

Caring Acceptance

Acceptance grows out of a genuine and sincere interest in children, a sensitivity to their rights, and a belief that they can assume responsibility for themselves. Children who experience such an atmosphere of acceptance in the playroom learn that they can depend on others for support while developing their own sense of adequacy and independence. Acceptance is communicated through the therapist's patience and willingness to trust the process. The therapist is always patient with children. Patience allows the therapist to see things from the child's perspective. The therapist's acceptance is reflected in refraining from offering advice, suggestions, or explanations, and in not questioning or interrupting children. The therapist's empathic responses communicate understanding and acceptance to children, thus freeing them to be more creative and expressive.

Whether or not a child's actions, behaviors, or feelings are good or bad simply does not occur to the therapist. They are accepted as they occur without being screened through any hint of judgmental attitude. By empathically reflecting these happenings and feelings, the therapist expresses respect for the child and affirms the child's right to have feelings and to express self through actions. Acceptance, then, occurs in conjunction with permissiveness, but does not necessarily imply approval of what the child is doing. An important dimension in the therapeutic process is the child's need to be accepted as a person of worth regardless of inadequacies, deficiencies, or behaviors. The creation of this kind of relationship allows the child to express self at his/her own pace without any hurry or pressure from the therapist. That is the epitome of respect, to be accepted just as one is without even the possibility of criticism, evaluation, judgment, rejection, disapproval, censure, condemnation, punishment, penalty, rebuke, reprimand or praise, compliment, reward, or accolade.

The therapist's accepting responsiveness encourages a child to explore thoughts and feelings further. When a child's

When a child's feelings are expressed and accepted by the therapist, they are experienced with less intensity by the child, and the child's acceptance of those feelings is facilitated.

feelings are expressed and accepted by the therapist, they are experienced with less intensity by the child, and the child's acceptance of those feelings is facilitated. The child then is more fully able to integrate and deal with feelings by expressing positive and negative emotions in a more focused and specific way. This is a central postulate of child-centered play therapy, and is the basis for the therapist's empathic responsiveness. Focusing on the child's feelings validates the person of the child rather than the importance of the problem.

Details of Therapeutic Responsiveness

I like my response to a child best when it fits smoothly into the child's expression without interrupting the flow. The response has been offered at just the right moment, interjected into the plane of the child's communication with no disturbance of the surface, and the blending has been so harmonious that the child hardly takes any conscious notice. I would like my responses to be like a world-class diver who, with seemingly little effort, gracefully springs off the diving board at just the right moment and gently intersects the surface of the water with hardly a ruffle to show that the diver's presence has been there. At such moments, I feel a oneness with the child, a genuine understanding, and a "living with" that transcends the circumstances of both our lives. We are here together, and a mutual acceptance exists.

Lengthy responses from the therapist disrupt the child's focus, result in the child being caught up in using energy to try to understand what the therapist is saying, and tend to change the direction of expression. **Responses should be short and interactive** with the child's affect. The flow should be like a conversation, not just simple reflections, and should have a rhythmic quality.

The therapist needs to be an involved verbally responsive participant with the child. The relationship will deteriorate when a child feels watched. A child's question of "Why are you looking at me?" typically means the therapist has not been verbally active enough. The child often will be engrossed in play and not talkative about what is being done, and no feelings are evident or sensed by the therapist. At such times the therapist can respond to what is being observed. These tracking responses communicate the therapist's involvement, and help the child to feel the therapist is participating with the child. Sitting and watching without responding to the child can result in the child feeling watched and may increase the child's anxiety. Feelings of security and warmth are promoted as the child hears the therapist's voice and the description of the child's activities. Tracking responses convey interest in the child and what is being done.

Some therapists have a tendency to raise the tone of their voice when around small children as though talking to a baby or talking down to a child. Such behavior projects a basic attitude about children being incapable and has no place in the therapeutic relationship. The therapist also should avoid slipping into a monotone; that can be deadly. Use voice inflection to convey meaning and feeling.

The therapist should avoid getting overly excited beyond the child's level of affect about little happenings such as, "Oh, my! Isn't that wonderful! You found a colored rock in the sandbox!" This kind of excitement may cause the child to feel something is wrong or to distrust his/her own reaction because the child does not feel equally excited.

The therapist should project a warm and friendly image with tone of voice and facial expression. This is not a time to be overly serious or stern. Smile. The therapist's facial expression should be animated and convey what words cannot.

Questioning a child about the reasons for behavior is generally not facilitative of exploration because the child is expected to verbally communicate cognitive insight and this is a contradiction of the rationale for placing children in play therapy. If the child was able to fully express self through verbal means, the child would not be in play therapy in the first place. Questions place the therapist in a leading, controlling position and are, therefore, seldom facilitative. Even questions asking for clarification usually are not helpful or needed. Generally, if the therapist has enough information on which to base a question, enough information is available on which to base an empathic statement. Questions designed to satisfy the therapist's curiosity such as, "How many times have you been sent to the principal's office?" or guesses such as, "Does your mother get angry when you do that at home?" are inappropriate. Likewise, questions that attempt to produce insight such as, "Have you noticed you use a lot of dark colors?" usually are beyond the level of the child's awareness and thus are ineffective.

At one point, a therapist asked five-year-old Aaron to make up a story and at the end of his story asked, "What is the moral of your story?" to which Aaron asked, "What does that mean?" A therapist sensitive to the developmental level of children should know a five-year-old probably will not know what the word "moral" means. In addition, such a question calls for abstract reasoning beyond the child's developmental level. Later, Aaron was acting out a loud fight between a dinosaur and a snake and the therapist asked, "Wonder what would happen if all dinosaurs and snakes were friends instead of fighting each other?" Aaron did not respond and no wonder! Even the ability of most adults to give an adequate response to such an abstract question is questionable. The therapist was completely out of touch with Aaron, and the child expressed frustration with the therapist by throwing the dinosaur at her. The therapist's following response was equally ineffective. "Aaron, seems like you're pretty mad at me. I'm guessing maybe that you don't like coming here. And maybe you're a little mad at Mom for making you come here. 'Cause, by making you come here, that means she's in charge, and you don't like it when she's in charge." The therapist completely avoided the personal issue between herself and the child and placed the blame on the parent with an interpretative response that was much too lengthy for a five-year-old and drew a series of abstract associations that were bewildering to the child. The therapist probably felt quite satisfied, but we must wonder how Aaron felt. The therapist gave very little indication that she understood Aaron.

Allowing a child the freedom to engage in the process of decision making provides opportunities for the child to project his/her own personal meaning onto the item or material. This inner experience of making decisions strengthens the child's self-concept and provides the child with experiences which can become incorporated into a changed perceptual view of self. This is a growth process which will enable the child to respond emotionally to future problems and situations in a more effective way. Therefore, the therapist refuses to accept responsibility for making decisions for the child, no matter how insignificant the decision may seem to be. Thus, the child is encouraged to accept responsibility for self, and, in the process discovers personal strengths.

Responses always should be personalized and address the presence of the child. Responding to David who is busy banging on Bobo by saying, "David really likes hitting that Bobo" denies the presence of the child, and causes the child to feel talked about as a nonperson. *"You really like hitting that Bobo"* addresses the child personally. Michael paints a picture, and the therapist responds, "Michael painted a picture" as though someone else is in the playroom. *"You"* gives the child credit and recognizes ownership.

Some therapists are prone to inappropriately include themselves in the interaction. Beth talks about playing soccer and how much she wanted to win but her team lost. The therapist responds with, "Sometimes it feels bad when we lose and want to win." The therapist was not a part of the happening, and the use of "we" shifts the focus away from the child. Nancy says, "Last year these people came to our house. . . Uh, I forgot their name," and the therapist inappropriately responds, "Sometimes we do forget people's names if they are hard names for us." Again, the therapist should use "you" to recognize the person of the child.

Facilitative Responses

The importance of making facilitative responses cannot be overemphasized. Just because a therapist is trying to be helpful to a child does not insure that the therapist will be, as can be seen in the following responses made by inexperienced play therapists when asked to respond to the same play therapy episodes.

Directions: Robert, a seven-year-old boy, won the second grade spelling bee in his school but exhibits socially maladaptive behavior. In his first play therapy session, Robert writes "skool" on the chalk board and asks, "Is this the right spelling?" Write the response you would make to Robert.

Response:

1. You tell me if that is the right spelling. (Response is not freeing to the child and places emphasis on right and wrong.)

2. You wonder if this is the right spelling. (A delaying tactic. Yes, that is exactly what the words say, but probably is not what the child is wondering.)

3. You're not sure if it's spelled right, so you want me to tell you if it is. (Response attempts to convey understanding but misunderstands

the child's reason for asking. Also does not grant the child freedom.)

4. You would like me to tell you how to spell, but I know you can spell "school." (Reflects the child's obvious request, places emphasis on the therapist, and pressure on the child.)

5. I think you can decide how you want to spell "school." (Focus is on the therapist and what she thinks.)

6. Sounds like you would like me to tell you if that is right or wrong. In here you can spell that word any way you would like to. (First sentence indicates the therapist is not sure of the request, restates the obvious and makes the response too long.)

7. You want me to tell you if that's right, but in here that's something you can decide. (A much more facilitative response by using the word "decide;" conveys to the child that this is a place where he can make decisions. First part of response is really not needed.)

8. You can spell any way you like in this room. (Very specific, to the point, and grants the child freedom.)

The first few responses seem to disregard the fact that Robert won the spelling bee in his school and thus probably knows how to spell "school." Another consideration is that the way he has spelled "skool" is correct if he is thinking about the way he has seen the word spelled on some toys by the Play Skool company. An objective in play therapy is to grant children the opportunity to set their own direction. Children do not need the therapist to be their spelling teacher or their math teacher. Must things always be the way the therapist thinks they should be?

Directions: Jim, an eight-year-old boy in his second play therapy session, picks up two large throwing darts with rubber suction cups and asks, "What do you do with these?" Write the response you would make to Jim.

Response:

1. You would like for me to tell you how to use those darts. (Another delaying reflection that is inappropriate. The therapist should say at this point what he would say after this. The response also labels the items as darts and thus interferes with the child's creativity. He may have been wondering if they could be used for something else.)

2. Those are for throwing at the dart board or the wall but not at me or the mirror. (Response potentially structures and limits the child's activity, inhibits creativity. Therapist's anxiety results in premature limit setting. There is no indication the child was even thinking about throwing at the therapist or mirror.)

3. You would like me to tell you what to do with those. In here, you can decide. (Again, the first sentence is not facilitative. The second sentence is freeing and allows the child to be creative.)

4. You may do anything you want with those in here. (The therapist is trying to make a freeing response but this is not a true statement. There are limitations. The child cannot smash the therapist in the face with the darts.)

5. In here, they can be whatever you want them to be. (A response that allows the child to be creative and to experience making a decision. A variation on this response would be "That's something you can decide.")

The therapist's response should not bind the child to the therapist's world of reality. The child might want to pretend the darts are rocket ships, people, or bombs. They can be whatever he wants them to be to express himself at that moment.

Directions: Connie, seven years old, in her second play therapy session, walks into the playroom, looks around the room and asks, "Is this room really for me?" Write the response you would make to Connie.

Response:

1. You can use this room during the thirty minutes each Tuesday we meet. (Does not respond to the child's emphasis on self.)

2. Some other children come here to play just like you. But right now this room is for you. You can play with the toys in a lot of the ways you like. (Attempts to provide too much information and does not respond to the child's potential feelings.)

3. This room is for you to use during our time together. (Response focus is on activity and ignores the child's potential feelings.)

4. It's just kind of hard for you to believe this is all just for you. (Response shows understanding of the child's feelings.)

Facilitative responses touch on feelings whenever possible. In this way, the therapist shows understanding of the inner child and avoids answering questions that have not been asked. The focus is on what the child is trying to say rather than on what the child is asking.

Directions: Kathy, eight years old, in her second play therapy session, says, "Today is my birthday . . . but . . . my mother said . . . she said I been too mean to my little brother . . . so . . . she's not going to bake me a birthday cake. (Kathy looks very sad, tears begin to form in her eyes, her head drops, and she stares at the floor.) Write the response you would make to Kathy.

Response:

1. Oh, so you've been too mean for a birthday cake. I bet that makes you feel sad. (Response is really off-base. First sentence states the child has been mean when, in fact, the child said, "My mother said I been too mean." That's the mother's perception, not a fact. This is a grossly insensitive response. The attempt to touch the child's feelings places emphasis on the therapist with "I bet . . . ," and also conveys the therapist is unsure and, yet, the child is standing there crying!)

2. You feel sad and wish you could have a birthday cake from your mother. You're so worried that your mother doesn't love you anymore because you've been so mean to your little brother. (First sentence is appropriate. Second sentence is too interpretative. Response confirms the child has been mean when that fact is not known, and besides, that is not the issue. How the child feels at this moment is what is important.)

3. Sometimes it hurts when people don't do what we want them to do. (Does identify the hurt but generalization to "people" weakens the impact. The therapist is not a part of this happening and so use of "we" is inappropriate, does not focus on the child.)

4. You seem disappointed that your mother is not going to bake you a cake. (A gross understatement of the child's feelings, ignores the child's obvious tears and sadness.)

5. Sounds like you're pretty sad that your mom won't bake you a cake. Sounds like you're angry with her. (Inappropriate use of common counseling phrase "sounds like." No, the child doesn't sound like she is sad and hurting. She is experiencing and demonstrating sadness and hurt at that moment. There is no indication the child is angry. That is a projection by the therapist.)

6. You're sad that your mother isn't going to bake you a cake for your birthday because she thinks you have been too mean to your little brother. (Better, but still does not capture the feeling of the child. No need to stick in the part about being mean because that detracts from the main focus of the child's feelings.)

7. There's something really sad about a birthday and no birthday cake. You just feel like crying. (Short, shows understanding by touching child's feelings.)

Children do not need explanations or lengthy discourses about their experiences. The most important part of the relationship is what the child feels and experiences in the relationship. An interesting point to note is that only the last response gave recognition to the child's tears which were the most obvious part of the child's feelings. The absence of therapist verbal recognition of obvious feelings may be interpreted by the child to mean such feelings or expressions are not acceptable.

Returning Responsibility to Children

Children cannot discover and develop their inner resources and, in the process, experience the power of their potential unless opportunities to do so exist. Responsibility cannot be taught; responsibility can only be learned through experiencing. When we make decisions for children which deprive them of the opportunity for potential use of their own creativity, we interfere with the development of responsibility. Most child therapists would readily state the development of children's self-responsibility as one of their major objectives in therapy but, in reality, limit children's opportunities to assume responsibility by making decisions for children which foster dependence. This does not happen in some major catastrophic way but, rather, in little, almost imperceptible parts of the interaction with children by giving answers, making choices for children, helping when help is not needed, and leading children when they should be allowed to lead. The ease with which the therapist can create dependence is recognized by a therapist who wrote,

> There were other times that my responses slipped into my old ways of making children dependent. April asked if she could play with a baby doll, and before my brain had turned on, I realized I had answered "Sure." I must eliminate that word from my vocabulary. This session again reinforced the need for constant connectedness with the child. A split second can mean the difference between a therapeutic response and one that encourages dependence.

Therapeutically facilitative responses return responsibility to children thus helping children to feel in control and to become intrinsically motivated. The child-centered therapist believes in the child, is willing to allow the child to make decisions, and is committed to providing opportunities for self-direction by avoiding interfering with the process. What is being described here is an understanding of self and a deep, abiding attitude that becomes a way of being with children. A play therapist described this process as

> I am beginning to grasp in a very small way that giving responsibility isn't something one does verbally, although responsibility may be facilitated in that manner. I think giving responsibility must also have to do with freeing myself from responsibility. The session certainly would have been different if I had not been so concerned with putting Christina at ease and with things being done right. I mean, "Who am I? What makes me so special that I can 'fix it' for her? And to what end? Whose needs would that satisfy? Who does that make feel adequate?"

At the beginning of the first play therapy session, a child often wants the therapist to say what to do, what things are used for, and how to "undo" difficult things. The child may hold up a toy which he/she obviously knows the name for and ask, "What's this?" This is a moment when the therapist does not know for sure the motivation behind the question. To name the item may inhibit the child's creativity, structure the child's expression, or keep responsibility in the hands of the therapist. Responsibility could be returned to the child by responding *"That can be whatever you want it to be."* Similar responses, depending on the child's request, might be, *"You can decide"* or *"That's something you can do."* If the child needs help to complete a task he/she is not capable of completing without assistance, the therapist can respond, *"Show me what you want done"* or *"Tell me what to do to help you."* These responses allow a child to assume responsibility and to make a decision, and, typically, by the end of the session the child is stating what things are without asking for the therapist's decision. A therapist's critique described the process as

> Throughout the session, Angelina wanted to give everything a name in the playroom. For example, she held up a Barbie doll hairpiece and asked "What's this?" Then she repeated this question with a Barbie doll dress, a compact, and an empty container. She wanted me to give each item a name. I responded by stating, "That can be whatever you would like it to be," and "You can decide what that is for." Each time she readily made her own decision. The hairpiece was a crown, the compact was something you put paints into, the Barbie dress was a dancing dress, and the small container was a holder for Barbie's hair rollers. If I had answered *for* her, I would have fostered dependence, and she could not have discovered the answers for herself. This approach to returning responsibility seems to be a real self-esteem booster. By the end of the first session, Angelina asked very few questions and made very decisive statements and actions. Her independence was showing, and she seemed self-assured. I think this was a direct result of redirecting the responsibility to her instead of the focus being on me being the answer source.

When responsibility is returned to children, they will think of creative solutions that might never occur to the therapist. When five-year-old Bert asked the therapist, "What do you want me to fix you for lunch," the therapist responded, "In here you can decide what you would like to fix." Bert chose "smushed spider pie." Later Bert held up a plastic round bracelet and asked, "Hey, what is this?" The therapist responded, "That can be whatever you want it to be." Bert decided it was a handcuff.

Children will often answer many of their questions if the therapist simply will not be so quick to reply. A thoughtful *"Hmmmm"* by the therapist may be all that is needed. Four-year-old Zack picked up the airplane and asked, "Why does it have two doors?" The therapist responded, "Hmmmm . . ." and Zack promptly stated, "Because if children bought it, more people could get out. That's maybe it." Rachel sat down by the paints and made a comment about painting. The covers were on the paint canisters, and the therapist started to take the covers off but checked herself and waited. Rachel easily removed the covers. The therapist can so easily take responsibility away from the child. Responsibility also can be granted to nonverbal requests as in the following account:

> Since Samantha talked so little, I couldn't be sure when she was looking for direction or help. When she was sitting next to the dollhouse, walking the teddy bear around the house, she took a piece of furniture from the box and put the bear and the piece of furniture into the house. Then she took both items out and gave me a quick look. I said, "You can decide what goes in the dollhouse." Samantha then proceeded to pile all the furniture into the house.

Typical Nonfacilitative Responses

The following excerpts from play therapy sessions are examples of typical responses that are not facilitative. How the therapist responds, the words used, can make a significant difference in whether or not the child feels understood, accepted, or restricted. The suggested responses are just that, suggestions, and are not intended to imply that these are the only responses that should be made. The objective here is to help the reader to become aware of his/her own response patterns to children.

Missed feelings

Child: Do people come here lots? (excited voice, eagerness in face)

Therapist: Sometimes. (Child is not asking for an answer.)

Suggested: You really like coming here. (Need to respond to feelings indicated.)

Child: My puppy got killed, and I cried.

Therapist: I'm sorry your puppy got killed. (Therapist focus is on his own reaction, ignores child's feelings, does not allow child to explore her feelings further.)

Suggested: You were so sad about your puppy dying. You just felt like crying. (Touches feelings and shows understanding.)

Child: (Therapist had just explained that the cassette tape recording was for her and the child to hear and no one else.) I know what you're gonna' do! You're gonna' give it to my mother!

Therapist: The tape will not go to your mother. It's just for me to hear, and I'll let you hear it if you want to. After that I will erase it. (Therapist is a bit defensive. Child needs to know he/she has been understood.)

Suggested: I know you're really concerned. You don't want your mother to hear the tape. It is just for you and me to hear and no one else. (Recognizes feeling and reassures confidentiality.)

Child: (What he is working on keeps coming apart.) No, it's not working right! (Sounds angry)

Therapist: Does that make you feel mad? (Therapist asks a question for which the answer is already known, and thus sounds like the therapist doesn't understand the child's feeling.)

Child: Yeah! What do you think it does! (Child doesn't feel understood and is justifiably angry at the therapist.)

Suggested: Just makes you angry when you can't make that stay fixed. (Recognizes feeling)

Child: My dog died, and we buried him right in our backyard. It was amazing! He died right by his old doghouse. (No observable affect about dog's death.)

Therapist: He died right by his old doghouse, and you buried him in the back yard? (Simple reflection of words and voice tone at end turns statement into question of what child has just said.)

Suggested: That was really surprising that he died right by his doghouse. (Shows understanding of feeling.)

Labeling Objects Ahead Of Child

Child: Vrrooom. Vrrooom. (Pushing block along on floor.)

Therapist: You are having fun with the car. (Child has not identified block as a car. Therapist projects an assumption.)

Child: That's not a car. That's a boat.

Suggested: That's sure making lots of noise. (Avoids labeling block and says "I'm with you.")

Child: (Places alligator puppet on her hand.)

Therapist: Now you have the alligator. (Child has not identified puppet. By naming the puppet, the therapist limits child's creativity and structures possible play activity.)

Suggested: Now you have put that one on. (Allows child to continue to lead and identify the puppet.)

Child: (Had been examining the spaceship but did not identify it. Then he picked up two male figures from the doll family on the table.)

Therapist: Looks like you picked out two things to go in your spaceship. (Therapist takes the lead and labels the spaceship. Child had not indicated what he intended to do with the two male figures, directs child's play.)

Suggested: Looks like you have something in mind for those. (Communicates involvement in what child is doing and allows child freedom to continue to direct his own play.)

Child: (Uses crayons and draws a picture of a cat.) This is my kitty. (Draws legs and puts several points on end of each leg.)

Therapist: I see you are putting toe nails on the kitten. (Child had not identified them as such; so therapist is leading.)

Child: No. (Proceeds to color over the cat. Child had been drawing toes on the cat, not toe nails. Child felt she had done something wrong.)

Suggested: Now you're putting some of those on your kitty right there. (Response conveys therapist is noticing what child is doing, conveys interest, allows child to identify what she is drawing.)

Evaluation And Praise

Child: (Child finds a comb, and combs the hair of two dolls.)

Therapist: You're making them so pretty. (Since children want to please, child may continue the activity to get more praise.)

Suggested: You know just how to comb their hair. (Reflects child's ability rather than making a judgement as to how the results turn out.)

Child: Maybe I'll paint after I finish this.

Therapist: That sounds like a good idea. (Child may now think painting is what the therapist wants him to do. Child is no longer free to change his mind.)

Suggested: You're thinking you might like to paint next. (Shows understanding. Child is free to decide.)

Child: I made an airplane. (She then flies the airplane around the room.)

Therapist: Oh, you made an airplane! That's a nice looking airplane. (Therapist excitement exceeds child's level of feeling. Value judgement.)

Suggested: And you can make it fly around. (Avoids simple word reflection and gives child credit.)

Child: (Pretends to cook eggs, gives all to therapist on a plate.) How do they taste?

Therapist: These eggs sure do taste good! (Evaluates and encourages external motivation.)

Suggested:	You worked hard cooking these eggs just for me. (Recognizes effort, encourages internal motivation.)

Inappropriate Questions

Child:	Me and Courtney played house and (goes into long discourse about activities, keeps mentioning Courtney.)
Therapist:	Is Courtney one of your friends? (Question meets therapist's need. Whether or not Courtney is a friend is irrelevant.)
Suggested:	Sounds like you and Courtney did lots of things together. (Shows understanding of content, and keeps focus on child.)

Child:	(Routinely hits on Bobo but with some vigor. No affect observable.)
Therapist:	How does it make you feel to hit Bobo? (Inappropriate because no affect is observable. Implies to child she should be feeling something.)
Suggested:	(A response is not needed to everything a child does in the playroom.)

Child:	(Tells about his baseball team and excitedly says) I know we're going to win this afternoon!
Therapist:	Do you like to win? (Asks question for which answer is obvious. Conveys lack of understanding.)
Suggested:	You really have fun winning. (Shows understanding)

Child: (Child finds a small container.) Where's the stuff that goes in here? (Then places Barbie's shoes into the container.)

Therapist: Do you think those go in there? (Questions child's decision, causes child to doubt self, does not communicate understanding.)

Suggested: You decided those go in there. (Gives child credit for making a decision.)

Statements Turned Into Questions

Child: The lightning's scary.

Therapist: The lightening is a little scary? (Use of word "little" underplays child's feeling, and question at end conveys therapist does not understand child's feeling and has to check.)

Suggested: It scares you when there's lightning. (Communicates understanding of feeling.)

Child: I'm going to cook supper now.

Therapist: You've decided it's supper time? (Questions imply lack of understanding.)

Suggested: You've decided it's supper time. (Avoiding voice inflection at end turning statement into question communicates understanding and gives child credit for making a decision.)

Child: I like puppet shows! Do you like puppet shows?

Therapist: You like playing with all the puppets? (Voice tone at end of statement turns statement into question and calls for yes or no answer.)

Suggested: You have fun with puppet shows.

Child: (Playing with several toys.)

Therapist: Wesley, we have five more minutes in the playroom, okay? (Last word implies child has a choice when no choice is intended.)

Suggested: (Same response, just take out last word.)

Tentativeness In Limit Setting

Child: (Starting to leave the room with thirty minutes left in session.)

Therapist: Let's stay in here for the rest of the time rather than going in and out, okay? (Therapist sounds unsure and asks for child's agreement.)

Suggested: Jason, our time in the playroom is not up for today. We have thirty more minutes, and then you can leave. (Sets a definite limit and indicates when the child will get to leave.)

Child: I want to go out there. (points to the offices)

Therapist: Let's wait a little longer before we leave. (Attempts to coax child into staying, hoping child will forget she wants to leave.)

Suggested: You want to go out where the other people are, but our time in the playroom is not finished for ten more minutes and then you can go out there. (Shows understanding of what child wants, sets a firm limit, and communicates what can be done later.)

Child: Can I put water in here? (gun)

Therapist: You would like to put water in there, but we won't do that now. (Does not set a definite limit, indicates there is the possibility of putting water in the gun later. Inclusion of "we" implies therapist will assist in putting water in the gun.)

Suggested: You would like to put water in that, but that's not for putting water into. The pan is for putting water in. (Acknowledges child's want, sets a firm limit, and communicates an acceptable alternative.)

Child: I think I'll throw this truck right through that window.

Therapist: Could you maybe do something else with it? (Implies that original plan is acceptable if child can't think of anything else.)

Suggested: You would like to throw that truck, but it's not for throwing. The truck is for playing with on the floor. (Recognizes the child's want, sets a firm limit, and states an acceptable use of the truck.)

Leading The Child

Child: (Uses plastic knife to scrape paint off jar lid. Works hard to scrape paint off.)

Therapist: Even though things are hard, you don't give up. (Child will now have great difficulty in stopping, even if some of the paint is hard to get off, because she may fear the therapist will think she is giving up and will be disappointed in her.)

Suggested: You're working hard to get that off. (Acknowledges child's effort.)

Child: This house is for you. What color do you want it to be?

Therapist: I like houses made out of red brick. (Child's focus will now be on trying to please the therapist. Child may think he is supposed to draw a whole house covered with individual bricks and spend an excessive amount of time drawing hundreds of individual bricks. What will happen if the child has difficulty drawing bricks?)

Suggested: A special house for me. You can choose what color you want it to be. (Allows child to make the decision and to lead, keeps focus on the child. Total design of the house can be the responsibility of the child.)

Child: (Plays in the kitchen area with the baby and the pots and pans. She picks up the coffee pot.)

Therapist: Are you going to have some coffee? (Therapist inserts his own reality and interferes with child's creativity and direction. What if the child was planning something else? Could child be about to pour orange juice or a glass of milk for baby?)

Suggested: Now you're going to use that. (Shows attentiveness of therapist and allows child to continue to lead.)

Child: What can I make for us to eat?

Therapist: Oh, there are lots of different things you could make. (Implies therapist knows what child could make and will result in child waiting for therapist to tell.)

Suggested: You can decide. (Grants child freedom and allows child to assume responsibility for deciding.)

This new language of empathic responding requires effort and commitment on the part of the therapist and a sincere desire to understand and to be fully with a child in nonobtrusive ways that sufficiently allow the child the freedom to be completely the person he/she is at that moment.

Chapter **11**

THERAPEUTIC
LIMIT SETTING

Limit setting is one of the most important aspects of play therapy and is also the most problematic for most therapists. Limits provide structure for the development of the therapeutic relationship and help to make the experience a real life relationship. Without limits a relationship would have little value. The fact that the therapist struggles with setting limits speaks loudly of the therapist's valuing of self, the child, and the relationship. Emotional and social growth is not very likely to occur in disorganized, chaotic relationships, and according to Moustakas (1959), no therapy can occur without limits. Limit setting seems to be the single most difficult area for play therapists. The inexperienced therapist often feels insecure and is slow to apply limits. Sometimes the therapist is reluctant because of a desire to be liked by the child.

Basic Guidelines in Limit Setting

Permissiveness in the child-centered play therapy approach does not mean the acceptance of all behaviors. Therapy is a learning experience, and limits provide children with an opportunity to learn self control, that they have choices, what making choices feels like, and how responsibility feels. Therefore, when limits should be set and are not, children are deprived of an opportunity to learn something important about themselves. In therapeutic limit setting, children are given the opportunity to choose. They, therefore, become responsible for themselves and their own well-being.

The therapist's belief that children will choose positive cooperative behavior is a significant and impactful variable in the therapeutic process. Children are more likely to comply when they experience respect for themselves and acceptance for their feelings and behaviors . . . both positive and negative. Therefore, the therapist will be most helpful by focusing on the child's unexpressed need for defiance, for example, while continuing to express fundamental understanding, support, valuing of the child, and a genuine belief in the child.

Limits in the playroom should be minimal and enforceable. Children cannot learn about themselves and cannot adequately express themselves in the face of a multitude of limits. Unenforceable limits do great harm to the therapeutic relationship by interfering with the development of trust.

In most cases, the establishment of total limits rather than conditional limits seems to work best. Total limits are less confusing to children and help the therapist to feel more secure. "You may pinch me, but you may not hurt me" leaves the issue wide open as to how much pinching is hurtful. "You may put a little water in the sand" would likewise not be acceptable. How does a child know what is expected if the therapist says, "You probably shouldn't smear so much glue on the Bobo." A total limit would be *"I'm not for pinching."* The child now knows exactly what is not permissible. Conditional limits, "You can't kick the door hard," can become the basis for arguments. What the therapist thinks is hard may not be perceived by the child as hard, and so the child may attempt to convince the therapist. The therapist should never engage in an argument with a child. The best procedure is to just restate the original limit or issue and then reflect the child's feelings or desire. "You would like to convince me that you didn't shoot the mirror, but the mirror is not for shooting."

Limits should be stated in a calm, patient, matter-of-fact, and firm way. Limits that are rushed or stated quickly reveal the therapist's anxiety and lack of trust in the child. If the therapist's attitude really is one of trust and a belief that the child will respond responsibly, then the therapist will respond accordingly with calmness. The fact of the matter is that if a child is standing ten feet away from the therapist threatening to shoot the theapist with the dart gun, the therapist cannot move fast enough to get across the room and stop the child before the trigger is pulled. Therefore, the therapist may as well sit there with calmness and trust that if she responds appropriately, the child will respond responsibly. If the therapist were to jump out of her chair and attempt to grab the gun, her behavior would communicate a message of "I don't trust you." The child is then left to carry out the original intent because "She really expects me to." Such moments of intense interaction can be anxiety provoking for the therapist and quickly reveal deeper attitudes, beliefs, and motivation. Inexperienced play therapists should not be discouraged, though, if they experience some anxiety or perhaps even a bit of rejection of the child who persists in pushing the limit, threatening or verging on actually breaking the limit. There is only one way the therapist can learn that children really can be trusted in such situations and that is to "weather the storm" and in the process discover children really can and will control their behavior if responded to appropriately. For this reason, supervised experience is a must in helping therapists to process their own deeper levels of feelings and attitudes.

In therapeutic limit setting, *the focus and emphasis is always on the child in order to clearly convey where the responsibility lies.* A response such as "In here we don't take our pants off" is inappropriate because the therapist has not the least inclination to undress. Yet the use of "we" and "our" implies the therapist is a part of the process. *Children should be allowed to be separate.* The response "In here we don't throw paint on the floor" does not focus on the child and so dilutes the impact of the limit. The therapist's inclusion of self in such responses is probably a function of cultural response habits but also may reveal a need and attitude of which the therapist is unaware.

When to Present Limits

A common question among play therapists is when to set limits. Should limits be set as a part of the general introduction to the playroom at the beginning of the first session, or should the therapist wait until the occasion calls for the setting of limits? Providing a long list of limits at the beginning of the first session is not necessary. This tends to set a negative tone and interferes with the therapeutic objective of establishing a climate of freedom and permissiveness. In play therapy, the therapist is always concerned with the attitude that is being projected about the child and the relationship.

For some children, a listing of limits only serves to give them ideas. For shy and fearful children, the early introduction of limits only serves to inhibit them more. Some children never need limits set on their behavior. Since play therapy is a learning experience for children, the best time to learn is when the limit issue arises.

RULE OF THUMB:

Limits are not needed until they are needed.

Self-control cannot be learned until an opportunity to exercise self-control occurs. Therefore, a limitation on the child leaving the playroom is unnecessary until the child starts to leave the playroom. At that moment, responding with *"I know you want to leave the playroom, but* (therapist glances at watch) *we have twenty more minutes in the playroom, and then it will be time to leave,"* allows the child to struggle with the responsibility of following or not following the limit. In this case, the therapist uses "we" to emphasize the relationship.

Rationale for Therapeutic Limits

Therapeutic limit setting is based on sound principles and a well thought out formulation of general areas where intervention through limit setting will probably be needed. Limit setting should not occur at the sporadic insecure whims of the therapist. **Limits are to be based on clear and definable criteria supported by clearly thought out rationale with the furtherance of the therapeutic relationship in mind.** Limits are not set simply for the sake of limiting behavior. Limits are applied because they are recognized as facilitating the attainment of accepted psychological principles of growth.

Although it may seem strange to say so and even more difficult to appreciate in the midst of confrontation by an aggressive, angry child, the child's desire to break the limit has greater therapeutic significance than the exhibited behavior. For here we are dealing with intrinsic variables related to motivation, perception of self, independence, need for acceptance, and the working out of a relationship with a significant person. Although the behavior being expressed is really secondary, the child's behavior too often captivates the unskilled therapist's attention and energy in an attempt to stop it. *All feelings, desires, and wishes of the child are accepted but not all behaviors.* Destructive behaviors cannot be accepted, but the child can be granted permission to express a personal self symbolically without fear of reprimand or rejection. The rationale for therapeutic limits is contained in the following seven statements and accompanying discussions.

1. Limits help assure the physical and emotional security of children. Although the atmosphere in the playroom is conducive to a greater feeling of permissiveness than usually exists in a child's relationships outside the playroom, basic common-sense health and safety limits prevail in the playroom. A child may not shoot a pencil in the dart gun because of the sharp point, drink water from a rusty can, use the hammer in a manner that would be potentially harmful, such as striking the block of wood violently with the claw side of the hammer which can act as a spring sending the hammer back into the face of the child, or cut himself with the scissors. A session in which the therapist is on edge because the child is engaging in potentially harmful activities would seem to have very little therapeutic value. A child should never be allowed to stick objects in electrical wall outlets. As a precaution outlets should be covered.

At times the child may need to be protected from potential guilt as in the case when a child is allowed to hit the therapist or smash the therapist over the head with a toy. The child may later worry about what was done to the therapist and become quite anxious, fearing the therapist was hurt or that the therapist wouldn't like the child anymore. Similar feelings and reactions can result if the child is allowed to paint the therapist's face, pour paint on the therapist clothes, or shoot the therapist with the dart gun. A child should not be allowed to hit, kick, scratch or bite the therapist. An emotionally disturbed child may often not be able to perceive the extent or result of behavior suddenly acted out on another person and may later feel guilty for what was done. An important point to realize is that the child is not to leave the playroom feeling anxiety about actions. Although a child may express a desire to hit the therapist, paint on the walls, or break equipment, such behaviors are limited in order to prevent accompanying feelings of guilt or anxiety. In responding to situations described here, the therapist always maintains an accepting attitude of the child's feelings and desires.

The growth potential in children cannot be maximized in settings where children feel insecure. When no boundaries, and no limitations on behavior exist, children feel insecure and usually experience anxiety in such situations. Limits provide a structure to the environment and the relationship in which children can feel secure. Some children have difficulty controlling their own impulsiveness and so need the security of experiencing limit setting which provides them with an opportunity to gain control of their own behavior. Limits, therefore, help to assure the emotional security of children. When children discover where the boundaries are in the play therapy relationship and experience those boundaries being adhered to consistently, they feel secure because there is predictability in the relationship and setting.

2. Limits protect the physical well being of the therapist and facilitate acceptance of the child. The therapist's physical safety as well as emotional and physical comfort are important dimensions in the therapeutic process. A therapist who is being bombarded with blocks of wood thrown by a child from across the room will experience great difficulty trying to focus on understanding the underlying reason for the attack, or what the child is feeling at the moment. The therapist who can sit through sand being poured over her head or watch patiently as the child cuts tassels off her new shoes and still concentrate on the needs of the child is rare. Physical comfort and safety are basic needs for everyone and will be attended to by the individual either consciously or unconsciously. Therapist self-awareness is essential to the appropriate handling and resolution of this issue.

The inherent growth potential in children is facilitated by the therapist's acceptance and warm caring, and it is limit setting which allows the therapist to remain empathic and accepting of the child throughout the therapy process. For the therapist to maintain a warm, caring, accepting attitude toward a child who is hitting the therapist on the knee with a hammer is virtually impossible. In this situation, the therapist will very likely experience feelings of resentment and rejection which will in turn be communicated to the child at some level. A child should not be allowed to pull the therapist's hair, throw sand on the therapist, paint the therapist's shoes or hit the therapist in any way. ***Any form of direct aggressive physical acting out or attack on the therapist should be prohibited.*** Such behaviors are not to be tolerated under any circumstances because they will interfere with the therapist's empathic acceptance, respect for the child, and objectivity in relating to the child.

Play therapist's are not some kind of superperson. They are subject to experiencing normal, sometimes uncontrollable, emotional reactions and once reactions of anger or rejection have been experienced, they will be sensed by the child. Therefore, appropriate timing in setting limits is crucial to maintaining an attitude of acceptance and positive regard for the child. Activities which are likely to arouse feelings of anger or anxiety in the therapist should generally be limited. However, some therapists experience anxiety and anger over what would be described as minor messiness by the child, and in such cases, it is strongly recommended that therapists carefully examine their own motivation. Are the limits being set to facilitate the therapeutic relationship or to accommodate the therapist's rigid code of neatness?

3. Limits facilitate the development of decision making, self-control and self-responsibility of children. One of the things children learn in play therapy is that their feelings, whether positive or negative, are accepted. Therefore, rejection or denial of one's feelings is not necessary. In the playroom, acceptable ways are available for the expression of all feelings. *Before children can resist following through and expressing feelings in ways dictated by first impulses, they must have an awareness of their behavior, a feeling of responsibility, and exercise self-control.* In the midst of experiencing the welling up of intense emotion, children are often unaware of their behavior and so are equally devoid of feelings of responsibility. Limit setting addresses the immediate reality of the situation and indirectly calls attention to the child's behavior through statements such as *"The wall is not for painting on."* How can children develop a feeling of responsibility if they are unaware of what they are doing? And how can they experience a feeling of self-control if they are too defensive to change their behavior? Therapeutic limit setting does not stir up feelings of defensiveness which often accompany attempts to stop a behavior because the child's behavior is not the focus. What is focused on are the child's feelings or desires and the recipient or object of the behavior. This can be seen clearly in the statement *"You would like to paint on the wall, but the wall is not for painting,"* as opposed to "Don't paint on that wall."

The child's need to paint on the wall, to be messy, to break the limit is accepted and communicated to the child in very specific and concrete ways by providing acceptable alternatives, *"The paper on the easel is for painting."* No attempt is made to stop the expression of the feeling or the need. Such a statement clearly indicates to the child a permissible way to express self. Now the child is confronted with a choice, to act on the original impulse or to express self through the alternative behavior. The choice is the child's and the therapist allows the child to choose. *The decision is the child's and responsibility accompanies decision making.* If the child chooses to paint on the easel paper, it will be because the child decided to and exercised self-control, not because the therapist made the child.

4. Limits anchor the session to reality and emphasize the here and now. Some children become caught up in fantasy play in the playroom and could spend the entire time absorbed in the enactment of fantasy scenes thus effectively avoiding any personal responsibility for actions or behaviors which may be socially unacceptable or destructive. When the therapist verbalizes a limit, the experience is quickly changed from fantasy to the reality of a relationship with an adult where certain behaviors are unacceptable as is true in the world outside the playroom except that in the playroom substantially fewer limitations are established on behavior. When the therapist interjects *"You would really like to dump that paint on the floor, but the paint is not for pouring on the floor. The sink is for pouring paint into,"* the child is confronted with the reality of having crossed an unacceptable boundary, has been presented the opportunity to choose what will be done next and experiences the accompanying responsibility. The child can no longer live in the enactment of fantasy because the therapist refuses to be ignored once the limit is set. The child must now focus on the reality of making a decision in relation to the playroom and the therapist.

Limits, then, assure the play therapy experience will have a real life quality. The therapeutic experience should not be so unlike life outside the playroom that no transfer of experiences and learning will occur. *Limits exist in every relationship that has any significance. A relationship without any limits surely would have little value to the participants.* When the therapist states a limit to protect self from harm, the therapist's personhood and respect for self are declared. At that moment, the experience with the child truly becomes a living relationship anchored in the dynamics of the process of the reality of the moment.

5. Limits promote consistency in the playroom environment. Children often come from homes and classroom settings characterized by inconsistency in behavior on the part of adults who have difficulty maintaining rules. What was prohibited today may or may not be prohibited tomorrow. What was allowed today may or may not be allowed tomorrow. An accepting attitude on the part of the adult this morning may or may not be evident this afternoon. Consequently, children in such environments are never quite sure just what to expect and often attempt to cope accordingly by being very cautious or by overtly acting out in an attempt to find out just where the boundaries are. Children need to experience consistency in their lives if they are ever to achieve some degree of emotional balance. Consistency of attitude and behavior on the part of the therapist helps children to feel secure, and this inner security enables children to move toward being the person they are capable of being.

One of the ways the play therapist establishes a consistent environment is through the introduction and use of consistent limits. Limits are presented in a consistently nonthreatening manner, and the therapist is consistent in seeing that the limits are adhered to—not in a rigid manner, but in a consistent manner. Rigid could perhaps imply punishment and the absence of an understanding and accepting attitude. On the other hand, understanding and acceptance does not imply license, unwillingness to follow through, or a "wishy-washy" anything goes attitude. The therapist can be patiently understanding and accepting of the child's wish or desire and still not accept the behavior. **Limits, therefore, help to provide the structure for a consistent environment.** What was prohibited last session is prohibited in this session, and what was allowed in the last session is allowed in this session. Thus, the sessions have predictability. Without consistency there can be no predictability and without predictability there can be no security. Consistent limits unwaveringly enforced help to make the play therapy relationship predictable and thus increase the child's feeling of security. Consistency in limit setting is a function of the therapist's attitude and is a tangible demonstration of the therapist's commitment to the welfare and acceptance of the child. Consistent limit setting is a concrete manifestation of the therapist's willingness to put energy into the relationship with the child. By being consistent in such a tangible way, the therapist assures the child of the realness of the therapist's feelings and attitudes in other less tangible areas such as acceptance.

6. Limits preserve the professional, ethical, and socially acceptable relationship. The very nature of the play therapy setting and age of the clientele are potentially more likely to result in uninhibited or acting out behaviors than other therapeutic settings. Although it is almost unheard of for an adult or adolescent to want to take their clothes off in the therapist's office, fondle the therapist, or urinate on the floor, such behaviors may not be uncommon in the playroom. The nature of the freedom, permissiveness, and structure of the playroom is more conducive to these behaviors than is the typical office. Sometimes a logical sequence to these behaviors occurs. First the child takes shoes and socks off to get into the sandbox, and later the child takes the rest of his/her clothes off to play in the sandbox, or to pretend to be a baby. Allowing a child to remove shoes and socks to play in the sandbox is appropriate. After all, this is a common practice on the school ground, in the park, and at the beach. Taking trousers and underwear off is neither common or socially acceptable at these same places, and is unacceptable in the play therapy experience. Urinating on the floor is also socially unacceptable and should be responded to with firm, consistent limit setting.

Some sexually abused children may attempt to act out on the therapist sexual or erotic behaviors they have been taught by perpetrating adults because the children feel safe in the playroom and/or in their attempt to perhaps unconsciously communicate to the therapist what they have experienced in their life. *The child should not be allowed to fondle the therapist or engage in other seductive behaviors.* Limits should be set on such behaviors. Any form of sexual contact between the therapist and the child is inappropriate, unprofessional, unethical and a violation of laws. As with many other acting out behaviors, therapeutic limit setting enables the child to express the behavior and accompanying feelings symbolically and allows the therapist to be an objective but involved participant, thus preserving the professional and ethical therapeutic relationship. These same limitations would apply to the group play therapy experience. Children should not be allowed to engage in these behaviors with each other.

7. Limits protect the play therapy materials and room. Most play therapy programs are not blessed with unlimited budgets for keeping the playroom supplied with toys and materials. Allowing random destruction of toys could become an expensive process and at the same time would not be helpful to the emotional growth of the child. Most play therapists probably cannot afford to frequently replace the triple thick, heavy gauge vinyl, canvas enclosed Bobo punching toy which costs over $100.00. Therefore, *"Bobo is for hitting, not stabbing with the scissors."* Although it might be great fun for the child to jump on the wood dollhouse and smash it to pieces, it would probably not be repairable and should be protected with, *"The dollhouse is not for jumping on."* Less expensive items also are not for breaking or smashing. Likewise, the room is not for destroying. The child is not allowed to knock holes in the wall or floor with the hammer. For that matter, the wall is not even for tapping gently with the hammer because that can lead to harder whacks, and who is to decide what is gentle and what is hard and should be limited? These are opportunities for limit setting and thus opportunities for the child to learn something valuable. The playroom is not a place of limitless freedom where the child can do anything. There are limits and they are a part of the therapeutic process.

Every playroom should have some inexpensive items that are for smashing, breaking, or throwing. Egg cartons seem to fit this purpose quite well. They can be stacked and kicked over, jumped on and smashed, broken apart, thrown, and painted. Clay or Play Doh can be suggested as an acceptable substitute for smashing or throwing on the floor. Play Doh also can be pinched into pieces as a way to express anger or frustration. Popcicle sticks can be snapped in two or poked into the clay with vigor.

Procedures in Therapeutic Limit Setting

The process of setting limits is a carefully thought out procedure designed to convey understanding, acceptance, and responsibility to the child. The objective of the therapist is not to stop the behavior but rather to facilitate the expression of the motivating feeling, want, or need in a more acceptable manner. *The play therapist is a facilitator of expression rather than a prohibitor of action.* Therefore, the objective is to facilitate the child's expression through actions and behaviors which are more socially acceptable. As will quickly be recognized, however, some actions in the playroom must be limited. The attitude and objective of the therapist at these times will largely determine the impact of the therapist's approach to limit setting. If the therapist is determined to stop the objectionable behavior, the approach to limit setting very likely will be a demanding statement such as, "Don't you do that." The child will then feel rejected or that the therapist does not understand. If the therapist lacks confidence and is unsure of the procedure, that too will be conveyed in statements such as, "I don't think you should do that." The child may then either feel insecure or continue the behavior because there is no good reason not to. Many practicing play therapist's will readily recognize that children persisted in the behavior the therapist sought to limit because the therapist's uncertainty or insecurity was communicated to the child. When confronted with a demanding or authoritarian attitude and approach, "I've told you before you can't do that," children seem to feel they must protect themselves by persisting in their original behavior. In such instances, to change would almost be a loss of self. The result then is likely to be a power struggle.

Rather than attempting to stop behaviors, the therapist's objective is to respond to the child in such a way that the child is left with the responsibility for changing his/her behavior. If the therapist tells the child what to do, then the therapist is responsible. When the therapist trusts the child's capacity to respond responsibly and communicates *The mirror is not for throwing at. The door is for throwing at,"* the child is then free to decide what to do next and is thus responsible.

The play therapist is encouraged to carefully examine his/her attitude and intent when faced with the need to set limits and to give thoughtful consideration to how best to communicate the actual limit. A different message is obviously communicated in each of the following statements to a child who is about to paint the wall.

"It's probably not a good idea to paint the wall."

"We can't paint walls in here."

"You shouldn't paint the wall."

"You can't paint the wall."

"I can't let you paint the wall."

"Maybe you could paint something else other than the wall."

"The rule is you can't paint the wall."

"The wall is not for painting on."

Steps in the Therapeutic Limit Setting Process

Several specific steps may be used in the therapeutic limit setting process. They are implemented to facilitate the process of communicating understanding and acceptance of the child's motives, to make the limit clear, and to provide acceptable alternative actions and behaviors.

STEP 1: Acknowledge the child's feelings, wishes, and wants. Verbalizing understanding of the child's feeling or want conveys acceptance of the child's motivation. This is an important step because it recognizes the fact that the child does have feelings that are being expressed in the play activity, and that these feelings are acceptable. Simply setting the limit without acknowledging the feelings might indicate to the child that emotions are not important. Verbalizing an empathic understanding of the feeling often helps to defuse the intensity of the feeling. This is especially true in the case of anger and is often all that is needed for the child to begin modifying personal behavior. Acceptance of the motivation seems to be satisfying to the child, and a need for the act no longer exits. *Feelings should be reflected just as soon as they are recognized.* Once the block of wood is in flight across the room, acceptance of the feeling can no longer be a deterrent.

STEP 2: Communicate the limit. Limits should be specific and should clearly delineate exactly what is being limited. No doubt should exist in the child's mind as to what is appropriate and what is inappropriate, or what is acceptable and what is unacceptable. Limits that are "fuzzy" or unclear interfere with the child's ability to accept responsibility and to act responsibly. Therefore, a therapist's statement, "You can't put very much paint on the wall," would be inappropriate. Such a statement is not explicit and is certainly unclear, especially to children who perceive themselves as always doing only a "little bit" of anything.

The therapist may not always be able to follow these steps in sequence. The urgency of the situation, the child is about to throw the hammer at the window, may necessitate stating the limit first *"The window is not for hitting with the hammer,"* and then reflect *"You want to throw the hammer at the window."* In this example, no feelings are evident, so the child's desire is reflected.

STEP 3: Target acceptable alternatives. The child may not be aware of any other way to express what is being felt. At that moment, the child can only think of one way to express self. At this step in the process of limit setting, the therapist provides alternatives to the child for the expression of the original action. This can involve pointing out a variety of different alternatives to the child. A more durable or appropriate object may need to be selected for the expression. *"The dollhouse is not for standing on. You may choose to stand on the chair or the table."* A different surface may be needed to paint on, *"The wall is not for painting on. You may choose to paint on the easel paper or the block of wood."* A substitute may need to be selected to replace the therapist as the recipient of aggressive behavior, *"Ellen, I'm not for hitting. The Bobo is for hitting."* A nonverbal cue, pointing toward the alternative(s), in conjunction with the verbalized alternatives is especially helpful in diverting the child's attention from the original source of focus and facilitating the process of choice making. Using the child's name helps to get the child's attention.

When limit setting is needed, the therapist can remember to **ACT** in instituting the steps in the process sequence.

A—Acknowledge the child's feelings, wishes, and wants.
C—Communicate the limit.
T—Target acceptable alternatives.

The following interaction shows how the steps are applied when six-year-old Robert is just as angry as he can be at the play therapist, picks up the dart gun and glares at the therapist as he begins to load the dart gun.

Therapist: Robert, I can see you are really angry at me.

Robert: Yes! And I'm going to shoot you good!

Therapist: You are just so angry at me you would like to shoot me. (Robert now has the gun loaded and begins to take aim at the therapist.) But I'm not for shooting. (Robert interrupts before the therapist can go on with the limit.)

Robert: You can't stop me. Nobody can! (points the gun at the therapist).

Therapist: You're so powerful no one can stop you. But I'm not for shooting. You may pretend the Bobo is me (therapist points toward the Bobo) and shoot the Bobo.

Robert: (swings the gun around, takes aim at the Bobo and yells) Take that! (as he shoots Bobo).

The important consideration here is that the feeling is expressed and the child has assumed responsibility for both feelings and controlling behavior. This is a significant step in the therapeutic process of learning self-control, self-direction, and that feelings are acceptable.

When Limits Are Broken

A broken limit can mean anything from mild testing behavior to a battle of wills. Breaking limits is often a cry for help from a child with low self esteem who really does want the security of knowing definite boundaries do exist. Therefore, at this time, perhaps more so than at any other time, the child needs understanding and acceptance. The therapist should stay right with the child with reflection of feelings and desires while stating with firmness the established limit. Debates and lengthy explanations should be avoided. Threatening the child with what may happen if a limit is broken is never acceptable. Limits are never used as a way to punish a child. This is a time for exercising patience, calmness and firmness. Even though the limit has been broken, the therapist is still accepting of the child.

When a child persists in expressing or pursuing the original behavior and continues to break an established limit, verbalizing an additional step to the limit setting sequence may be necessary. Before explaining this step, a caution is in order. Too often therapists become overly involved in trying to force the acceptance of the limit and move much too quickly to implement this final step. *Patience is the rule of the day.* In most instances, the first three steps should be gone through in sequence at least two or three times before verbalizing the final step. This final step should rarely be used.

STEP 4: State final choice. At this point, an ultimate or final choice is presented to the child. The therapist either indicates the item will be placed off limits for the rest of the session or presents leaving the room as the ultimate choice. This step must be carefully stated so the child clearly understands he/she has a choice and that whatever happens will be the result of his/her choice. *"If you choose to shoot me again, you choose (not to play with the gun anymore today) (to leave the playroom)."* Limits presented in this manner are neither punishment nor rejection of the child. If the child shoots the therapist one more time, the child has clearly indicated by action the choice to leave the playroom or to stop playing with the gun, depending on which choice was presented. In this process, leaving the playroom or having the gun removed is not the therapist's choice. Therefore, the child is not rejected.

Children need to realize they have a choice and that consequences are related to their behavior. Therefore, once this final choice has been presented, and the child has indicated the choice by his/her behavior (either stops shooting or shoots one more time), the therapist must follow through and see that the child's choice is carried out. Guerney (1983) pointed out that limits and consequences should be as predictable and consistent as a brick wall. Therefore, if the child chooses to break the limit again, the therapist stands up and says, *"I see you have chosen to leave the playroom for today."*

The therapist's selection of which final condition to present will depend on the situation, the child, and the therapist's tolerance. Leaving the playroom should not be presented as a choice to a child who is manipulative and already wants to leave.

Other considerations are that every possible effort should be made to protect the child and therapist from harm or to keep valuable property from being broken. The therapist would not stay seated and go through the limit setting steps two or three times while the child banged on the observation mirror with the hammer. The shattered glass could severely injure the child. On the other hand, the therapist could tolerate being shot with the vinyl dart while going through the limit setting sequence two or three times in order to give the child an opportunity to assume responsibility for self and to limit his/her own behavior. Assumption of responsibility for self is a major objective and the opportunity to exercise that responsibility may be more important than the therapist being shot one more time with a dart, but is not more important than the possibility of personal injury.

Situational Limits

Taking Toys or Materials from the Playroom. This experience can really tug at the therapist's emotions when a child begs ever so pitifully "Can I please just take this little car home to play with. I don't have any cars to play with, and this is my most special one." The therapist's first reaction may be "Sure, why not? There are lots of other toys here and even another one just like that one." There are four basic reasons for not allowing toys to be taken home. First play therapy is based on an emotional relationship, and what the child takes away internally is more significant than what is carried away externally. In far too many homes, children have been taught by parental behavior that material sharing is more important than emotional sharing. Gifts are given as a substitute for the sharing of self, and children have learned, inappropriately, that tangible items express a relationship. Second, equally important is the fact of budgetary considerations. Most playrooms operate on a very limited budget. A third factor involves consideration for other children, and the basic rationale for selecting the toys and materials in the first place. They are the child's means for self-expression. Allowing toys to be removed from the playroom can interfere with other children's freedom of expression. Therefore, toys also should not be taken to the waiting room by other staff members for babysitting purposes. A fourth factor is the issue of what to do if the child is allowed to take a toy home and does not bring it back. The therapist would then be placed in a different role of trying to get the toy back.

To a child's request to take a toy home, the therapist could respond *"Having that car to play with at home would be fun, but the toys are for staying in the playroom so they will be here when you come back next time."*

If a child wants to show a parent a special item in the playroom, the child can invite the parent to the playroom to see the item after the session is concluded. Children are allowed to take their paintings home, but the therapist does not suggest they do so. If the therapist wants a record of the child's paintings, the therapist could ask the child's permission to keep the painting until the next session and during the intervening time take a picture of the painting. Several therapists have reported that some children seem to paint pictures just to take home as gifts to parents and siblings. In these cases, the therapist felt little, if any, exploration or self-expression was evident in the activity so they requested the child leave all paintings until the last session and then take them all home. Fewer paintings were produced after the limit was set which seemed to confirm the therapists' hypothesis. Limits may or may not need to be set on taking home items created with the clay or play dough depending on the budget. Most play therapists will probably need to set a limit with the clay and play dough and that can be perfectly acceptable.

Leaving the Playroom. Allowing a child to go in and out of the playroom at random during the session is not advisable because that severely restricts the development of the relationship and prevents follow through and completion of some interactions, especially when a limit has been set or the child has just expressed some angry or frightening feelings. *Children need to learn that they cannot run away from the responsibility of seeing things through, that commitment to a relationship means staying and working things out.* Allowing children to leave the room and return at will can turn the experience into little more than a game. The therapist may want to inform some children that if they choose to leave, they choose not to come back to the playroom for that day.

In most cases, the preferable procedure is not to allow children to leave the playroom until the scheduled time is up, except to get a drink or to go to the bathroom. Usually a rule of one trip out for a drink and one trip out to the bathroom is sufficient. However, this cannot be adhered to rigidly because some children may genuinely need to go to the bathroom more than once, as many inexperienced therapists have discovered when a puddle suddenly appeared on the floor, and then the child felt awkward and embarrassed. To help avoid this problem, *parents can be given the responsibility of taking the child to the bathroom prior to each session.* Two of the playrooms in our Center for Play Therapy have a small bathroom that opens into the playroom, thus eliminating these problems.

The following interaction in the playroom illustrates the process of setting limits about leaving the playroom.

> Kathleen: I don't like any of your stuff in here. I'm leaving (moves quickly toward door).

> Therapist: Kathleen, our time is not up in the playroom. You just don't like anything here and want to leave, but our time is not up. (Therapist glances at watch). We have fifteen more minutes and then it will be time to leave.

As pointed out earlier, the therapist uses "our" and "we" because each of them is a part of the relationship, and both will be leaving the room. Adding the last part of the statement, "and then it will be time to leave" conveys to the child that he/she will eventually get to leave. Otherwise the child, especially the very young child, may be afraid he/she will never get to leave and "Mommy and Daddy will never see me again."

Time Limits. A forty-five minute session is sufficient and the fifteen minutes between sessions is often needed to get the room ready on time for the next child. In some settings such as elementary schools or women's shelters where the counselor is burdened with huge case loads, thirty minute sessions may be quite sufficient. Whatever time span has been communicated to the child, should be adhered to. The therapist should remind the child when five minutes are left in the session. Young children who do not have a clear conception of time and children who are completely immersed in their play also may need a one minute time "warning." These reminders help children to get ready to end the experience and give them an opportunity to complete the task at hand or to move quickly to something else they had planned to do. This latter behavior is typical of many children and speaks of their planning ahead in their play or even before they come to the session, as shown in Paul's comment "I was gonna play with that truck before I came, right?" Ginott (1961) suggested another possible explanation for children moving quickly to some other play activity is that they know they will soon leave the playroom and so feel safe to engage in play activities that touch more directly on their basic difficulties. This process is not unlike what is experienced with adults who sometimes wait until the last few minutes to discuss significant problems.

The objective is not to get the child out of the room but rather to provide the child with an opportunity for the child to assume responsibility for leaving the room. Therefore, the therapist's patience and understanding are continued with the ending of the session. The therapist experiences no feeling of being rushed to get the child out of the room. When the therapist announces *"Our time is up for today. It's time to go to the waiting room where your mother is,"* the therapist stands up to give a visual cue and respects the child's need to finish a task by waiting the necessary few seconds or minute. The attitude of returning responsibility to the child is continued by allowing the child to precede the therapist out the door.

Limiting Noise. Generally all noise in a playroom is acceptable. Children may yell, scream, bang on the block of wood as loud as they wish and as long as they want. Noise level may have to be limited in some clinics and schools, however, where people and activities in adjoining rooms and offices will be interrupted. This is certainly situational and, although not desirable to have to do so, is necessitated by practicality. I once worked in a playroom on the third floor of an office building, and in that setting, when children banged extra hard on the block of wood, the sound reverberated throughout the steel structure of the building. We solved the problem by placing several layers of an old rug under the block of wood to cushion the sound. Noise level in play therapy can be a major problem in elementary schools because the counselor's office is usually located near the administrative offices. Limiting the noise level would be far better than to have an administrator prohibit the use of play therapy.

Personal Items are not for Playing. Prohibiting a child's play with the therapist's watch, glasses, appointment book in a shirt pocket, and other personal possessions will significantly increase the therapist's comfort level and acceptance of the child. Allowing a child to try on and wear the therapist's glasses can lead to disaster and feelings of anger and rejection toward the child. A simple *"My glasses are for me to wear"* is sufficient. If the child persists, the therapist can add *"My glasses are not for playing with."*

In situations where a tape recorder is taken into the playroom to record the session, the recorder should be placed near the therapist's chair in an inconspicuous place and turned on prior to bringing the child into the room. This will avoid calling attention to the recorder. If the child begins to play with the recorder, the therapist can say *"The recorder is not one of the toys for playing with."*

Limiting Water in the Sandbox. Children delight in pouring water into the sandbox and can get caught up in pouring bucket after bucket of water until the sand is soupy. Even though the therapist may be comfortable with soupy sand, several points may need to be considered. The next child in the playroom may have been planning to play in the sandbox but does not because the sand is too wet thus limiting the second child's expression. Soupy sand may take weeks to dry out, and if the sandbox is made of wood, will quickly rot the bottom. It seems best to limit the amount of water to a specific number of containers of water rather than trying to limit a certain volume of water. "James, the rule is three containers of water in the sandbox" should be stated as the child heads back to the sink for the third pan full of water.

Urinating in the Playroom. Allowing a child to urinate in the sandbox or on the playroom floor is highly questionable and shows little regard for other children who will play in the sandbox, unless the therapist plans to empty the sandbox and put in fresh sand. Children need to learn to control such acting out behaviors. Likewise, children should not be allowed to urinate in the nursing bottle and then drink the urine.

Beginning Play Therapists' Reactions To Setting Limits

Joanna: I was very apprehensive about being able to handle unexpected situations in the playroom. I was afraid I would become too nervous to react appropriately and assuredly. In the first play therapy session, the child put his hand on the door knob as if to open the door and leave. I surprised myself by responding, 'I know you would like to go now, but our time is not up.' I did not become overanxious as I expected. In the second session, the child obviously did not want to leave the playroom at the end of the time. I was able to remain patient and calm and to follow through in getting the child to leave. In both instances the children followed my expectations without direct instruction.

Carmen: When Laura ran for the tape recorder, I overreacted. Instead of stating a limit and allowing her to decide, I pulled her hand away. However, when Sarah saw the microphone, I did not touch her, I simply said it was a microphone, and not a toy. She accepted this easily. I guess I learned more from Laura and Sarah than I could have learned from a book or journal article.

Research on Limit Setting

Ginott and Lebo (1961) found that therapists of different orientations were similar in their patterns of limit setting. Of the 54 limits listed, few were never used, and statistically significant differences were found between therapists of different orientations for only seven of the 54 limits. Using the same sample of therapists, Ginott and Lebo (1963) investigated the most and least used play therapy limits. They found that the most widely used limits related to protection of playroom equipment, safety and health, and physical attacks on the therapist. The least used limits were those associated with symbolic expression. A replication of their study by Rhoden, Kranz, and Lund (1981) resulted in similar findings.

McDougal (1988) selected 22 items from the Ginott and Lebo list for her survey of play therapists in school and clinical settings. She found that an astonishing 45% of the clinical therapists allowed parents to review films of their children's sessions. She also found that the most widely used limits related to protection of playroom equipment, safety and health, and physical attacks on the therapist.

The list of limits used in the Ginott and Lebo (1961, pp. 153-154) study is included here for the reader's consideration as possible areas in which limits may need to be set.

1. Taking home a playroom toy
2. Taking home a painting he made
3. Taking home an object he made of clay, etc.
4. Deciding whether or not to enter the playroom
5. Leaving the playroom at will
6. Turning off the lights for a long while
7. Pouring a generous amount of water in sand box
8. Spilling sand any place in the room

9. Spilling as much sand as he wants
10. Painting inexpensive toys
11. Painting expensive toys
12. Painting or marking walls or doors
13. Painting or marking furniture
14. Prolonging his stay at the end of the session
15. Bringing a friend
16. Bringing drinks or food to the playroom
17. Lighting matches brought with him
18. Smoking
19. Starting small fires
20. Reading books he brought with him
21. Doing his schoolwork
22. Breaking inexpensive toys
23. Breaking expensive toys
24. Damaging furniture and fixtures
25. Breaking windows
26. Opening door or window and talking to passers-by
27. Using terms such as nigger, mick, or kike
28. Verbalizing profanities in the playroom
29. Yelling profanities at passers-by
30. Writing four-letter words on blackboard
31. Drawing, painting, or making obscene objects
32. Painting his face
33. Painting his clothes
34. Exploding a whole roll of caps at once
35. Climbing on window sills high above the ground
36. Hitting the therapist mildly
37. Squirting water on the therapist
38. Painting the therapist's clothes
39. Throwing sand at the therapist's shoes
40. Throwing sand at the therapist's person
41. Throwing rubber objects around the room
42. Throwing hard objects around the room
43. Tying the therapist up playfully
44. Shooting suction-tip darts at the therapist
45. Attacking the therapist with some force
46. Sitting on the therapist's lap
47. Hugging the therapist for long periods of time
48. Kissing the therapist
49. Fondling the therapist
50. Completely undressing

51. Masturbating openly
52. Drinking polluted water
53. Eating mud, chalk, or finger paints
54. Urinating or defecating on the floor

REFERENCES

Ginott, H.G. (1961). *Group psychotherapy with children*. New York: McGraw-Hill Books.

Ginott, H., & Lebo, D. (1961). Play therapy limits and theoretical orientation. *Journal of Consulting Psychology, 25*, 337-340.

Ginott, H., & Lebo, D. (1963). Most and least used play therapy limits. *Journal of Genetic Psychology, 103*, 153-159.

Guerney, L. (1983). Client-centered (nondirective) play therapy. In C.E. Schaefer & K.L. O'Conner (Eds.), *Handbook of play therapy* (pp. 21-64). New York: John Wiley & Sons.

McDougal, P. (1988). A comparative analysis of limits in play therapy in school and clinical settings. Unpublished Thesis, Texas Woman's University.

Moustakas, C. E. (1959). *Psychotherapy with children: The living relationship*. New York: Harper & Row.

Rhoden, B.L., Kranz, P.L., & Lund, Nick L. (1981). Current trends in the use of limits in play therapy. *Journal of Psychology, 107* (2), 191-198.

CHAPTER 12

TYPICAL PROBLEMS
IN PLAY THERAPY
AND
WHAT TO DO IF . . . .

The relationship with a child in the playroom is always new, creative, exciting and different with each child. Therefore, predicting what an individual child will do in a given session is not possible. Trying to anticipate some of the things children might do and to formulate a response ahead of time can be helpful, though, to the inexperienced therapist. Knowing how to respond when confronted with an unexpected occurrence can help the therapist to remain calm and accepting of the child. Planning what needs to be done and how to respond ahead of time should not diminish the therapist's creative and spontaneous use of self. No matter how often certain responses, verbal and otherwise, are used, they should never become perfunctory or routine. The therapist should always be responding with compassion, understanding and the utmost concern for the child's feelings. With that in mind, the following common problems in the playroom and possible responses are presented for the therapist to consider.

What to Do If the Child Is Silent

The silent child presents an interesting paradox for the therapist and a perplexing problem. The therapist uses play therapy because of the belief that children communicate through play, and yet when confronted with a child who is verbally silent, experiences thoughts and feelings that the child should talk. Therapists, who feel awkward with children's silence or secretly wish children would talk, should examine their own value system, expectations of children, and their willingness to allow children to be children.

Is there ever a time when a child is not communicating? Must a child verbalize for communication to occur? Whose needs are being met by trying to get the child to talk? An honest answer to this last question requires courage on the part of the therapist to look deep within self. Does the child need to talk to complete what he/she wants to accomplish? How accepting is the therapist who wants the child to talk? A reasonable assumption is that a therapist who feels uncomfortable with a child's silence is not very accepting of the child. Children are remarkably sensitive to these inner feelings and attitudes of the therapist, and often resist being verbal because they sense being nonverbal is unacceptable to the therapist, and they, therefore, feel rejected. Acceptance means accepting the child as he/she is—being silent. Acceptance that is contingent on the child's talking is not acceptance. **Acceptance is not conditional**—there is no "if."

In play therapy, the child is continually sending messages, whether they are verbalized or not. Therefore, the therapist must maintain an attitude of responsiveness that communicates verbally and nonverbally acceptance of the child's silence. The therapist must listen carefully to the child, whether the child speaks or not. The key to establishing contact with the silent child is to respond verbally to what the child is doing at the moment or to what is sensed within the child at the moment. **A responsive attitude is not dependent on the child talking.** The facilitative quality of this kind of responsiveness can be seen in the following interaction with a child who was verbally silent.

> Michael:　(sat in sandbox methodically spooning sand on his shoes)

> Therapist:　You're putting lots of sand right on top of your shoes.

Michael:	(no response, doesn't even look up, continues to spoon sand concentrating on completely covering one shoe)
Therapist:	There, you got that one completely covered up. That one can't be seen.
Michael:	(shifts activity to carefully spooning sand on top of his left hand which is resting on the side of the sandbox, spills a little sand on the floor, glances at the therapist)
Therapist:	Looks like you are wondering what I might think about your spilling sand on the floor. Sometimes accidents happen in here.
Michael:	(returns to covering other shoe with sand, completes the task)
Therapist:	Now they are both covered up and can't be seen.
Michael:	(whispers) Nobody likes them; so they are hiding.

Michael had been referred for play therapy because he was an isolate on the playground and seemed to have no friends in his second grade. Other children did not seek him out in the classroom.

As this episode demonstrates, the therapist proceeds at the child's pace, allowing the child to continue to provide direction for the interaction. Patience is the rule of the day. The therapist must be careful to avoid trying to respond to every single thing the child does. That can be very irritating to the child and also can result in the child feeling self conscious. The therapist needs to avoid any behavior that might result in any pressure for the child to talk. After enduring a long silence, the therapist might ask, "Do you know why you are here?" in a not so subtle attempt to get the child to say something. Also, the question implies the child has problems and needs to get on with the business of working on those problems. Such efforts only serve to alienate the child.

What to Do If the Child Wants to
Bring Toys Or Food into the Playroom

Sometimes children bring a favorite toy or doll with them to the first session and this may indicate the presence of some anxiety. Therefore, the child's desire to take a special doll to the playroom would be recognized and accepted. If the child cradles a special truck under one arm and accompanies the therapist down the hall toward the playroom, this would be permissible and could be used as a point of contact with the child as they walk down the hall. *"Robert, I see you brought something with you to take to the playroom. That must be a special toy. It's all green with big black wheels."* This response accepts the child's desire to take the truck to the playroom, implies permission, recognizes the importance of the truck, and shows appreciation or prizing of the truck.

Does this mean that all items that are special to children are allowed in the playroom? Absolutely not. The general rule is to allow only those items that approximate what would normally be selected for the playroom. Remote control toys, highly mechanical toys, wind up and watch games, cassette players with head sets, glass items, etc. do not facilitate interaction with children or their expression and, therefore, would not be allowed. Favorite books also are not allowed in the playroom because defensive, shy or withdrawn children can retreat into the book and spend the entire time avoiding interacting with the new environment or the therapist. Books seldom facilitate building a relationship with a child in the playroom.

Children may come to the waiting room munching on all sorts of snacks. Excluding food from the playroom is generally best because of the distraction precipitated by eating. Munching on chips is not conducive to involved or intensive play and also presents problems when children offer the therapist some of the food. If the therapist doesn't take a drink of the child's Coke, will the child feel rejected? Allowing food in the playroom usually results in the child later insisting that the therapist go get Cokes or snacks. If the child shows up with a half eaten ice cream bar, the therapist can show compassion and understanding by allowing the child to finish eating before going to the playroom. The same suggestion does not apply to waiting for a child to drink all twelve ounces of a can of Coke. Have you ever watched a four-year-old drink a can of Coke? That can take hours!

In responding to a forbidden item, the therapist should be sensitive to the child's feelings. *"I know you would like to take that game with you to the playroom, but it stays here in the waiting room. It will be here when you come back from the playroom."* The therapist is then responsible for helping the child to remember forty-five minutes later that the item is in the waiting room. Likewise, children are prone to forget they brought a special item into the playroom; so the therapist will need to remember at the end of the session.

What to Do If the Child Is Overly Dependent

Many children who are referred for play therapy have learned to depend on adults for getting their needs met. Parents and care givers are notorious for doing things for children thus fostering dependency and affecting children's feelings of competence and responsibility. ***The objective of the therapist is to return responsibility to children and to facilitate their self-reliance.*** Some children deluge the therapist with requests for help or insistence that the therapist make a decision for them. Children are quite capable of making decisions for themselves in the playroom, and can only discover that strength by being allowed to struggle with making decisions. Children also must be allowed to struggle with doing things for themselves.

The therapist is not the child's servant to run and fetch items for the child, or dress the child, or open containers the child can easily open, or choose colors, or decide what picture the child should paint, or decide what the child should play with first. Such behaviors only perpetuate the child's dependency and confirm an already existing perception of self as being inadequate and incapable. The therapist's responses should convey confidence in the child and return responsibility to the child.

The following examples are comments made by children and the therapist's response returning responsibility:

Robert: Go get those scissors for me.

Therapist: If you want the scissors, you can get them.

David: I want to play in the sand. Will you take my shoes off?

Therapist: You have decided to play in the sand and want your shoes off first. You can take your shoes off if you want them off.

Sally: (without trying to open the paste jar) Will you open this jar for me?

Therapist: In here that's something you can do.

Janet: I'm going to paint a picture of a fish. What color are fish?

Therapist: You can decide what color you want the fish to be.

Timothy: I like to draw pictures. What pictures do other kids draw?

Therapist: Oh, so you like drawing pictures. Well, in here, the important thing is the kind of picture you like to draw.

Mary: I don't know what to do. What do you want me to play with first?

Therapist: Sometimes it's hard to decide. What you play with first is for you to decide.

These responses clearly convey the parameters of the relationship and return responsibility for action and direction to the children who now must struggle with the process of self discovery. If children are not allowed to struggle with doing things for themselves, how can they discover their worth, and if no one believes in them enough to allow them to set their own direction, how can they ever believe in themselves?

**What to Do If the Child
Persists in Seeking Praise**

As in all interactions with children, when confronted with a child who persists in wanting the therapist's evaluation or judgement, the therapist should be sensitive to the child's feelings and perception of self. Is the child's persistent demand to know if the therapist likes the child's picture an indication of insecurity and poor self-esteem or a need to control the interaction? Dealing with a child who angrily demands a specific answer can severely test the therapist's feelings of adequacy and acceptance of the child.

When confronted with "Just tell me. I want to know. Do you think my picture is pretty or not," the therapist may have a tremendous temptation to stall by giving the question back to the child in order to buy time to think of a good response. A faltering "You're wondering if I think your picture is pretty," has little or no facilitative value in such situations and usually only frustrates or confuses the child who is left to wonder if he is being understood and so insists all the more for an answer. Children also will sense the therapist's hesitating, tentative quality and try even harder to force a direct answer. Although it might seem to be a simple matter of just giving the child an answer such as "I think your picture is very pretty," praise directs children's behavior, restricts their freedom, creates dependency, and fosters external motivation.

In child-centered play therapy the objective is to free children to evaluate their own behavior, to appreciate their own creative beauty, and to develop an internal system of reward and satisfaction. Praise does not contribute to the development of a therapeutic relationship and usually indicates the therapist is not in touch with the inner dynamics of the child, due to the therapist's need to have the child feel good. In this situation, the therapist's response should either clarify the relationship in the playroom or facilitate the child's prizing of the picture as in the following excerpt.

> Martin: (shows therapist a picture he has painted) Do you think my picture of a house is pretty?
>
> Therapist: (pointing to the picture) You painted a red house right there, and hmmm, (thoughtfully studying the picture) you put three windows right there (pointing to the windows) and, oh, you made this whole top blue all the way across here. And I see you painted a whole bunch of orange in this corner. (said with genuine interest and a real prizing shown in tone of voice)

When the child's productions are responded to in this nonevaluative, careful attention to detail, esteeming manner, the child tends to forget the original question asked and begins to study his/her work, getting caught up in noticing what the therapist notices, and feeling good about what has been produced. Often the child will take over the therapist's role of prizing and will begin to make comments like "And up here I painted a big yellow sun, and these birds right here were kinda hard to make" to which the therapist could respond "Yes, I see that big yellow sun, and those do look like birds alright. They were hard to make but you made them." The child is now free to evaluate and appreciate his/her own work. When the therapist judges or evaluates something the child has done or created and pronounces it pretty or some other positive response, the therapist also communicates that the therapist has the power to judge something to be ugly or negative. Therefore, evaluative responses are to be avoided.

Some children will persist in their demand for the therapist to say whether or not they think the picture is pretty. When this occurs, the therapist can clarify the relationship in the playroom by saying *"In here the important thing is not whether or not I think your picture is pretty, but what you think about your picture."* This response is too long for some children and the therapist may want to say *"What is important is what you think about your picture."* The child is now free to say whether or not he/she thinks the picture is pretty. Evaluation belongs to the child. Therefore, the therapist returns the power of judgement back to the child.

Although the above example deals with cognitive evaluation, the same approach is used when feelings about a picture or some other object are the focus.

Jimmy: See what I am doing.

Therapist: You are playing with the clay.

Jimmy: What should I make?

Therapist: You may choose to make whatever you wish.

Jimmy: All right. I'll make a hippopotamus.

Therapist: You have decided to make a hippopotamus.

Jimmy: (shapes the clay with much care and holds up a form that somewhat resembles an animal) What is it? Do you like it?

Therapist: You worked hard on that. It can be whatever you want it to be. (said because once into the actual construction or shaping of an object, children sometimes change their mind about what they have created)

Jimmy: But do you like it . . . do you think it is good?

Therapist: What is important is how you feel about it.

What to Do If the Child Says You Talk Weird

That the therapist does not ask questions, offer suggestions, or tell what to do, may seem strange to a child. In some ways, the therapist may sound to the child as though the therapist is speaking a foreign language because the child is not accustomed to hearing his/her expressed thoughts and feelings verbalized by anyone. When a child says "You talk funny," the child is often referring to the fact that the therapist's responses or manner of responding does not sound natural. Often a stilted or rote quality is evident and the interaction doesn't sound at all like a conversation.

When the therapist merely parrots the child's words or verbally tracks the child's play activity in a perfunctory reporting way, the child has good reason to take notice and to be irritated. The child may feel the therapist is just telling, reporting what is being done, which is an insult because the child already knows what is being done. The objective is to *be with* the child and to convey understanding, not to report what is seen or heard. "Now the car is on top of the table" and "You put that car—just—as—close—to the edge as you could get it" convey entirely different messages. One is objective, takes note of the facts; the other communicates a feeling of being with.

A statement of "You talk strange" should be accepted and could be responded to with *"Oh, so I sound different than other people to you"* or could be responded to with an explanation *"I'm just trying to let you know I'm interested in you and what you are doing, I guess maybe what I say does sound different."* Sometimes the statement "You talk weird" is the child's negative "put down" of the therapist or an expression of resistance and could be responded to with *"You don't like the way I talk"* or *"Sounds like you might want me to stop talking."* How to respond would depend on the child's meaning as sensed by the therapist.

What to Do If the Child Wants the Therapist to Play a Guessing Game

"Guess what I'm going to do" or "What do you think this is?" are frequently asked questions by children in play therapy. The tendency of many therapists when faced with these requests or questions is to become involved in a game of guessing and in the process they restrict children's freedom and assume responsibility for direction. "Guess what I'm going to do" may not be a request but rather an excited child's way of including the therapist in the activity with no expectation for an answer. "What do you think this is?" may indeed be a request for the therapist to identify an object or a painting by the child. Even so, what are the potential consequences of engaging in a game of guessing with a child who has a poor self-concept, is dependent, or has a strong need to please? The child may very well take the therapist's guess to mean that is what the picture should be or that is what is expected next and as a result change the original intent. If the therapist guesses the picture is a tree and the child intended it to be a nuclear explosion, the child may think the therapist's message is that drawings of people being blown up are not acceptable. After the therapist has made an identification, the child may have difficulty changing the content of the picture or continuing the play activity because the child may feel that doing so would be going against the therapist, and that the therapist would not like him/her. **Play therapy is not a time to get caught up in guessing games.** This is a time when the therapist must be consistent in intent, attitude, acceptance, objective, and approach. The child is responsible and capable and that message must be clearly communicated in all interactions. Therefore, when the child says "Guess what I'm going to do next," an understanding and freeing response would be *"Sounds like you have something in mind"* or *"Sounds like you have something planned."* We can assume that if a child says, "Guess what I'm going to do next," the child must have something in mind to do. If the child asks "What do you think this is," the therapist could respond simply *"You can tell me."* Responsibility for leading is then returned to the child.

What to Do If the Child Asks for Expressions of Affection

Some children in play therapy may have experienced very little direct expression of affection and are often emotionally needy. They may be unsure of just where they stand in the relationship and may need reassurance that the therapist does indeed care for them. When a child asks "Do you like me?" is no time to reflect with "You're wondering if I like you." Yes, that is exactly what the child is wondering and is exactly what was asked. Therefore, telling the child what was just asked is not necessary. This is a time for sharing on the part of the therapist in the developing of a personal relationship. In the following interaction, the therapist avoided the child's emotional need and the child quickly changed the focus of the interaction. This was eight-year-old Frank's sixth session.

> Frank: (sitting in sandbox) I want to tell you something but . . . (sits silently for a moment, sifting sand through his fingers)

> Therapist: You have something to tell me, but you're not sure if you want to say it.

> Frank: Yeah. It might hurt your feelings, and you might cry. (buries his fingers in the sand and looks down)

> Therapist: You don't want to hurt my feelings.

> Frank: Yeah, and . . . (avoids eye contact and digs his hands deeper into the sand, sits silently for a time, glances at therapist) It's about your children.

> Therapist: So it's something about my children.

> Frank: Yeah, and . . . Well . . . (then quickly, breathlessly) It's . . . do you love me?

> Therapist: You're wondering how I feel about you.

> Frank: Yeah . . . Well, do you?

> Therapist: It's important to you to know how I feel about you, if I love you or not.

Frank: (continues to sit in sand, eyes averted, hands deep in the sand, his fingers touch something) Hey, what's this? (pulls a nail out of the sand)

This emotional moment with Frank is lost for now. The opportunity to respond to his emotional needs will probably come up again because such issues are so important to children, but this particular moment is gone forever.

The therapist always hopes that his/her genuine caring for and prizing of the child will be received and felt by the child. Some children, though, may need more concrete verification and may ask "Do you like me?" At such moments, the therapist needs to be very warm, caring, and personally responsive because the child's feelings of self-esteem are vulnerable. If the therapist really does care for and values the child, expressing that would be appropriate. In our society, the words "like" and "love" are tossed around like confetti often with little meaning or significance. Therefore, in responding to the child, the therapist may want to convey his/her feelings with *You are special to me and this is a special time together.* The same response would also be appropriate if the child asked "Do you love me?"

What to Do If the Child Wants to Hug Or Sit in the Therapist's Lap

When children seek confirmation of caring, a verbal statement should be sufficient. In some cases, the most appropriate response might be to remain neutral, accepting and noncommittal, especially in the case of a manipulative child. Requests for hugs, to sit in the therapist's lap, etc. should be responded to with caution about the underlying motive. Of course if the child hugged the therapist, it would be inappropriate for the therapist to sit there rigid as a board. The therapist would want to return the hug, but there is a need to be cautious. Is this a sexually abused child? Has the child been taught that if you like or love someone you will show the person sexually? Does liking to the child mean seductive behavior expressed by touching, fondling, rubbing? What if a girl suddenly hops into the male therapist's lap and begins to wriggle playfully? Surely the therapist would be aware of the possibilities of such behavior and would respond accordingly with *"I know that's fun for you, but I know you like me without your sitting on my lap,"* as he gently lifts the child off his lap.

For some children, the most natural thing is for them to lean against the therapist's leg as they take in scenes in the playroom. They are comfortable and this is an unconscious behavior. They are just being spontaneous and free. If the therapist reached out and hugged the child, then one could ask whose needs are being met? The therapist would then be taking over the direction of the relationship and the session.

Another child might get the nursing bottle, begin sucking on it, crawl into the therapist's lap, and want to be held like a baby. The therapist's own comfort level here may best determine the appropriate response. If the therapist senses that this is an innocent request, no subtle underlying motive, simply a child acting out a sequence or reexperiencing feelings of being a baby, a natural response might be to hold the child for a few minutes. The therapist must be prepared, however, for additional requests to sing, rock, and change the baby's diaper. At some point, a limit may need to be set on the role the therapist is asked to play.

This situation may truly be one of the most awkward times in the therapeutic process. If the therapist doesn't allow the child to crawl onto the therapist's lap, will the child feel rejected or will this help the child to move toward self-reliance? Will cradling a child on the therapist's lap stimulate parental feelings of rocking his/her own children and thus interfere with the therapist's acceptance of the child's separateness?

Physical and sexual abuse have reached such epidemic proportions and have become such emotionally charged issues in our society that no longer can a clear suggestion be given as to the appropriate response except to be very cautious. If in doubt about the child's needs or intent, perhaps a response could be *"I know you want to pretend to be a baby and suck on the bottle. You can do that in the baby bed there."* This response is included here with much reservation because it may be misunderstood. However such a response also may be necessary in order for the therapist to maintain the conditions necessary for growth by the child. Just because cuddling a child feels natural for the therapist may not justify the behavior if the therapist has not carefully examined his/her own needs in this area. In most cases, cradling and rocking a child would be very natural and appropriate.

What to Do If the Child Tries to Steal a Toy

Justin is five years old, and this is his second time to be in the wonderful playroom. The playroom contains more toys than he has ever seen in any place except where you buy them. He can't remember the last time his parents bought him a toy, but now here is all this neat stuff with no price tags. He pretends to play with the truck while he crams a small car into his pocket with the other hand, making sure the therapist can't see what he is doing. But she does see the car being shoved into his pocket. Justin continues to play with the truck until the therapist announces time is up.

Now, what is the therapist to do? Wait for Justin to be honest and confess? Allow him to take the car, and hope he will bring it back? Use this as an opportunity to teach him about honesty? Don't worry about the car because it cost less than a dollar anyway? None of the above! We must be concerned about the potential guilt Justin may feel after taking the car home. The value of the car is immaterial. The child's behavior and feelings are what we are concerned about, not the cost. The playroom is a place where values are learned by the child, not taught by the therapist.

Some inexperienced therapist's might ask "Justin, have you forgotten anything?" They might respond with "Justin, can you think of one more thing you need to do before you leave today?" Some might ask "Did you take the car?" Questioning of this nature presents a mixed message to Justin because he senses by the insistence that the therapist knows, but the question implies that the therapist does not know. Could it be that in such cases the therapist is really being dishonest? This does seem to be the case. Questions about what is already known are seldom helpful.

RULE OF THUMB:

Don't ask questions when you already know the answer. Make statements.

This is a time to be straightforward, understanding, and firm.

Therapist: I know you would like to take the car with you, but the car in your pocket (points to pocket) stays here so it will be here for you to play with next time.

Justin: What car? I don't have any car. (pats an empty pocket)

Therapist: You would like to pretend you don't know where the car is, but the car in that pocket (points to pocket) stays in the playroom.

Justin: (puts hand into pocket, retrieves car)

Questioning Justin about why he wanted to take the car, moralizing with "You know you shouldn't take things that don't belong to you" or trying to get him to discuss related happenings by asking "Wonder what happens when you take things at school" increases the intensity of the episode and the possibility of guilt feelings. These responses also take responsibility for leadership and direction away from the child and put the therapist in charge to decide what is important. In addition, asking a child to verbally engage in insightful comparisons ignores the developmental reasons for placing children in play therapy. The child's play in play therapy is not merely preparation for the presumed more significant activity of verbal exploration.

What to Do If the Child
Refuses to Leave the Playroom

Some children may express their resistance or need to test limits by refusing to leave the playroom at the end of the session. The child's reluctance to leave may be manipulation to see how far the time limits and the patience of the therapist can be stretched. An indication of possible manipulation is that usually when the child is being manipulative, the child tends to observe the therapist's reactions. The child's facial expression lacks intensity and body language indicates an incomplete and superficial involvement in the play in which the child is engaged at the moment. Other children may want to stay longer because they are having so much fun. In this instance, the importance of the project to the child is conveyed in intensity and sincerity of facial expression as the child concentrates on the project. Regardless of the reason, sessions should not be prolonged. *A part of the therapeutic process for the child is developing enough self-control to stop, to say no to one's wishes or desires.* Therefore, the following procedure is recommended for ending a session with a child that is reluctant to leave.

> Therapist: Our time in the playroom is up for today. (therapist stands up) It's time to go to the waiting room where your mother is.
>
> Jessica: But I haven't played in the sandbox yet. (she runs over and begins to play in the sand)
>
> Therapist: You would like to stay longer to play in the sand, but Jessica, time is up for today. (takes two steps toward door, while continuing to look at Jessica)
>
> Jessica: (big smile) This is neat stuff. Can't I just stay a little longer? (begins to pour sand through the funnel)
>
> Therapist: (takes two more steps toward door) That's really a lot of fun for you, but it's time to leave.

Jessica: You don't like me. If you really liked me, you would let me stay. (continues pouring sand)

Therapist: Oh, so you think if I liked you I would let you stay. I know you really want to stay longer, but it's time to leave the playroom. (takes two more steps reaches out and turns door knob, pushes door open a couple of inches)

Jessica: (looks up and sees therapist holding door open) I'm almost through. Just one more minute.

Therapist: (opens door wider) Jessica, I know you want to stay for as long as you decide, but time is up. (takes a step through door while looking expectantly at Jessica)

Jessica: (slowly stands up, drops the funnel, and shuffles toward the open door)

This episode took approximately four minutes, which can seem like forty if the therapist gets caught up in the pressure of trying to make the child leave. Even if Jessica had taken five or six minutes to leave the room, the most important consideration is that she took herself out of the playroom even though she wanted to stay, and in the process her dignity as a person and her self-respect as an individual were not only preserved but enhanced.

What to Do If the Therapist Unexpectedly Cannot Keep an Appointment

Children deserve just as much consideration and courtesy as adults with respect to making, keeping, and informing about the canceling of appointments. Preferably the therapist would inform the child at the beginning of the session prior to the anticipated absence, followed by a reminder at the end of the session with a clear statement that the child will get to come back to the playroom in two weeks or whenever the next regular appointment time would be. The anticipated coming absence should be mentioned at the beginning of the session so the child will not think the absence is some kind of punishment for something the child just did in the playroom. A general statement about the reason for the absence, *"I'm going to be in another town at a meeting"* also helps the child to understand that the reason for the absence is not something the child has done.

If an unexpected occurrence between sessions prevents the keeping of the next appointment, a post card or telephone call informing the child about the absence would be a warm expression of the importance of the relationship. In those rare instances when an emergency prevents the keeping of an appointment, and notifying the child prior to the appointment time is not possible, the therapist could leave a personal message for the child on a tape recorder or a printed note for the child to read or to be read to the child. ***Concern for the child's feelings is always the rule of the day.***

CHAPTER **13**

ISSUES IN
PLAY THERAPY

The therapeutic relationship in play therapy probably raises more questions about procedures and process than any other relationship in the helping professions. Although the therapist could not possibly anticipate all the issues that may arise in the playroom, thinking through issues prior to beginning relationships with children can help the therapist to react with assurance so as not to confuse children by indecisiveness. The issues discussed here can provide a starting point for that kind of self-exploration. The therapist will need to ask the what and why of his/her position held on these issues.

Participation in the Child's Play

Whether or not to participate in children's play is an important decision the therapist must make prior to the onset of therapy, and although largely a function of the therapist's personality, should be based on a rationale consistent with the therapist's objectives. The child-centered play therapist is committed to a belief in the child's capacity for self-direction and avoids intrusion of his/her personality into the child's play. This is the child's special time to direct his/her own life, to make decisions, to play without unnecessary interference, to bring forth in play whatever is yearning to be expressed. The session belongs to the child, and the therapist's needs and directions are to be kept out. This is not a social time, and the child does not need a playmate. The therapist is there to help the child hear self, see self, understand self and be self in the safety of an accepting relationship.

Although the child invites the therapist to play, the child may not particularly want a playmate. Some children feel obligated to invite the therapist to participate. The child may be asking for the therapist's participation because of a belief that doing so is what is expected or because the child wants to be liked by the therapist. An invitation to play could mean the child is looking for approval or for the security of having someone determine the direction of the play. Such a request could be the child's way of testing the therapist's level of permissiveness.

The therapist must struggle with the question of what is the objective of participation and what will be accomplished. Is the real motivation to make contact with the child or to meet the therapist's need to be included? When faced with a nonverbal child who stands in the middle of the playroom, the therapist may pick up a doll, begin to straighten the doll's clothes and put a shoe on the doll's foot. By such action the therapist is indicating a willingness to participate in play. Is the therapist's motivation to free the child or to have the child do something so the therapist will feel comfortable?

Participation in the child's play does not guarantee the child will feel more included. **The attitude of the therapist is the crucial variable, not the actual play participation.** When the therapist is fully involved and experiencing with the child and is successfully communicating that involvement to the child, the child seldom asks the therapist to overtly participate. When the therapist is asked to participate, sometimes an underlying message is present. Perhaps the central issue is whether or not the child feels the therapist is participating. Could the child's message be "I don't feel I have your attention. You don't seem to be involved with me, or interested in what I am doing."

The therapist can be actively involved with the child without playing. The attitude of the therapist is more important than the participation. Choosing not to be directly involved in the child's play does not necessarily predispose the therapist to be only a passive observer as some writers state. A non-playing involved relationship with the child in which the therapist indirectly participates in the child's play is quite possible. Just as words are sometimes not necessary for two people to be involved with each other, so too, participation in play is not necessary for involvement. The therapist's genuine involvement and feeling with the child will be sensed by the child, just as a lack of involvement and interest also will be sensed and felt by the child.

Although the therapist must guard against intruding in the child's play or inhibiting the child, participation in the child's play does not automatically impede the therapeutic process. Some experienced play therapists do an artful job of participating in an unobtrusive way. Guerney (1983) maintained that the therapist can participate in play without abandoning the adult role as long as the therapist is clear on the setting of limits. If the therapist chooses to participate in the child's play, such would be done as a following participant, taking cues from the child. Asking the child to define the role or activity of the therapist allows the child to lead the way. The therapist's participation in the child's play can facilitate the therapeutic relationship only if the therapist's participation facilitates and promotes independence and not dependence in the child.

Even when following the child's directions for play, an ever present possibility is that of influencing or inhibiting the child's play. When Susie tells the therapist to draw a picture of birds, sits watching, and then tries to copy the therapist's drawing, the needs of the therapist seem to be being met rather than the therapist facilitating opportunities for the child's positive growth. Confirmation for this conclusion comes from Susie's statement on the way home. "She draws better pictures than I can."

The potential influence of the therapist's participation in the child's play is a subtle but powerful force, and the therapist should be ever mindful of this fact. Five-year-old Carmen is playing with the doctor kit in her third session.

Carmen: Take off your shirt. I'm going to give you a shot.

Therapist: My shirt is not for taking off. You can pretend the doll is me and take the doll's shirt off.

Carmen: Okay. (takes the female doll's shirt off, then completely undresses the doll, uses the syringe to act out on the doll very explicit sexual activity)

Children can act out behaviors and express feelings on inanimate objects that could never be expressed on the person of the therapist. Therefore, the presence of the therapist in the play can be a structuring or inhibiting factor regardless of the therapist's intent. Following Carmen's activity with the doll, the therapist later learned she had been sexually abused. Would the therapist have discovered that if the therapist had removed her jacket which covered her shirt? Possibly not, but one cannot be sure.

The therapist must be sensitive to her own potential feelings which may be aroused as a result of playing. Chasing and retrieving darts for twenty minutes may result in the therapist feeling irritated, frustrated, or even angry toward the child. Therefore, the skilled therapist would stop long before negative feelings emerged or would refuse participation in such a game altogether. Attempting to respond with understanding while running around the room can be very difficult. Participation in a child's play may be most effective when the therapist's participation is limited in a controlled manner, allowing one's self to be handcuffed, for example, but not to be led endlessly around the room.

The skilled therapist who is ever mindful of the risks of influencing the child or of being manipulated is not likely to compromise therapeutic effectiveness by limited participation in the child's play. However, reservations about the subtle influence of the presence of the therapist in the play still hold.

The question of whether or not to participate in a child's play depends on the child, the situation, and the therapist.

A non-playing or limited play relationship may be the most effective way to assure non-structuring and that the time together belongs to the child. If the therapist chooses not to play, the suggestion can be made for the child to act out the therapist's part.

Accepting Gifts from Children in Play Therapy

What an awkward situation this can be. In many homes, children have been taught by their parent's behavior that love, affection and appreciation are expressed by giving presents. Parents returning from a trip bring gifts home for the children. Special toys are purchased by parents as a way of asking forgiveness or to try to restore a damaged relationship. Consequently children learn to express feelings through gift giving. The natural result then is that they may sometimes bring the therapist a gift to express their liking for this special person in their life or to try to win the therapist back after giving the therapist a particularly difficult time in the playroom.

When a child appears with a present in hand, the therapist will very likely experience an emotional tug to accept the present. After all, the therapist does not want to disappoint the child. But what are the potential consequences of accepting a gift? "If I do this what will the child learn? Will this help to strengthen our relationship? Will this facilitate the child's inner growth as a person? Will this help the child to become more independent?" These are important questions the therapist always should be examining in relation to his/her own behavior. Accepting gifts may help perpetuate a kind of external giving that is separate from self. The play therapy relationship is an emotional relationship and what is shared emotionally is more significant than what could be shared in some tangible way. In play therapy children learn to share themselves emotionally. Sharing a gift may blur the significance of emotional sharing. *Emotional gifts are more powerful and more satisfying than tangible gifts.*

An important factor affecting the decision to accept a gift is the kind of gift presented by the child. Art work or something created by the child is an extension of the child and therefore, can be viewed as an extension of emotional giving because it is a part of the child, what the child has created. Accepting nonpurchased items would be acceptable in most cases, a flower picked by the child, a drawing. The therapist should receive such gifts with warm appreciation, prizing with tone of voice, commenting on details, but, as in the playroom, avoiding overt expressions of praise. "Oh, what a beautiful picture" would be unacceptable. Prizing and appreciation can be shown by reaching out and gently, tenderly taking the object, commenting on it, and carefully placing the object on a nearby table or shelf.

Gifts that are accepted should not be displayed because this might foster competition or encourage other children to bring gifts. These special items should be kept in a special place until termination of play therapy. They can be a great source of satisfaction if the child asks to see the item later. Some children will hand the therapist a painting and state "You can hang this on your wall" to which the therapist can respond "I have a place in my office where I keep special things like this so they will be safe."

Accepting purchased items, even though they may be inexpensive such as a candy bar, can restrict the possibility of emotional sharing by the child and may subtly obligate the therapist in some unconscious way. A determining factor also is whether or not the purchased item is given as a preplanned present or is spontaneously shared as in the case of unwrapping a stick of gum, breaking it in two pieces and sharing one-half. Among my prized possessions are two tiny little round pieces of pink and yellow candy spontaneously shared by a three-year-old from a batch clutched in her fist just before she popped the rest into her mouth.

The issue of accepting a gift could perhaps most easily be dealt with by a blanket rule of no gifts which were purchased regardless of cost. However, I feel very awkward about that. So much depends on the child's intent and the spontaneity of the moment. Declining a gift can be a very awkward and trying moment for the therapist, but it is so important for children to learn they can give of themselves and that presents are not necessary to express emotional meanings. At such moments, the therapist will want to convey sensitive understanding and appreciation. In declining the gift, the therapist can respond with *"You bought this just for me. That says you were thinking about me. I really appreciate that, but here you don't have to give a gift to say you like me. I would like for you to have this"* or if the item is a present purchased at the store just for the therapist *"I would like for you to take this and get something for yourself."*

No hard and fast rule prevails in regard to the issue of gift giving. A sensitive, empathic therapist should be able to handle the situation with a minimum of frustration by using the best judgement in considering (1) the timing of the gift-giving, (2) the nature of the gift, and (3) the implications of accepting or not accepting the gift.

Asking the Child to Cleanup

Some children seem to need to be messy to fully express themselves. They play with toys and quickly move on to other toys without putting the first items back on the shelf. Some children may be like Jerry whose home situation was chaotic, and his play expressed what his life was like, disorganized and messy. At the end of the sessions, toys were all over the floor. Should these children be asked to cleanup? What are the implications of such a request? Whose needs are being met by asking the child to cleanup? Some therapists feel they are "letting the child get away with something" if the child walks out of the playroom leaving a mess. Some therapists may ask the child to cleanup because they are irritated or angry at the child for being so messy, and they personalize the child's behavior, feeling the behavior is an act against them.

Some therapist's rationalize that if the child is to be helped to function outside the playroom, then the child must learn there are consequences associated with her behavior in the playroom. Therefore, the child must be made to cleanup. If the therapist is doing an adequate job of setting therapeutic limits in other areas of play when they are appropriate, then the question of learning to control self should not be an issue. In examining this issue, the therapist should reexamine the rationale for placing children in play therapy. Children need the toys and materials to fully express themselves and the totality of their life experiences. ***Toys are children's words and play is their language.*** If that is the case, then a request that the child cleanup is a request to cleanup what has been expressed. Would a therapist with adult clients ever ask them to cleanup their language or talk less graphically about a topic? Probably not. What therapist would ever ask an adult client who had smoked excessively to clean the ash tray, or dispose of the styrofoam coffee container, or sweep up the mud tracked in on the carpet, or an emotional client to gather up the tear soiled tissues before leaving? When this kind of comparison is made with adults, it becomes clear we are saying children are less respected than adults if we ask them to cleanup. After all, if learning the consequences of one's behavior really is the issue, is it not also important that adults learn the consequences of their behavior?

After observing a play therapy session, a graduate student wrote, "I wonder at what point it becomes appropriate to help James recognize the consequences of his messy behavior. Granted, he didn't break things, but the room was in total disarray when he left. Is there a point in the therapy where this freedom and release of energy needs to be modified? James, you can decide what you want to do in here, but at the end of our time we will put everything back the way it was.'" Would such a statement ever be made to an adult who was being verbally aggressive, distraught, and loud? If play is the child's language, why can't the play language be accepted?

Another graduate student wrote, "I have made a few attempts at involving the child in the cleanup process. Twice this has been with a very messy child. I suspect my motive was more for punishment than therapy." This student's honesty is a good reminder of the importance of asking whose needs are being met by asking the child to cleanup.

In the play therapy relationship, what is expressed and experienced in play is much more significant in the therapeutic process than learning how to cleanup. Requiring a child to cleanup or beginning to cleanup in an effort to model for the child will inhibit a child's expression in the next session because the message most likely to be internalized by the child is that making a mess really is not permissible. Also the child may very well feel punished for having made a mess. The therapist is faced with a dilemma if the child refuses to cleanup. What is the therapist to do now, engage in a physical battle to make the child cleanup or allow the request to be ignored? Neither option is acceptable. What choice can be presented to the child, no session next week or place all the toys that are left on the floor off limits for the next session? What if all the toys in the room are left in the middle of the floor? These options are just not acceptable. Trying to get the child to cleanup takes the therapist out of the role of acceptance and understanding which the therapist has worked hard to try to communicate throughout the session. The therapist also should avoid trying to encourage a child to cleanup with responses such as "Boy, you remembered just where to put that back on the shelf" or "You do such a good job of cleaning up."

Since cleaning up is not the responsibility of the child, that leaves the therapist or some other adult to do the job. The proposed solution by some authors of having a neutral third party or a maid cleanup is financially unrealistic. I know of no play therapy room anywhere in the United States that has a maid or neutral third party who cleans up after each session. That leaves the therapist to clean up, and although not ideal, it is workable. A child who is being messy can severely test the limits of the therapist's acceptance of the child as the therapist watches tinker toys being spilled all over the floor, the doll house furniture dumped and all the toy soldiers left scattered in and around the sandbox.

Since the therapist will need time to put the room in order for the next child, forty-five minute sessions are sufficient. If a child is especially messy and additional time is needed to return the room to order, the session can be shortened by a few minutes without announcing the change to the child. To announce the change would cause the child to feel punished for being messy.

Informing Children of the Reason
They Are in Play Therapy

Some therapists inform children of the specific reason they are in play therapy believing the child's knowing is necessary for behavior change to occur. The child is then expected to work on the identified problem, and the therapist assists by structuring to keep the session content focused on the problem. This poses the problem of placing the therapist in the lead and the sessions becoming problem focused rather than child focused. This approach also assumes that the identified problem is indeed the dynamic to be dealt with and overlooks the possibility of other or deeper issues the child may be concerned about.

Since the child-centered approach is non-prescriptive and is not based on diagnostic information, the therapist may often not know a great deal about the specifics of an individual referral, especially in terms of diagnostic testing. Therefore, the therapist may not have specific reasons to relay to the child.

The child-centered position is that informing children of the specific reason they are coming to the playroom is not necessary. Such information is not necessary for change and growth to occur. Children's behavior can and does change without them knowing what they are working on or indeed without working on trying to change anything. If an understanding of the reason for referral was necessary before change could occur, how could a depressed four-year-old or a manipulative three-year-old or a two-year-old who tries to injure her baby brother ever be helped to change? What would seven-year-old Ryan who had terminal cancer have been told he needed to work on? Should he have been told "You are coming to the playroom because you are dying, and you need to accept death." Certainly not! Ryan focused on issues of living just like the rest of us. Impending death was only a part of his living. What therapist is omnipotent enough to know what a dying child should work on in therapy? This may be viewed as an extreme example, but perhaps an extreme example is sometimes necessary to force us to examine the essence of an issue. If a proposition for change is really necessary for change, then it should be necessary in all cases irrespective of age or presenting problem.

To volunteer a reason why children are coming to the playroom is to imply that something about them is unacceptable. The child-centered therapist avoids any implication that something is wrong with children or that something is needed to correct or change their behavior or themselves. Acceptance by the therapist promotes self-acceptance by children and both are a prerequisite to change and growth.

Bringing a Friend to the Playroom

Prohibiting the bringing of a friend to the playroom is practiced by play therapists, although not universally, from all theoretical approaches (Ginott & Lebo, 1961). Within the client-centered approach, differences in approach to this question range from Ginott's (1961) serious reservations about allowing children to select their own group members for play therapy to Axline's (1969) conclusion that "If the therapy is truly child-centered, the child-chosen group should be more valuable to the child choosing the group than a group chosen by the therapist" (p. 41).

According to Dorfman (1951),

> If therapy can be effected when it is not solely a relationship between two people, as in group therapy, then perhaps allowing a child to bring a friend to an individual therapy session need not hinder the process . . . . Surely, it cannot always be a mere accident that a child brings one person rather than another to his play contact. Sometimes a child may bring in, one by one, those people who represent his areas of difficulty, and then dismiss each one as his need disappears. (p. 263)

Allowing a child to bring a friend to the playroom would be contraindicated for children who are shy, need the therapist's complete acceptance, and are sensitive to comparisons with other children. When another child is present, the therapist must be extra careful not to imply by his/her response that what one child is doing or has accomplished is better. If a shy child brings a friend who is more active, the therapist may unintentionally respond verbally more to the active child simply because more observable activity is present. Responding to one child more than another also can be perceived as comparative and critical. "Sally, you stacked those blocks just like you wanted them to be" is a natural tracking response, but what kind of response is likely to made to a child who is sitting holding a doll or sitting in the sandbox sifting sand through his/her fingers? Will the absence of a similar response imply that what the active child is doing is better? Perhaps it would be best for this kind of child to bring a friend at a later date when the relationship with the therapist is well established and can weather some storms.

Consideration also must be given to the timing of the child's request to bring a friend. Does the request follow a particularly difficult session in which numerous limits were set? Does the child fear he/she is no longer liked? Will the presence of another child interfere with the rebuilding of the relationship? Has the child just revealed something the child feels awkward about, is embarrassed, or is afraid that what was said should not have been?

The presence of another child changes the dynamics of the relationship rather dramatically. Some children may be reluctant to share very personal material about self or family with an invited friend present who has not been a part of the developing relationship as in group play therapy. Children may compete with each other for the therapist's attention or one child may spend most of the session bringing toys to show the therapist, piling things in the therapist's lap to capture attention, or standing near the therapist trying to keep attention through conversation.

The skill of the therapist is a major consideration in determining whether or not to allow a child to invite friends because the dynamics of the interaction increases geometrically with the addition of another child. Everything is potentially intensified. The situation is not simply the addition of one more child. Children stimulate each other, challenge each other, and activities requiring limit setting are exacerbated. Unique skills and training are required to be effective in group play therapy.

Inviting friends is not a typical request and when allowed, after consideration of the needs of the child and the therapist, can be beneficial to children. If group play therapy is determined to be the most effective way to meet the child's needs, then compassionate concern for all children who hurt would dictate that those children in need of therapy should be given priority in the forming of a group.

Inviting Parents or Siblings to the Playroom

The playroom is usually such an exciting place to children that they may want to show their parents or siblings this special place. However, the request to do so may come in the middle of a session. Just what the child has in mind should be determined before allowing a parent or sibling to join the session. Generally, parents are not allowed in sessions. Usually allowing a child to show parents and siblings the playroom after a session has ended is sufficient. If the child requests again at a later time and the request is not associated with wanting to show something that has been made or manipulation to get Mom into the playroom, then the child may want to communicate some important message to the parent. The concerns related to inviting a friend also hold true for inviting parents. The presence of a parent in the playroom can severely restrict the development of the relationship between the therapist and the child. The presence of a parent in a play therapy session should be a rare occasion. Once in the playroom, an anxious child's request to go get a parent would be denied with careful attention to responding to feelings.

If siblings are invited in at the end of a session to see the room, care must be taken to see that they do not use this as a play time. The playroom is a special place for building relationships, and what goes on in the playroom is always consistent. If at a later time the sibling needed play therapy, a new kind of relationship would have to be established.

REFERENCES

Axline, V. (1969). *Play Therapy*. New York: Ballentine.

Dorfman, E. (1951). Play therapy. In C.R. Rogers (Ed.). *Client-centered therapy*, (pp. 235-277). Boston: Houghton Mifflin.

Ginott, H. G. (1961). *Group psychotherapy with children: The theory and practice of play therapy*. New York: McGraw-Hill.

Ginott, H. & Lebo, D. (1961). Play therapy limits and theoretical orientation. *Journal of Consulting Psychology, 25*, 337-340.

Guerney, L. (1983). Client-centered (nondirective) play therapy. In C.E. Schaefer & K.J. O'Connor (Eds.) *Handbook of play therapy* (pp. 21-64). New York: Wiley.

Chapter **14**

CHILDREN IN
PLAY THERAPY

Cases described in this chapter were selected to present a cross section view of the child-centered approach to play therapy. The sentence structure and language used in the sessions has been left exactly as the children expressed themselves to provide a realistic picture of what the sessions were like. Before presenting these five cases, a summary review of the child-centered approach to play therapy seems to be in order to make clear the purpose of the therapist's behavior in facilitating an accepting emotional climate.

In the child-centered approach, the play therapist consistently conveys a deep and abiding belief in the child's ability to make appropriate decisions in the playroom. The child is encouraged to make decisions, and the play therapist listens actively with tenderness and concern. The child's capacity for self-direction is respected. No attempt is made to direct the child's activities or to change the child to meet some preconceived expectations or standards of behavior. The child is given the freedom to express and explore self in an accepting climate of faith and trust.

Although actively involved emotionally in experiencing with the child the child's world at the moment, the play therapist is not a playmate; this would potentially interfere with the child's freedom of expression. Children are allowed to lead the way, to determine their own direction, and to fully express feelings, interests, and experiences within acceptable limits. Although a feeling of permissiveness exists, all behaviors are not permissible. For example, a child's attempts to pour sand in the middle of the floor would be responded to with a statement such as, *"The sand is for staying in the sandbox."*

In the safety of the emotionally accepting climate of the playroom, the child is free to express confusion, insecurity, hostility, or aggression without feeling guilty about having done so. As children feel more secure, they feel more adequate in coping with their own attitudes and feelings. Positive feelings and attitudes are expressed gradually, and children come to view themselves as neither completely good nor bad, but rather as a balanced, acceptable whole. This enables children to feel adequate and to express themselves in terms of their unique, positive potentials and abilities. This seems to be an accurate description of the process for the children described in this chapter.

Nancy: From Baldness to Curls

Nancy stood in the middle of the waiting room, in the midst of a new and strange environment known as the Center for Play Therapy on the University of North Texas campus. The fingers of her left hand made small circling movements over her head as if entwining strands of hair, while two fingers of her right hand completely filled her mouth. For the most part, Nancy looked like any other four-year-old. There was one distinguishing characteristic though, that could not be overlooked. She was completely bald! The circling movement of the fingers of her left hand left little doubt that she once had hair.

Nancy's parents reported that as a 3-year-old, Nancy had curly blonde hair, but during the past year she had begun to suck her thumb, pull her hair out, and eat it. Nancy's parents had decided that she needed counseling. After diagnostic interviews with her mother, the counseling staff concurred and determined that play therapy, accompanied by periodic parent interviews, would be the most efficient therapeutic procedure.

Family Background

Although family background is not essential information for the play therapist at the onset of play therapy, Moustakas (1982) suggested that a parallel exists between early emotional development in the family and emotional growth in play therapy. "Childhood emotions develop and grow in and through family relationships, reflecting the variety and intensity of interpersonal attitudes within the family. During the first five years of life, the most dramatic and formative emotional learning takes place" (p. 217).

To better understand Nancy, her play, and the changes she exhibited in play therapy, a description of her family and their interaction is important.

Nancy, age 4, lives with her mother, father, and sister, age 4 months. Nancy was adopted when she was a few days old. Her sister is the biological child of the two parents. Both parents are college graduates; the father is a technician for a major corporation, and the mother is a homemaker. There are several complicating factors in Nancy's family background that are directly related to the themes of Nancy's play.

Nancy and her parents had lived with the maternal grandparents for the first 2 years of her life. The family then moved into their own household. The mother's relationship with the new baby was one of overprotectiveness and little mother-child separation. Nancy seldom had her mother to herself, even for short periods of time. Nancy may have seen herself as "dethroned" from her position as the center of attention.

Nancy's father has a son from a previous marriage who visits and then returns to his mother. This situation may validate Nancy's fear of the lack of anything permanent in her life. Adding to this possible fear is the fact that Nancy's mother suffers from an illness that results in frequent hospitalization for periods of several days. The mother also must receive daily injections at home for her illness.

Nancy's mother and grandmother take an instructional approach with Nancy, which results in restrictive limits being placed on almost all of her behavior. Areas that are stressed constantly are neatness, manners, learning, and performing what she has learned for others. The environment is loving. Nancy's mother tries diligently to be the good mother, even though many limits are set for Nancy. The results manifest themselves in Nancy's fear of separation from her mother, competition with her younger sister, and rebellion against the overwhelming number of limits and demands placed on her.

NANCY IN PLAY THERAPY

A Cautious Beginning Turns Messy

In the waiting room before the first session, Nancy sucked her thumb and called for her mother to pick her up. Since her mother was already holding her baby sister Mary, Nancy contented herself with sucking her thumb and standing to one side, warily eyeing the play therapist. The family was invited to walk down the hall together to the playroom. At the door, Mary and her mother were asked to return to the waiting room, and Nancy began her play therapy experience. She turned slowly around and looked at all of the toys, much like a china doll revolving in a department store window. After carefully exploring the room with her eyes, she began to tentatively touch and examine the toys in the room. Making contact with most of the toys seemed important to her.

By the middle of the second session, off came the shoes and Nancy daintily put a little sand between all her toes. The water faucet caught her eye. Sand and water trips became the order of the day, with each trip adding water and sand to the floor. The play therapist said, "The sandbox can hold two more cups of water, Nancy, or the sink can hold 20 cups of water." She laughed and chose to continue playing in the sand without additional water. The play therapist sensed that Nancy felt more trusting in this session.

Being Free and Accepted

During the third session, Nancy shoved two baby dolls into the stove and doused them with water. She then proceeded to take their place in the baby bed and suck on their water-filled bottle.

Baby play continued as the primary act in the next three sessions. For the first time, Nancy felt free to push back the restrictive boundaries set for her by her mother and grandmother. The therapist was always given at least one, and sometimes two, babies to hold in her lap while Nancy played with other babies and surreptitiously sucked on the baby bottle. She climbed inside the doll house and the refrigerator to spend more time sucking on her bottle.

She further released her emotions by crumbling Play-Doh and walking in it and spilling paint. When she spilled the paint, she said, "I'm going to tell my mommy, and she will be so mad," verbalizing her awareness of her boundaries. Whereas her paintings formerly were straight lines and structured, now her paintings became free, flowing, and expressive. This movement to be more free carried over to the Play-Doh. At first, she would only touch it; now she willingly stuck her fingers in it.

Whatever Nancy produced or felt was accepted by the therapist. No value statements were made. Nancy's reactions to her own behaviors were supported. The play therapist conveyed acceptance of Nancy's thoughts and decisions in the playroom. This kind of unconditional acceptance seemed to be freeing to Nancy and to help her trust herself.

In the fifth session, Nancy threw clay, painted the riding car, and then carefully dumped her brand new shoes that her grandmother had just bought her into the water-filled sink. After this outburst of anger, she threw the babies out of their bed, got into their bed, covered up, sucked the bottle, and said "You come get me when I cry." The therapist responded "You want to be held and loved." Nancy got up out of the baby bed, walked over, and climbed onto the therapist's lap with the baby bottle. They rocked and crooned for about three minutes. Nancy's eyes glazed over as she got back into the baby bed and acted out the baby role.

Nancy more or less staggered out to her car that day. She could not quite shake the intensity of her role as the baby. She angrily said "no" to instructions given her by her mother.

Although Nancy had never attempted to pull her hair during the play therapy sessions, this was the first day that she did not pull her hair in the waiting room in the presence of her mother. The play therapist noticed wisps of fine baby hair covering her head.

Even though she continued to suck on the bottle for short amounts of time in later sessions, Nancy never returned to her baby role with the intense emotion as was displayed this day. Being the mother of these babies was a new and rewarding role for Nancy. Painting, cutting up Play-Doh, sticking her hands into the paint, and using lots of glue and paper began to develop as the primary activities. Babies were a thing of the past.

Nancy with Curls

When Nancy came bouncing in for the seventh session, her head was covered with short, naturally curly, blonde hair. She continued to play with a wide variety of toys, especially the expressive arts and crafts materials. She began to play "mother and Nancy" with the play therapist. Nancy, who was the mother, said "No, no, no, this is mine. You can't have it. Play with your toys." The therapist, who was asked to play the role of Nancy, whispered, "Tell me what Nancy does when Mother says no, no, no." She said, "You suck your thumb and pull your hair and eat it." The therapist demonstrated to make sure the procedure was correct and asked, "Now what?" Nancy, in a mother's voice, said, "Don't do that," and laughed. She was aware of her habit.

In the waiting room, her grandmother was trying to manage Nancy and wanted her to put on her coat. Nancy said "no" instead of retreating to her former behavior of sucking her thumb and pulling her hair. This ability to resist was short lived. Grandmother's attempt to control Nancy was to recite a poem: "I'll tell you of cabbages and kings." Nancy's response was to freeze and stare into space as she began to suck her thumb and pull her hair. With both of them shuffling out the door, the grandmother took Nancy's thumb out of her mouth and stated, "Wet thumbs get chapped in the cold air." Even though Nancy occasionally succumbed to this instructional pressure, her hair continued to grow.

In the eighth session, Nancy was reminded that this would be the final session. Nancy did not respond verbally, but began her usual play, which no longer included crawling into holes, sucking on the bottle, acting like the baby, or asking the therapist to hold the babies. Nancy's play with the babies during the last three sessions was characterized by assigning the role of "mommy" to herself. With the paints, Play-Doh, and sand, her play was free but not so messy. Knowing this was her last session, Nancy's usual goodbye to the toys was given an added dimension; she took the bottle of water and poured just a little bit on each of her favorite toys. She smiled again and sauntered out of the playroom.

In the waiting room, dialogue about this being her last session, with an invitation for her to visit anytime, met with silence and basic refusal to acknowledge the conversation. There was, however, no anger, thumb sucking, or hair pulling.

Parent Consultation

Consulting with parents in conjunction with the child's play therapy experience can enhance the therapeutic process by facilitating communication in the home. When consulting with parents, the play therapist must explain to parents that the child's play therapy sessions are confidential. Therefore, the consultation sessions will not revolve around the specifics of the child's play. In Nancy's case, the play therapist met with her parents every other week for approximately a half hour, and on two occasions, full 1-hour sessions were conducted. During these consultation sessions, the therapist's goals were to provide insight for the parents with respect to Nancy's feelings and, perception of her world and to develop communication skills, which would enhance the parent's relationship with Nancy, and parenting skills, which, if adopted, would benefit both Nancy and her parents.

Discussion

Nancy's play can be described in the following observable stages outlined by Guerney (1983):

1. Children begin by acclimating themselves to the playroom situation and the play therapist.

2. Children begin to test limits, express anger, and experience freedom.

3. Children deal with the independence/dependance relationship.

4. Children begin to express positive feelings about themselves and the world. Children also begin to make decisions about how they will deal with their world.

The play therapy experience provided Nancy a way in which to organize her experiences, express her feelings, and explore relationships. The development of the relationship between Nancy and the play therapist grew from one of caution to one of trust and acceptance. As a result of Nancy's environment and her perceptions of it, she began her play as she would any other new experience. She was guarded to protect herself from *dos* and *don'ts*. Nancy had never experienced an atmosphere in which she could decide, without fear or disapproval, what she wanted to do. This atmosphere created by the play therapist, the single most important factor, enabled Nancy to feel what she had never felt before: the freedom to express herself.

Axline (1982) believed that "the intensity of the feelings that some children hold at very early ages, as these are revealed through a series of play therapy contacts, are often surprising" (p.49). Through her play, Nancy acted out her feelings of frustration and anger. These became apparent in relation to her apparent confusion concerning her place in the family and her mother's attachment to her younger sister Mary. Nancy's play with babies, bottles, and baby bed provided her a unique experience through which she experimented and began to resolve this inner conflict. Nancy's anxiety related to separation from her mother, and her anger toward sharing her mother with her sister seemed to be resolved as the play therapy progressed. She began to accept and live the role of older sister, not baby. This change was evident in the playroom and at home.

The second apparent frustration with which Nancy was struggling was her constant anger at the vast array of limits placed on her by her mother and grandmother. In trying to fulfill the role of the good mother and the good grandmother, Nancy's elders had discouraged her from learning to set her own limits. One symptom of this anxiety was Nancy's baldness. Nancy chose to experiment with limit setting through water play, paints, and getting her shoes and clothes wet or dirty. After some time, she found a nice balance for herself. She enjoyed the water play and the paints, but she no longer needed to go to extremes.

More intense emotional behaviors seemed to often be preceded by a well-planned testing of limits by Nancy. Reflections of her feelings, accompanied by limit setting in a matter-of-fact way, resulted in allowing Nancy to work through the intensity of her feelings.

Sometimes important actual events in children's lives fail to enter either into their play or into their associations, and the whole emphasis, at times, lies on apparently minor happenings. But these minor happenings are of great importance to children because they have stirred up their emotions and fantasies. Nancy never sucked her thumb or pulled out her hair in the playroom. Only once did she express an interest in the wig, which was one of the toys in the playroom. When she was in the waiting room outside the playroom, she occasionally did suck her thumb, and once or twice pulled her hair when she was overwhelmed with parental instructions.

Finally, the playroom atmosphere provided Nancy with a relationship other than the usual teaching relationship that she had with her mother and grandmother. The play therapist had no preconceived expectations of Nancy and did not direct her play. Nancy soon learned that the therapist believed that she could make her own decisions. Nancy's newfound courage to make her own decisions became apparent in play therapy and also in Nancy's world outside the playroom.

Nancy was able to use her experiences in the play therapy sessions to reorient herself to her world. This process can only take place in an atmosphere where the child feels unconditionally accepted, encouraged to make choices, and emotionally safe. The regrowth of Nancy's hair seemed to be dramatic evidence that these conditions were met.

The case of Nancy—From Baldness to Curls is from Barlow, Strother, & Landreth (1985). Child-centered Play Therapy: Nancy from Baldness to Curls. *The School Counselor, 32,* (5), 347-356. Reprinted with permission of the American Association for Counseling and Development.

Case 2:
Paul—A Fearful Acting Out Child

Paul had a very close relationship with his grandfather. They went just about everywhere together in an old pickup truck. When Paul was four-years-old, his grandfather died, and although grandfather's death did not seem to be a traumatic experience for Paul, he did miss his grandfather. Two months after grandfather's death, Paul insisted that Mother take him to the cemetery to visit Paw Paw. At the cemetery, Paul ran over to the grave site, got down on his hands and knees and began to talk to Paw Paw through a hole in the flat headstone. Evidently the hole was intended for a flower vase. After talking to Paw Paw for several minutes, Paul was ready to go home. Two weeks later Paul insisted Mother take him to the cemetery again to talk to Paw Paw. This, then, became the pattern for the next two years, every other week an hour drive to the cemetery to talk to Paw Paw. During the following two years, Paul developed an obsessive fear of death. As a six-year-old in first grade, Paul was not learning to read, was very aggressive with other children on the playground, and was fearful. Paul was referred to the Center for Play

Therapy by his mother. The following protocol is from Paul's second play therapy session.

Paul: (Paul opened the door to the playroom, walked into the room and immediately began hitting the bop bag, punching-return toy) What was that? Bam. (Hits bop bag).

Therapist: You really whammed him one.

Paul: I'm the policeman. I'm the policeman now.

Therapist: You're the policeman for a while.

Paul: Ah huh. (Hits bop bag) God! Did you see that?

Therapist: You made him spin all the way around.

Paul: I, you know who I really am? The police. No. I'm gonna play with the home (doll house) for awhile. I kind of like it.

Therapist: You kind of liked that last time.

Paul: Yea. (Playing with dollhouse, arranging furniture) What happened to Batman (bop bag)? He's marked on.

Therapist: Looks like somebody marked on him.

Paul: Guess somebody did. (Returns attention to doll house.) Oh, they have a television. What's this? (Discovers toy soldier someone left in doll box.) Somebody was in here before.

Therapist: You discovered someone was here before you came today.

Paul: Who?

Therapist: Other boys and girls come here some times.

Paul: Oh. (Satisfied, returns to doll house.) This one. This must be the children's room for a little while, ain't it? Where's the car? I need the car. Oh. (Walking around the room, looking for car, finds it and brings it to the dollhouse.) Here it is.

Therapist: That's the one you had last time.

Paul: Yea. (Pinches himself with car.) Ouch! Ouch! Oh darn! Daddy has to buy a new television. He bought one. This one's for his bed. They just moved in. (Referring to doll family.)

Therapist: So they're just now moving into this house.

Paul: Again, didn't they? The television . . . They use to live in here, didn't they?

Therapist: And now they're going to live here again.

Paul: Yeah. Oh, know what they're gonna do? They're gonna take a trip. They've got to get on. (Gets large Fisher Price airplane and begins to put family dolls in the airplane.)

Therapist: They're going to fly somewhere.

Paul: Do you know where they are going really? They're going to . . . (Pretends to turn off cartoon.) And now it's time to go to New York.

Therapist: A long way away.

Paul: I'll bet it's fast. Wonder what the kids think of flying. They are going to be happy, aren't they? Aren't they?

Therapist: So they will really like that.

Paul: I know cuz they are going on a plane trip. I'm going to make them sit down, right?

Therapist: You're going to put them in there just right.

Paul: If they don't sit down and put on their seatbelts, you know what's going to happen? They're gonna have to stay home. They won't get to go on a plane trip, right?

Therapist: So they have to do just what they are supposed to or they won't get to go.

Paul: Right. The baby won't cry cuz she is going to be happy too, I bet. The mother's gonna . . . (laughing). The mother and family is too big for the plane, ain't they? (Said even though all the doll family members were inside the plane.) They're back. (Plane never left original spot.) They parked right by their home, didn't they?

Therapist: So they're just real close to their house.

Paul: (Removes dolls from plane. Returns to dollhouse) God! That was pretty fast. Guess what? You know what the Daddy's gonna do? Buy a new truck.

Therapist: So he's going to buy a new truck.

Paul: Yeah. They got two of them. They might move in this truck. They're getting ready to move. (Playing with dolls in the dollhouse.)

Therapist: And they could move in their truck.

Paul: They might. They might move. The kids are watching cartoons. The baby's, the baby's playing. Know what? After cartoons they get to go outside.

Therapist: So they are going to watch TV and then go outside.

Paul: The Daddy's gonna get a new truck. So she's (mom) staying here cooking supper. Daddy couldn't find a new truck. (Gets another truck, returns to dollhouse.) Here's one. He's gonna buy this one. (moves truck around) Golly, that's a big truck, ain't it? He might not buy that truck. Oh. Ahhh. Look now. Look at this now. Daddy's at work. He can't buy a truck. He didn't find one.

Therapist: He didn't find one he liked.

Paul: (Going to sandbox.) He's going to find something he likes someday, ain't he? Do you have another truck? Now stay tuned for Batman. (Runs over to bop bag, punches bop bag fiercely nine times in face, wrestles him and pushes him down.) He's down for a little while. I'm gonna put him on this chair. (Puts Batman bop bag on a chair). He's gonna. I'm gonna shoot him. I got these many guns. I'm gonna shoot at him. (Picks up guns and small plastic TV.) Ooooo! This can be a different TV.

Therapist: Uh huh.

Paul: (Paul puts TV in the dollhouse). I guess that's Daddy's TV.

Therapist: So he's going to have a special one.

Paul: Yea. (Picks up rifle that shoots Ping Pong balls) Hey where's those round balls? (Picks up Ping Pong ball.) I'm gonna shoot him (Batman) for good, ain't I? Ain't I?

Therapist: So you know just what you're going to do. You've got it planned.

Paul: Look! Ready for Batman? Batman's gonna be in big trouble, ain't he? (Shoots.) I got him, didn't I?

Therapist: You got him the first shot.

Paul: I'm gonna kill him more. (Aims, shoots and misses.) Hmmm, better try another gun. (Tries dart pistol.) There's another. I got it. (Shoots to side of bop bag.) I missed him, didn't I?

Therapist: It went right past him.

Paul: (Shoots again to side of bop bag.) It's a hard shot, ain't it?

Therapist: It's hard to hit it from way over there.

Paul: (Shoots again and misses). I missed him a bunch, didn't I? (Picks up the darts.) When I get him, guess what I'm gonna do? I'm gonna tie him up and kill him. I'm gonna cut him up.

Therapist: You're really going to kill him.

Paul: (Shoots and misses again. Shoots bop bag again.) Got him! (Runs over and puts bop bag on the floor, head under a chair so that bop bag is horizontal.) Supposed to be dead for a little while. You know what I'm gonna do to Batman? Ahhh. (Gets rubber knife and cuts the middle of Bobo. Goes to kitchen and looks through the dishes.) You know what I'm gonna do?

Therapist: You've got something planned now.

Paul: I'm not gonna poison him. (He cooked poison last session and fed it to Batman.) You know what I am going to do this time. Na. I'm not going to. I'm gonna kill him again. I'm gonna poison him. That's what I was gonna do. Let's see. (Picks up hand gun, walks over to Batman, aims gun right next to Batman's face and shoots.) Ha. Ha. (Goes to sandbox, stands in middle and fills bucket with sand.) Guess what I'm gonna do?

Therapist: You can tell me what you're going to do.

Paul: Well, I'm gonna put Batman in this. (Drops bucket, starts sweeping in the sandbox and outside the sandbox.) Sweep the blood off. Ha. Ha. Sweep the blood. Batman's gonna be really dead this time cuz I'll really kill him.

Therapist: This time you'll make sure you kill him.

Paul: You're right. This time I'm going to make sure you're gonna get killed.

Therapist: Oh, I'm going to get it too.

Paul: I know. You're Robin.

Therapist: You're going to kill both of us.

Paul: Bet you're right. Hope I don't miss ya. (Said with lilt to voice and big grin)

Therapist: I'm not for shooting. (Paul aims way over therapist's head and shoots wall.) I know you would like to shoot me. You can shoot Batman. (Paul again shoots over therapist's head. It is obvious he does not intend to shoot the therapist.)

Paul: Ohhhh. I missed you. (Shoots again.) Ahhhhh, gosh. (Begins to play with phone.) You know who I'm gonna call? Mmm ammm. (Gets other phone and dials.) Yeah, Batman's dead. Hum hum ok. (Leaves phone and goes across room.) Hey I'm gonna make a little song to wake Batman up, ain't I? (Plays xylophone and looks expectantly at Batman.) He's almost woke up. (Walks over to Batman.) Chop his neck off, ain't I? (Hits Batman.) Now he's dead. Now I'm going to play with Dad again, Mr. old Dad. (Plays in dollhouse and with the scooter truck.) Here's his new truck. That's gonna work better. He bought a new television, didn't he?

Therapist: So now they have two televisions.

Paul: Right. Hey, does this work? You put it in there? (Examining TV and figures out where a piece goes.)

Therapist: There, you figured it out.

Paul: Does it move? (Tries to make picture screen move.)

Therapist: I guess you're wondering, does this thing really work like a real one?

Paul: It didn't move. Daddy bought a new television didn't he? Mr. Dad, for them.

Therapist: Dad brought it home for them.

Paul: To watch . . . to watch. The kids saw the new truck Daddy bought. Daddy . . . The kids didn't know it yet. They start running.

Therapist: Oh, he sort of surprised them.

Paul: The kids didn't see nothing like it, didn't they?

Therapist: So it was a special surprise.

Paul: Dad's gonna, he's gonna have to take it back someday.

Therapist: So Dad can't keep it.

Paul: (Puts the dolls in the truck.) They're gonna have a ride. Where's the baby? Oh. Get in there. (Puts doll family in scooter truck.) They're gonna have fun, aren't they?

Therapist: So they're all going together in that new truck and have fun.

Paul: (Paul pushes the truck slowly around the doll house, makes motor noise, stays very close to doll house.) They're almost home, aren't they?

Therapist: They're coming back.

Paul: Time for them to get out. (Takes dolls out and puts in the house.) Oh, the kids say, "Oowh! Oowh!"

Therapist: They didn't want to.

Paul: They didn't want to go home. They liked their ride, didn't they?

Therapist: They were having lots of fun.

Paul: Guess what? He might buy a tractor. He gets to go to work.

Therapist: So, he bought a TV, and then a truck and he might even buy a tractor.

Paul: They might move.

Therapist: Hmmm. They might move.

Paul: Yeah, they're gonna miss cartoons in a little while, aren't they? Daddy has to go. Mamma has to put baby in bed, don't she? (Picks up baby.) I bet this baby's gonna be baldheaded, don't you.

Therapist: No hair on his head.

Paul: I know. That means he's gonna be baldheaded someday.

Therapist: Hmmm.

Paul: This baby sure is, ain't it. We don't want no baby to be baldheaded. It's like a little boy being baldheaded. They're gonna do something. Daddy has to go to work. He might move something. He might get a new tractor. I bet he is. He needs one. Then he might move. Ahh Oh! Here they come! Here comes the new tractor. (Plays with a tractor.) I think the kids are gonna be happy with the tractor. Oh, God! It's too big with the steering wheel. (Tries to put tractor inside scooter car.)

Therapist: It won't quite fit in there.

Paul: I guess he has to buy another tractor. I got it. Turn it over. Na. (Can't make it go inside truck.) Do it backwards? Na. I guess he can't buy one today. Here's a tractor for him. (Finds another that fits.) Watch the tractor. Here's the tractor now. Let's get going. The cartoons are over. They got to watch it, didn't they? (Said with glee.)

Therapist: That made them happy to get to watch cartoons.

Paul: (Begins loading furniture into scooter car.) Yea, but poor mom can't cook any more (as he loads kitchen stove). She was hungry. The dad was hungry. You know something, they can move that bathroom.

Therapist: Uh huh. They can move just about everything in that house.

Paul: In the truck. Oh God! And they moved, didn't they?

Therapist: Moved everything out of the house.

Paul: Yeah. They decided to live here again. (Puts furniture back in dollhouse.)

Therapist: So they moved out and then decided to move back in.

Paul: Know why? They were missing some more cartoons.

Therapist: So they wanted to get back and watch some.

Paul: Know what Dad has to do. (Moves to the sandbox with father doll.)

Therapist: You can tell me what he's gonna do.

Paul: Ok. He's gonna . . . he died.

Therapist: Oh, Daddy died.

Paul: Yeah. So they're gonna bury him in the sand. (Scoops out hole in sand and begins to bury father doll).

Therapist: He died and now he's getting buried right there.

Paul: I know. I guess they have to have a new Daddy, right? (Continues covering doll with sand.)

Therapist: So if that daddy died, they'll need to get another one.

Paul: Ooooh. He's all buried.

Therapist: Now he can't be seen.

Paul: There's where he's at. (Places funnel upside down on top of grave with spout pointing up.) The kids came to see him. The baby's still asleep. (Goes to dollhouse, gets boy and girl dolls.)

Therapist: Hmm, so they're going to go and see where he is buried.

Paul: (Placed boy doll's head at funnel end.) They heard something. Uhhhhhhh. (Sound coming from grave.)

Therapist: They heard something where Daddy is buried.

Paul: Yea. And guess what. They are going to unbury him. (Pulls doll out of sand.) Oh, God! He's alive!

Therapist: So he really wasn't dead. Now he's alive.

Paul: They were surprised at him. (Sounds really excited and glad.)

Therapist: They were surprised but happy.

Paul: Oh my God, look! They're having a tornado in this area by their home. They better hurry home, right?

Therapist: Tornados are dangerous.

Paul: I know. It can blow houses down. One of them's, one of them's in the graveyard. That's the girl (Buries doll in sand. Therapist can't see doll being buried.)

Therapist: So the girl got left in the graveyard.

Paul: Uh uh, she's buried.

Therapist: Oh, she's buried in the graveyard.

Paul: She does not want . . . She does not want the tornado to get her.

Therapist: So the tornado can't get her there.

Paul: The tornado's past. Oooh. Look what happened! (Knocks over toys near the dollhouse.) God!

Therapist: The tornado wrecked some things.

Paul: Yea, some but it didn't wreck this. (Points to Scooter Truck.) All the kids have to get in the house fast, lay down and rest.

Therapist: So they're hoping they'll be safe in the house.

Paul: And she told her to get in and rest too, while Daddy got the pick up truck over. (Pulls truck over.) Ah, oh. The tornado's out. Guess what. Daddy's gonna be surprising. Guess what. Stay tuned for Batman!

Therapist: Now its time for Batman again.

Paul: (Goes over to Batman and attempts to put handcuffs on himself.) Uh, oh, they caught me, didn't they?

Therapist: You got caught by somebody.

Paul: The police. (Continues trying to handcuff his hands behind his back.)

Therapist: Oh, the police caught you. Hmm.

Paul: For killing Batman.

Therapist: So you killed Batman, and then the policeman caught you.

Paul: Yea. Batman is alive now. Ouch. No wonder I can't put these on when I have my hands behind my back. Here. (Brings handcuffs to therapist for aid, therapist fastens them behind his back.) OK, I'm in jail.

Therapist: So the policeman handcuffed you and took you to jail.

Paul: I know. First he has to do something. He can't kill nobody. The police surrounded him, and he has to put this (knife) back.

Therapist: So they fixed him up so he can't kill anyone.

Paul: Yeah. They have to put the knife back. The Batman's alive. Better get him up. (Stands Batman up.)

Therapist: So he's ok now.

Paul: But first wait. (Moves Batman around.) There. Uh oh, I'm out of jail now. Help me. (Tries to take handcuffs off.) Ouch, ouch. (Handcuffs pinch his wrists.)

Therapist: Sometimes those things pinch.

Paul: Yea. (Takes handcuffs off.)

Therapist: But you got them off.

Paul: Guess what. I'm the police now. I'm going to get to be a police, didn't I?

Therapist: So now you're going to be the one with the handcuffs.

Paul: I'm the police now. I'm Batman and I'll bring you in jail, ok?

Therapist: You can pretend that someone is doing that, and I'll watch.

Paul:	Ok. That. Mr. Policeman is having trouble, ain't he? (Trying to hook handcuffs together.)
Therapist:	Looks like he's having a hard time getting those on there just right.
Paul:	Oh, no. He got it. Now he don't have trouble.
Therapist:	You figured it out.
Paul:	Uh huh, I found the way. (Hooks handcuffs on pocket.)
Therapist:	Hhmmm. You found a way to do it. Paul, we have five more minutes in the playroom today.
Paul:	Oooh. (Doesn't want to end. Makes shooting noise, runs over and dives on floor. Pretends to wrestle someone.) Got him, didn't I?
Therapist:	You caught him right there.
Paul:	(Wrestles imaginary person for several minutes.)
Therapist:	You're really working hard.
Paul:	Yeah, I know. He's a tough one.
Therapist:	He's really tough but you're wrestling him.
Paul:	I got him down.
Therapist:	You won. Paul, our time is up for today. It's time to go to the waiting room where your Mom is.
Paul:	AAAAh! OK. (Walks to door and opens it.)

As is often true in play therapy, several themes were evident in this second session. Television seemed to be very important to Paul as noted in his numerous references to TV. A theme of moving and leaving the security of home was evident in the scenes involving the airplane trip in which the people didn't fly away, the auto trip in which Paul stayed very close to the dollhouse, and his announcing the family was going to move, followed by loading all the furniture and fixtures into the truck and promptly stating, "They decided to live here again." Another theme was his play and statements indicating death is not permanent, "Supposed to be dead for a little while." The culmination of this theme was the burial of the father figure in the sandbox and the boy doll figure talking to the buried father doll. This scene was dramatically similar to Paul's trips to the cemetery, to "talk" to his grandfather. After Paul began play therapy, he only asked one time to go to the cemetery indicating a significant change in Paul. In the fifth session, Paul announced, "My Paw Paw died you know." This was the first clear indication of his acceptance of the death of his grandfather.

CASE 3:
Ryan—A Dying Child

Two brothers, ages 7 and 5, were wrestling, and the 7-year-old suffered a broken leg. A trip to the hospital resulted in a surprising and traumatic finding. Cancer had weakened the bone, necessitating immediate, radical surgery to amputate his leg at the hip. The diagnosis: Ryan had only a few months to live.

Play Therapy

My first contact with Ryan came as a result of play therapy sessions with his five-year-old brother who had been referred to me by wise parents who recognized the potential emotional trauma for the five-year-old and the possibility of deep personal guilt. Prior to the eighth session with the five-year-old, his mother called to say the five year old wanted to invite Ryan to come with him to the special playroom. I viewed this as a significant positive development in the five-year-old's growth, that he was willing to share the playroom experience; that he perhaps recognized at some level that something here might be helpful to Ryan; and in our relationship, that he felt secure enough to bring Ryan.

The five-year-old showed Mom and Ryan the way to the playroom. Mom carried Ryan, sat him down in the middle of the playroom, and left. This was the first time I had seen Ryan, and I was overcome with a deep sadness and an ache that welled up in me as I watched this underdeveloped little boy try to scoot over to the toy shelf, but strength failed him. Ryan's condition so captured my attention, and I was so caught up in my own emotion that the five-year-old's offer to hand Ryan a toy jarred me back to the reality of his presence too—he needed me as much as Ryan.

Ryan took the ten-inch-tall dinosaur, stuck a toy soldier in the wide open gaping mouth, and with his finger slowly pushed the soldier all the way into the mouth until the soldier fell down the dinosaur's throat into the hollow body. He then stood the dinosaur on the floor and lined up three rows of thirty toy soldiers facing the dinosaur. Ryan very carefully made sure all the weapons were pointed toward the dinosaur, then leaned back and studied the scene for several minutes. Not one shot was fired—all that strategic placement of soldiers and they just stood there unexpectedly impotent facing the huge monster. No, the feeling was more clear now. This was not a monster, this was the enemy within Ryan. The enemy that could not be stopped. The soldiers were powerless, their weapons useless. The monster was too powerful. He could not be stopped! Ryan did not say one word or make any kind of sound during this entire process and did not need to. I was in touch with him, and he was communicating.

This was one of those rare experiences in the living relationship of the playroom when, for a few brief moments, time and the reality of everything outside the fleeting experience of the moment, did not exist in consciousness for either one of us. I was sensing Ryan's inner experiencing, captivated by the awesomeness of the scene before me. A moan of anguish moved slowly through my soul—"He knows. He knows." Then the moment was gone, broken by Ryan asking his brother for the can to put the soldiers in. Thus began my brief but extraordinary journey of learning about living as Ryan shared living with me.

I conducted play therapy sessions with Ryan during the last two months of his life. Ryan's condition deteriorated rapidly over the next few weeks, necessitating several trips to the hospital, and each time the pronounced diagnosis was "He has only a few hours to live." A kind and sensitive mom asked a friend to call me on these occasions, and after I hung up the phone, I wept for a dear, little friend I would not see again. Then I would receive word that Ryan had rallied, and a few days later he would be back in his home, asking to see me again.

During the last month of his life, Ryan was too weak to leave his bed, so I carried my traveling play therapy kit to his home. I was eager for the opportunity to be with Ryan, but each time I parked in front of his home, I sat there a few minutes fully experiencing a rush of sadness, a lump in my throat, and an urge not to go in, because so much about Ryan reminded me of his impending death—purple marks on his face from the radiation treatment, the protruding growth on the side of his head, his large stomach, the thinness of his whole body. I experienced each session as probably our last one. Uttering a deep sigh of resignation to the feeling and acceptance as my problem, not Ryan's, I would prepare myself to meet Ryan, to be open to his world of experiencing, to share in what he wanted to share.

Although weak and emaciated, Ryan delighted in our sessions together. While I held the newsprint tablet, he drew pictures of Mickey Mouse with huge hands and 40 fingers thrust outward, a porcupine and a buzzard which seemed to me to represent his struggle against cancer. Ryan was delightfully uninhibited. I had never imagined I would need to assist a child with a urine bottle in the middle of a play therapy session; thus, my initial reaction to his request to "use the bathroom" was an awkward and fumbling "I'll go get the nurse." Ryan's reaction was, "We don't need her." And indeed we didn't. Ryan trusted me and was patient with my awkwardness.

The next week Ryan was in the hospital again, made another dramatic recovery, and asked to see me again the next week. In this session, Ryan drew the Mickey Mouse figure again but with a smaller body and hands. He colored Mickey dark purple and the face looked hollow with very dark eyes. It did indeed look like death. Ryan then chose an egg carton from the kit, colored each of the egg cells a bright color, closed the carton and colored it black all over. Yes, beauty and color and brightness and hope are on the inside. Next, Ryan drew a picture of a straw house, a stick house, and a brick house, talked about the straw house and stick house being blown down and the three pigs being safe in the brick house. An interesting feature of the houses was that the brick house had the very largest door. I believe Ryan somehow intuitively felt death was near and that he would be in a safe place. Ryan then announced that he was tired; so I left.

That was the last time I saw Ryan. During our times together Ryan had led the focus and exploration of the sessions into those areas important to him, had walked down the road he had chosen, and had played in the way he wanted to play. In our relationship, I discovered that even under the most personally stressful of circumstances, children can experience the pleasure of playing and can feel in control even when circumstances seem to be out of control.

WHAT I LEARNED ABOUT ME

I know so little about what it is like for a child to face death.
> Therefore, I will be open to learning what Ryan taught me.

I experience sadness when I think of a child dying.
> Therefore, I will need to protect children from my feelings.

I know so little about life.
> Therefore, I will be open to the continuous wonderment of living as experienced by children.

I sometimes focus too much on problems, what is not working out.
> Therefore, I shall work hard to look beyond to the experiential world of the child.

I am not capable of knowing what should be significant or
   important for another person.
      Therefore, I will resolve in my relationships with children
      to discover their needs.

I like it, too, when another person "sees" my world.
      Therefore, I will struggle to be sensitive to the child's
      world.

I am more fully me when I feel safe.
      Therefore, I will, with all that I am capable, try hard
      to help children to feel safe with me.

WHAT I LEARNED ABOUT RYAN

I wanted to withdraw from the reminder of his pain,
      But Ryan wanted to be with me.

I could not solve his problem,
      But he did not expect me to.

I thought about him dying,
      But he focused on living.

I experienced deep sadness as I approached our times together,
      But he was eager and excited.

I saw an emaciated body,
      But he saw a friend.

I wanted to protect him,
      But he wanted to share with me a relationship.

RYAN LIVES

   Society will report that Ryan died, but I have recorded
in my heart his struggle to live, the oxygen mask, the bright
splotches of color he chose, the pain he endured, the fatigue
laden with delight in his squeaky little voice, the enthusiasm

and vigor with which he drew pictures. So, he lives. Not the part they see, but what I see! This dying little person taught me lessons for living.

I remember Ryan saying, "This is our special time, just for me and you. No one will ever know about it, Garry. It's just for us." I wonder what Ryan remembers.

THE RELATIONSHIP

This very special relationship with a special little person at a crucial time in his life gave me an unusual perspective on allowing children to lead the relationship into areas important to them rather than in a direction I might think important. I experienced a genuine prizing of this unique child, an appreciation for his expressive eagerness, which was only temporarily dimmed by overwhelming fatigue from the physical struggle. Our times together seemed to be an oasis in his life, a time when he was free to be in control of the direction of his experiences, even though reality dictated that he could not control what he was experiencing in his body. Ryan died three days after our last play therapy session. During our times together, Ryan focused on living rather than dying, on joy rather than sadness, on creative expression rather than apathy, and on his appreciation of our relationship rather than on the loss of relationships. It was with wonder and awe that I experienced with this dying child the shared joy, release, and excitement of the moment as he played out our living relationship. Play was special to Ryan, and our relationship was prized by him. I learned that success, then, may not be what I perceive to be needed, or the correcting of a problem. It may indeed be the brief momentary experiencing of a caring, safe relationship where the child is free to be all that he is capable of being at that time. Ryan, a child who was dying, taught me lessons for living.

The preceding case is an expansion of The Case of Ryan—A Dying Child from Landreth (1988) Lessons for Living from a Dying child. *Journal of Counseling and Development*, 67 (2), 100. Reprinted with permission of the American Association for Counseling and Development.

Case 4:
Cindy—A Manipulative Child

Mrs. M described her five-year-old daughter Cindy as, "She is careful to take care of her toys and things, always puts things back and cleans up her room when I ask her to. She's a good child, but I don't know . . . (long pause). I'm always angry at her and I don't know why. I know it's not good for me to be so angry at her, but I am. (pause) That's hard for me to admit, but it's true. I don't know what could be wrong. I'm just angry at her a lot. She's not a problem or anything at home. We do have a conflict when I have to discipline her. She tells me I'm stupid. She seems to say that a lot. She wants her way all the time."

An exploratory play therapy session with Cindy seemed warranted to formulate a picture of Cindy on her own terms and to decide whether or not play therapy was needed, so an appointment was scheduled for the next week. During the session, Cindy attempted to manipulate and control the therapist, insisting that he get items for her even though they were within her reach, asking him questions and then making decisions for him. She was not able to tolerate even the slightest mistake in her paintings, kept saying, "I can do one better" as she wadded the paintings up and threw them into the trash can. When the therapist announced the five minute warning, Cindy said, "I don't care. I'm not leaving." At the end of the session, the therapist indicated the time was up, and Cindy said, " I told you I'm not leaving. I'm going to do some, uh, art." She moved over to the art materials and began painting. The therapist responded, "You would like to be the one who decides just how long you stay, but our time is up. It's time to go to the waiting room where your mother is." The therapist took a couple of steps toward the door. Cindy continued to paint and to verbalize her resistance. The therapist continued to reflect her wants and to set the limit on ending the session. His patience paid off when Cindy voluntarily walked out under her own steam.

Cindy exhibited so much manipulative behavior that it was strongly suspected this was typical of her behavior at home. An interview with Mom confirmed that Cindy was doing a lot of subtle manipulative things of which Mom was unaware and that this was the basic reason for her anger toward Cindy. Additional sessions were scheduled with Cindy. Her second play therapy session is very revealing of manipulative behavior and her efforts to build a relationship with the therapist.

Second Play Therapy Session

Cindy: (Cindy enters playroom goes directly to sandbox and begins playing. Sits on side of sandbox, sifting sand. Cindy talks about the new house her family has moved into.) I know how long . . . a, uh, long time . . . more weeks . . . uh, I just don't know how many days that has been.

Therapist: You can remember how long you've been there. You just don't know how many weeks that makes.

Cindy: (Continues playing with sand.) I kind of like you better today.

Therapist: You like me better than last time.

Cindy: Yes. (Moves from sandbox to table where paints are.) Come on let's paint . . . . You may help me if you want or you may watch if you like. What do you want to do, watch?

Therapist: I'll watch.

Cindy: (Goes into bathroom, begins washing brushes and paint jar in sink.) A black sink.

Therapist: You made the sink black?

Cindy: Yes, with black water.

Therapist: Oh.

Cindy: (Continues mixing water with paints.) You hear that water?

Therapist: Uhhmm. I can hear it all the way in here.

Cindy: Well, here it goes again. Better watch out. (Turns water on full force. Stays in bathroom running the water for several minutes. Comes from bathroom and gets large piece of paper.) Watch what I'm going to put on this.

Therapist: You're really going to work on that.

Cindy: First thing I was going to do was paint. I did, right?

Therapist: You decided that before you came.

Cindy: Yes, I did. It was yesterday. My birthday was day before yesterday, etc. (Selects Play Doh can.) Is it alright to put . . . I'm going to put water in this so I can rinse this out. (Goes into bathroom. Her sandals slip on sand on floor and make scraping noise.) These are slippery sandals.

Therapist: They look slippery.

Cindy: They are slippery. (Comes back and starts painting. Therapist is sitting directly across table from Cindy.) Are you interested in art?

Therapist: I like art, and it looks like you like art.

Cindy: I like to make it. Yesterday, I think I made . . . uh, yeah, I made a tree with some flowers with a kitten in it, and uh, a fountain in it by the kitten.

Therapist: So you put lots of things in that picture.

Cindy: And some birds and a sky . . . some white birds and a blue sky and some leaves . . . and . . . grass and then I hung it on the bulletin board I got for my birthday. It was on the 4th of July.

Therapist: So that made it a real special birthday.

Cindy: When the people celebrated. I was a firecracker.

Therapist: Lots of things happened on your birthday.

Cindy: Uhhmmm, . . . and the reason was the police were out and they were looking for people who were doing firecrackers.

Therapist: Hmmm.

Cindy: Maybe they were after people because you don't supposed to do that. You get hurt.

Therapist: So they were trying to keep people from getting hurt.

Cindy: Uhhmmm. (Continues to paint. As she moves brush from painting to dip into paint jar, therapist turns his head to follow brush.) Without moving your head you can watch me paint at the same time.

Therapist: Sometimes some of the things I do bother you.

Cindy: Yes. (Moves paint brush back and forth rapidly in front of therapist's face. Taunting look on her face.) Giggles.

Therapist: I guess you were wondering then if I would play a game with you.

Cindy: Uhhmmm.

Therapist: And I just decided I would watch you.

Cindy: (Sticks paint brush toward counselor's face and giggles.) I fooled you didn't I. You thought I was going to paint on you.

Therapist: You like to fool me sometimes.

Cindy: Yes, I just like to fool you.

Therapist: Oh, you just like to fool me.

Cindy: Right. I can't fool Debbie. She's my cousin because she don't like it.

Therapist: She doesn't like for you to play games with her.

Cindy: No. Uh, see she don't like me playing tricks on her.

Therapist: Uhhmmm.

Cindy: But Robin don't mind.

Therapist: So with some people it's OK and with some people it's not.

Cindy: Uhhmmm. Robin's my favorite because Janie won't let me do that.

Therapist: You really like the people who will let you play tricks on them.

Cindy: Uhhmmm. Robin's my best one because anyway she was (Continues to paint.) Blue and red. (As she draws house with blue and red windows)

Therapist: A blue window and a red window.

Cindy: And a purple house with a black door.

Therapist: You used lots of colors.

Cindy: Is time almost up?

Therapist: We have 30 more minutes today. (She is painting a black door on the house and the black runs into the other colors.)

Cindy: Good. I can mess my picture up. Next time I won't splash it. I can make something better. I can make a little something better.

Therapist: You think you can make one better than that.

Cindy: I can! I just . . . I can. (Wads wet picture up into a ball and throws it into trash can.)

Therapist: You just know you can.

Cindy: (She discovers finger paints and decides to finger paint.) These smell like finger paints don't they?

Therapist: You've played with finger paints before.

Cindy: Yes, in Sunday School. Do you water finger paints?

Therapist: In here you can choose what you want to do.

Cindy: (Goes into bathroom, puts water into finger paints, returns, and begins to paint carefully with brush. It is obvious she doesn't want to get paint on her hands. Uses brush to paint finger paints for a while, then dips brush into finger paints and starts to transfer brush to other hand but notices paint on brush handle just as her fingers are about to close around the brush and quickly moves her hand away.)

Therapist: Just not sure whether or not to put your fingers into that.

Cindy: Yes I can. It's finger paints. (Goes into bathroom and washes brush, comes out and continues to paint finger paints with brush, uses all the colors to paint circles, goes back to bathroom, washes brush, comes out leaving water running. Mixes several colors of fingerpaint on her painting.)

Therapist: Now it has lots of colors all mixed up.

Cindy: Would you be quiet so I can do this.

Therapist: When I talk that bothers you.

Cindy: Yeah.

Therapist: You just don't like for people to bother you when you are doing things.

Cindy: It's all right except for the talking because I don't want, like to be bothered when I'm doing art. Rhonda's all right because she's just a baby, and she don't know better but you do! And you better be quiet!

Therapist: I should know better.

Cindy: Yes.

Therapist: And I should do what you tell me to do.

Cindy: Right. (Continues painting and then goes into bathroom, washes hands, comes out and begins to paint with just the tip of one finger, draws a tree.) There. A tree. I can do a better tree than that.

Therapist: A lot of times it just seems to you like you could do it better.

Cindy: Well, I can.

Therapist: You keep telling yourself, "I can do one better."

Cindy: Well, I can.

Therapist: Uh hmmm, and you just know you can.

Cindy: That's right. I know. Now would you please be quiet. Remember what I said?

Therapist: And you'd like for me to do what you tell me to.

Cindy: Well, I sure do. (Continues painting, hums a tune while painting vigorously with both hands—really leans into the activity of swirling her hands around on the paper.) I'm going to put a little glue in there. OK? . . . OK?

Therapist: I guess you're wondering, "Can I use that glue?"

Cindy: Uh huh. May I?

Therapist: You're just not sure whether you should or not.

Cindy: Can I? (Talks about Bobo the punching toy and goes into bathroom, washes hands. Returns and begins mixing paste with her finger painting. Gets double handfuls of paste from quart jar.)

Therapist: You got just as much as you wanted.

Cindy: (Gets huge handful of paste.) It looks like ice cream.

Therapist: Just reminds you of ice cream.

Cindy: Yes. It's going to be purple ice cream.

Therapist: So you know just how you want it to look.

Cindy: Purple is a pretty color.

Therapist: That's a color you really like.

Cindy: Uh huh, it's my favorite. (Gets more large scoops of paste and mixes with finger paint on paper.)

Cindy: Are you Mister Rogers? (giggles)

Therapist: I guess I remind you of somebody else.

Cindy: Yes, you do . . . He likes art. I like him too.

Therapist: So you like both of us.

Cindy: Yes I do.

Cindy: Now I've got purple hands.

Therapist: Uh Humm.

Cindy: (Goes to bathroom, washes hands for a long time, comes out and says.) One more time of it and then I will be through. But first I'm going to use a little teency bit of sand in it.

Therapist: So you know just how you want it to look, and you know just what you want in it.

Cindy: (Gets a little bit of sand, adds it to her painting and announces.) That's not enough. (Goes back to sand box and gets two huge handfuls of sand and dumps it onto picture, glances up at therapist to check his reaction.)

Therapist: You got just as much as you wanted.

Cindy: (Smooths sand out, adds more paste to sand, mixes it up and says.) This will stick on.

Therapist: You kind of know how that will turn out.

Cindy: Yeah. (Mixes more paste, has paste and sand all over her hands and arms) It's some kind of an art . . . that I made up . . . just for you. (Adds more sand.)

Therapist: So you made it up just for me.

Cindy: And you may have it if you want it. Do you want it?

Therapist: If you want to leave it for me that will be fine. You made it just for me.

Cindy: You can take it home with you.

Therapist: You would just like for me to have it.

Cindy: Uh hmmm. (Goes to bathroom, washes hands.)

Therapist: Cindy, we have five more minutes in the playroom today and then it will be time to go to the waiting room where your mother is.

Cindy: (Gets pan full of sand from sandbox and adds to art project, pats it down, begins to add finger paint to the sand and paste art project and says,) I'll have to use all of the blue, OK?

Therapist: You just decided you are going to use every bit of it.

Cindy: I'll need to. (Empties all the blue finger paint and mixes with sand. Throws empty paint container in trash, goes to bathroom and washes hands, leaves water running, comes out and says,) I've been painting all day haven't I?

Therapist: Seems to you you've been painting a long time.

Cindy: (Continues to stir and mix all the colors of finger paints into the sand project, announces,) I'm finally through.

Therapist: Finished.

Cindy: For the day. (Goes to bathroom, washes hands and turns water off.) Now it's going to be a

	taco. (Folds sheet of newsprint over, smears paste on edge of paper to stick edges together.
Therapist:	Just like a big taco.
Cindy:	(Tries to lift the "taco" up by holding edges of paper. Sand, paste, paint mixture is too heavy, paper tears.) Oops! I thought I needed a lot. Looks like we're gonna have to do it like this. (Folds ends of paper over.)
Therapist:	Have to do it a different way.
Cindy:	Yes. It's like a sandwich. (Looked like one.)
Therapist:	Uh humm. A big sandwich.
Cindy:	Uh huh. Finished for the day. There we go. There's your . . . art. (Hands "art" to therapist.) You may have it.
Therapist:	You made it just for me. (Shows prizing and appreciation in tone of voice. Gently takes "art" and carefully places it on table.) Cindy our time is up for today.

In this second session, Cindy made an immediate move to make amends for the difficult time she had given the therapist in the first session by saying, "I like you better today." Her motivation seems obvious in view of the fact that this statement was made in the first couple of minutes of the session, hardly enough time for the therapist to demonstrate he was different in any way. Cindy continued, though, to test the therapist's patience and acceptance of her by insisting that he not move his head and that he stop talking. Her anxiety and need to do things just right were expressed in her destruction of her first painting. Cindy's increasing inner freedom is evident as she becomes more involved, free, and expressive with the finger paints and then was able to cope and adjust when her taco art project ripped apart. The making of an art project for the therapist was Cindy's way of building the relationship. By the end of this second session, Cindy was more self-assured, able to tolerate a mess, expressed herself more creatively and no longer needed to try to manipulate the therapist.

Case 5:
Amy—An Elective Mute Child

Brown and Lloyd (cited in Kolvin & Fundudis, 1981) reported that for every 1,000 children, there may be as many as 7.2 who do not speak at school at the age of 5. Kolvin & Fundudis (1981) defined this phenomenon, elective mutism, as "a strange condition where talking is confined to a familiar situation and a small group of intimates" (p.219). They further reported that parents of elective mute children observed normal speech development when the children began to talk, but as they were placed in more social situations, shyness became prevalent.

ELECTIVE MUTISM AND ENURESIS

In this section, the case study of Amy, a 5-year-old elective mute is described. Her mother referred her to the center because she was concerned about Amy's refusal to talk at school or in any situation away from the home. Amy also exhibited excessive shyness and suffered from enuresis, nighttime bedwetting. Amy was the middle child in her nuclear family. She had two brothers, She seemed especially close to and dependent on her mother, which is common among elective mute children (Kolvin & Fundudis, 1981).

Elective mute children seem to be very dependent on their parents, especially their mothers. This seemed to be true in Amy's case. Her mother initiated the process of play therapy and was the parent who followed through during the entire treatment period. Amy's father was never involved, but he was reported to be cooperative in the process at home. When counseling children, it is ideal for counselors to have both parents involved and informed. This case, however, demonstrates that play therapy can have positive results even though both parents are not involved in the parent consultation process.

In addition to being concerned with the elective mutism, Amy's mother also reported a concern over Amy's nighttime bedwetting. Amy's brothers also suffered from this condition. In a study of 24 elective mute children, Kolvin & Fundudis (1981) reported a significantly high level of enuresis among the participants. They also found that these children had a higher ratio of behavioral problems, suffered from excessive shyness, exhibited more immaturity (especially in speech development), that more girls than boys were elective mutes, and that elective mutism proved to be rather intractable. The American Psychiatric Association (1987), in *The Diagnostic and Statistical Manual of Mental Disorders*, has also described elective mute children as suffering from excessive shyness, social isolation, behavioral difficulties, and, possibly, enuresis.

BEHAVIORS EXHIBITED

Amy's behavior and development paralleled that of children in the Kolvin & Fundudis (1981) study. According to Amy's teacher, she did seem to be developmentally behind and still suffered from enuresis at age 5. She was extremely shy and, according to her mother and teachers, exhibited some behaviors that were not normal for a child of her age. No distinguishable clues were identified as to the events that led to Amy's elective mutism. In their review of the literature, Kolvin & Fundudis (1981) found no specific or conclusive causes for elective mutism.

Amy did not speak one word during the first 5 months she was enrolled in the early childhood program at her school. She passed all the nonverbal items at the appropriate age level on an early childhood screening test and was put in a special education transition class. Amy's teachers observed her to be a passive little girl, who sat and observed activity around her. Her social skills were virtually nonexistent. She did not play with groups of children, but preferred to play alone or with an adult. When a new quiet girl took a special interest in her, Amy did accept her. Initially the new girl talked to Amy, but later she just followed Amy's gesturing. As the school year progressed, Amy became more active and her facial expressions became more animated. She even smiled and laughed occasionally.

Outside, Amy would linger on the playground and trail her classmates. She did not interact with the other children. When the teacher would take her hand to lead her to the sandbox or swings, Amy would pull away.

Amy displayed some additional unusual behaviors. She grasped the teacher aide's neck with her hands in a strong-hold, smiling while she did it. She repeatedly stabbed the playhouse doll with a fork. She would wet her pants if the teachers forgot to ask her if she needed to go the bathroom, although she had been told that she could go to the bathroom anytime.

Her mother reported that Amy did not show pain. She once sat in a tub of very hot water and just looked at her grandmother blankly when she asked Amy why she was still in the water. Amy had her pierced earrings pulled through her ears while playing and did not complain to the teacher, although her ears were bleeding. She fell in the gymnasium at school, which caused her mouth to bleed, and when the teacher asked her if it hurt, she shook her head from side to side. She did not show excitement or happiness on field trips or party days.

TEACHER'S EFFORTS

Amy's teachers used several techniques to try to elicit some type of verbal response. She was accepted as a nonverbal participant. On other occasions she was ignored when she would not respond verbally. When this failed, she was required to sit in a "time out" chair if she did not speak, but Amy seemed to take pleasure in sitting in the chair. According to her teacher, she was as sassy as anyone could be without saying a word. She did respond to being touched and on several occasions initiated sitting on the teacher's lap, following the lead of other children in the class. Amy was described by her teachers as passive, resistant, voluntarily nonverbal, occasionally hostile, compulsive and controlling, and emotionally unexpressive, as well as accepting of some people, responsive to affection, and willing to copy other children's behavior.

PLAY THERAPY

For a child exhibiting elected mutism, it is imperative that therapeutic communication be based on a means of expression with which the child feels comfortable. The therapist who relies exclusively on verbal means of communication with such children is often defeated in efforts to establish an effective relationship. The elective mute child easily controls the interaction with silence, thus also controlling development of the relationship with the counselor. Efforts to entice, encourage, cajole, or trick such children into a verbal exchange typically result in continued silence and a frustrated therapist.

The elective mute child has discovered from previous experiences what adults want—verbalization—and how to easily thwart their efforts by resisting through silence. Therefore, because play is the natural medium of self-expression for children, play therapy was selected as the preferred therapeutic approach with Amy. Her therapist believed Amy needed a therapeutic setting in which she could feel comfortable, a place where she could be in charge, within limits, of the relationship with an adult, and could communicate on her own terms without using words, as expected of her by other adults.

Regarding the value of play, Conn (1951) stated, "Every therapeutic play method is a form of learning process during which the child learns to accept and to utilize constructively that degree of personal responsibility and self-discipline necessary for effective self-expression and social living" (p. 753).

A SILENT BEGINNING

During the initial session in play therapy, Amy was totally nonverbal. She hid under the paint easel and gestured for forty five minutes. The therapist responded with similar gestures and verbal comments, hoping to communicate understanding of feelings. If the therapist remained motionless and silent for even a short time, Amy would look out from under the easel to make sure she still had the therapist's undivided attention. At the end of the session Amy readily emerged from under the easel.

Amy's cousin Susan accompanied her to the center for the second session. When Amy resisted returning to the playroom the therapist invited Susan to come into the playroom too. Susan began talking as soon as the playroom door opened, and Amy returned to her hiding place under the easel. Susan played with many of the toys and after about 10 minutes, Amy joined her. They chatted back and forth and played contentedly for the hour. One would not have believed that there was anything unusual about Amy at this time.

This was such an unexpected turn of events that the therapist decided to add Amy's 9-year-old brother Ben to the third session to better understand the dynamics of Amy's interpersonal interactions. In this session, Susan and Ben played together and ignored Amy, who finally retreated into her hiding place under the easel. After the third session, Susan returned to her home in another town. The therapist had to decide whether to see Amy by herself or to include her older brother in the session. Amy also had a younger brother, Ned, who was very eager to come into the playroom.

SIBLING GROUP PLAY THERAPY

The question of placing siblings together in group play therapy has received little attention in existing literature on play therapy. Ginott (1961) has been one of the few authors to even mention the issue of siblings; however, he has done so only in the context of recommending that children experiencing intense sibling rivalries be excluded from group play therapy. Consideration of placing siblings together is not mentioned.

The possibility of placing siblings together in group play therapy is often ruled out by requiring children selected for group play therapy to be the same age. According to Gazda (1989) and Ginott (1982), children in group play therapy should not differ in age by more than 1 year. Ginott (1982) did suggest that other considerations may take precedence over age, such as when aggressive children are placed in older age groups or immature children are placed in groups with children younger than themselves. Ginott further restricted the possibility of having siblings together in play therapy by recommending that school-age children be separated by sexes. We have found little need to separate children by sex until approximately the age of 8 or 9.

It seems reasonable to assume that the basic reasons for placing children in group play therapy may be equally as important for sibling group play therapy. If the presence of several children in the playroom helps to anchor the experience to the world of reality (Ginott, 1961), this would seem to be even more true for siblings together in group play therapy. If, as Ginott (1961) proposed, children help each other assume responsibility in interpersonal relationships, the impact on siblings would be even more significant because of the opportunity to naturally and immediately extend those interactions with siblings outside the setting of group play therapy.

SEARCHING FOR THE RIGHT COMBINATION

In Amy's case, a combination of sibling play therapy, individual play therapy, and brief family consultation was found to be the most appropriate approach. When Amy played in the playroom with Ben, he was the responsible one—for himself and for Amy. She did not have to do anything; Ben talked and played for both of them. When Amy played in the playroom with Ned, she was the teacher and helper, although, Ned was independent. When both boys came into the playroom, they played together and ignored Amy. When the children came into the room with their mother, they all tended to act out somewhat, but behaved with fairly equal exchanges.

When Amy played alone in the playroom, she remained shy, yet verbal. She would hide in her usual place under the easel for 10 or 15 minutes until she felt safe enough to emerge. Her play was often inappropriate, in the sense of periodic bursts of hostility or lengthy laughter or destructiveness. Modeling play behaviors that she had experienced with her brothers did generalize, however, to her individual play.

Amy's Need to Control

One theme continued for most of the play sessions. Amy wanted to be in total control and used silence to accomplish it. When the therapist continued to reflect her feelings verbally, Amy resented the loss of control. She repeatedly said, "Don't look at me. Don't talk to me." The therapist use a compromising approach on this issue. Amy was given control of "looks" and the therapist was given control of "talk." Amy seemed satisfied to have a well-defined area of control and was willing to let the therapist have one too. Gradually, Amy began to accept partial control in other areas. Ben and Amy divided the room into two parts. Each had to obtain verbal permission from the other to play in their respective control zones. Practicing, even in a structured way, the "give-and-take" that occurs naturally with many children seemed to give Amy the confidence she needed to develop her social skills, rather than to turn inward.

As Amy became more independent, Ben dropped his role as protector and responsible member of the family. He acted out to the extent that his mother had to discipline him publicly— a first in this family. Ben gradually was able to let Amy be her own person and retain his significant position of being one of several responsible members of the family. The mother encouraged this shift in communication at home by giving Amy more responsibility and not allowing Ben to take over her tasks, even when he could do them better and faster. Ned also maintained a balanced independence, rather than adopting Amy's role of being helpless and in total control or Ben's role of being responsible and in total control. Amy began to express feelings more frequently. Raising her closed fist was her way of saying, "Don't come close to me," or "This will keep me safe when I have to walk close to you."

A DIFFERENT AMY

Amy's new confidence extended into the classroom. Talking, singing, and participating in class became fun for her. Her play sessions shifted to depict the school setting. She loved to be the teacher. When Amy would forget some mathematical fact or how to spell a new word she had learned, she would report what this word would be in Spanish. The therapist reflected the idea that sometimes only Amy would be able to tell what the word really meant. Amy's love of learning became evident in the safe environment of the playroom. She had initially concentrated on receiving information and not expressing.

In later sessions Amy actively participated in expressing each new learning situation. The pace of Amy's progress was like a door bursting open. She even read a Christmas story over the loud-speaker at school. After 9 months and 36 sessions of combining sibling and individual play therapy, the final reward was Amy's assignment to a regular first-grade classroom in the spring of the year. As Amy became more verbal and more actively participated in her world, the enuresis occurred less frequently.

SIGNIFICANCE OF SIBLING PLAY THERAPY

What was gained by having Amy's brothers in play therapy with her? As in family therapy, ideally, the focus shifts from intrapersonal to interpersonal patterns of communication. In this particular case, lack of verbal communication skills and underdeveloped social skills were paralyzing Amy's efforts to function in society beyond her immediate family.

It was obvious in sessions with Amy and her younger brother, Ned, that Amy had some basic social and communication skills. Observation of Ben and Amy in the playroom revealed that Ben had assumed responsibility for both himself and Amy. By helping Ben and Amy shift their ways of communicating, the therapist helped Amy to gain confidence to try a new way of entering the world of people instead of having someone take responsibility for her. Although individual play therapy might have eventually produced similar results, the sibling play therapy approach in this case seemed to bring faster results because the issues could be defined immediately, and work in sessions and at home could begin on the shift in the communication pattern.

We are not suggesting that sibling play therapy be used exclusively in every situation, or that it is the answer to cases in which the child has experienced trauma, but it can add a dimension to play therapy that previously has not been seriously considered. In fact, Amy definitely needed some time by herself to try out new behaviors learned in the setting that included her brothers, but the sibling setting served as a diagnostic tool for the therapist and as an intimate environment in which Amy could interact safely.

SUMMARY

Kolvin and Fundudis (1981) stated that elective mutism is rather intractable. This case study of Amy demonstrates that play therapy seems to have been a viable treatment for an elective mute child.

Because elective mute children have a purpose for their behavior, verbal prodding by adults usually reaps few benefits. It only widens the gap between themselves and the child. The elective mute child has chosen not to communicate verbally with those outside the immediate family for reasons that may revolve around fear of social situations in which he or she is expected to interact verbally with others. It seems valuable, consequently, to provide an alternative for the child. With group and sibling play therapy, the therapist can provide an atmosphere in which the child feels safe and where there is no pressure to talk.

The case of Amy—An Elective Mute Child is from Landreth (1986). Sibling Group Play Therapy. An Effective Alternative with an Elective Mute Child. *The School Counselor, 33*, 164-6. Reprinted with permisssion of the American Association for Counseling and Development.

REFERENCES

American Psychiatric Association. (1987) *Diagnostic and statistical manual of mental disorders* (3rd ed.). Washington, DC: Author.

Axline, V.M. (1982). Entering the child's world via play experience. In G.L. Landreth (Ed.). *Play therapy: Dynamics of the process of counseling with children* (pp. 47-57). Springfield, IL: Thomas.

Conn, J.H. (1951). Play interview therapy of castration fears. *American Journal of Orthopsychiatry, 25,* 747-754.

Gazda, G.M. (1989). *Group counseling: A developmental appraoch.* Boston: Allyn & Bacon.

Ginott, H.G. (1961). *Group psychotherapy with children: The theory and practice of play therapy.* New York: McGraw-Hill.

Ginott, H.G. (1982). Group play therapy with children. In G.L. Landreth (Ed.), *Play therapy: Dynamics of the process of counseling with children* (pp. 327-341). Springfield, IL: Thomas.

Guerney, L.I. (1983, April). *Play therapy conference.* Conference held at North Texas State University, Denton.

Kolvin, I., & Fundudis, T. (1981). Elective mute children: Psychological development and background factors. *Journal of Child Psychology and Psychiatry and Allied Disciplines, 22,* 219-232.

Moustakas, C.E. (1982). Emotional adjustment and the play therapy process. In G.L. Landreth (Ed.), *Play therapy: Dynamics of the process of counseling with children* (pp. 217-230). Springfield, IL: Thomas.

CHAPTER 15

DETERMINING THERAPEUTIC PROCESS AND TERMINATION

The topic of trying to determine whether or not progress is being made within sessions or assessing children's readiness for ending play therapy sessions has received little attention in the literature. Perhaps these topics have not been dealt with because the answers are not easily determined. The void also may be the result of therapist's difficulty themselves in dealing with the ending of relationships. Typically therapists do not enter into relationships with a conscious goal to move toward ending the relationship. After all, we are in the business of building and facilitating relationships. The ending of the therapeutic relationship, though, is just as important as the beginning of the relationship and should be dealt with openly. The issue of on-going change or progress is actually more significant to the therapist than to the child and is a result of the therapist's need to know rather than being a prerequisite for the child's growth. Seldom do children wonder if they are making progress. They are simply and completely engaged in the continual process of the unfolding of the wonder of living. The therapist should appreciate that with children. But, at the same time, practical issues must be dealt with such as the therapist's own feelings about needing to know change is indeed occurring and the reality of not keeping children in therapy forever. At some point in time, decisions must be made. Hopefully, children will always be a part of these decisions.

Determining Therapeutic Movement Within Sessions

During the process of play therapy, changes within children are not always easily determined or observable in the context of the child's expressions in the playroom. Children may continue to demonstrate similar kinds of play session after session with no immediately observable change in pattern or content of play. At the same time, changes in children's behavior outside the playroom may indeed be observable. This can be accounted for by recognizing that as children's needs to express themselves in negative ways are met in the playroom, they have less need to express those needs in inappropriate ways outside the playroom. These negative behaviors can be discarded and creative energy focused on more positive behaviors. At the same time, children may continue to express similar previously exhibited behaviors in the playroom because this is a safe place to do so, and also because the need to express and examine those feelings has not been completed.

When children continue to demonstrate the same behaviors session after session, the therapist may begin to experience some anxiety because of the therapist's need to have things happen more quickly and the need to see observable change. The therapist may begin to experience some doubt about his/ her own adequacy and the adequacy of the approach. We all want to know we are doing well, that we are being helpful to children. When there is a lack of concrete observable change in children's playroom behavior, the therapist may experience doubt about self as a therapist, begin to lose faith in the process and decide that a more directive approach is needed. What the therapist needs to be aware of is that this is usually a move to meet the therapist's own needs to feel more adequate and is not really an attempt to meet children's needs. The responsibility of children in play therapy does not include satisfying the therapist's schedule for change in behavior. Children have their own inner developed schedule, and the therapist must wait patiently for each child's self to emerge.

Seldom do children make gigantic insightful breakthroughs in play therapy. Growth is a slow process and so is change in behavior. The therapist must be patient with the process. The therapist who expects momentous and dramatic changes by children will probably be disappointed and, if unaware of this need, will very likely become inconsistent in his/her approach to the child by trying first one technique and then another in an effort to bring about more rapid change. When the therapist is feeling the greatest urge to do something different, may very well be the time when the therapist needs to be most consistent, patient, and understanding. To do otherwise may result in the child feeling rejected and wanting to please the therapist.

Children's nonverbal behavior can provide significant cues to understanding the totality of their way of behaving or functioning and useful information in understanding the therapeutic process in play therapy. Change is occurring in hundreds of little ways, and the therapist just has to look for those indications of the process of change.

Dimensions of Change

That movement in the therapeutic process is indeed occurring can be determined by carefully noting in each session those behaviors that the therapist can recall as having occurred for the first time in the relationship with the child. For example, this may be the first time in the initial five sessions that Jason has played near the therapist, or perhaps Jason played very near the therapist and this is the first time he has ventured to play in another part of the room away from the therapist. Perhaps Kathy has painted pictures at the easel every session, and in this session she does not paint. The therapist needs to recognize that a reason does exist as to why Kathy has not painted. Something is different. A change has occured. This may be the first session in which the therapist has had to set a limit on Kelly's behavior or the first session in which limits have not had to be set. Such changes signal changes within the child.

RULE OF THUMB:

Look for firsts.

A dramatic first in one of my experiences with five-year-old Scott, an extremely withdrawn, shy child, occurred in our fourth session together when he handed me the alligator puppet to hold for him while he went looking for something else. For some observers, the significance of this behavior might go unnoticed. For Scott to approach me in this way indicated a change for him in how he felt about our relationship. This happening seemed to indicate he now felt more comfortable in the relationship and safe enough to approach me directly. This was also his way of including me in his play for the first time. To approach me in this way required courage on his part and a feeling that he could direct his own play. Could this be the beginning of becoming self-directing, of taking care of himself? Change for children begins in little ways like this, not with some magnificently insightful verbalized pronouncement of a decision to forevermore be independent and selfdirecting. Perhaps such meaningful change begins with Carol going through an entire sixth session without once asking the therapist for help or trying to get the therapist to make a decision for her as she had done in the previous five sessions. Could significant meaning be associated with the fact that Robert plays out elaborate scenes of cooking food and feeding every single doll in every session and now does not cook or feed any dolls in this session? I think so, just as there is significance in the fact that this is the first time Tammy has played in the sandbox in six sessions. A careful examination of such firsts across sessions can help the therapist become aware of significant movement in the therapeutic process.

A second dimension which can provide insight into the inner emotional dynamics of the child is the development of themes which occur in the child's play. Emotional experiences and happenings which are important to children or have contributed in some way to significantly impact children will often show up as repeated behavior in their play. A theme is the recurrence of certain events or topics in the child's play either within a session or across several sessions. A key point here is the recurrence of the play after some lapse of time or an intervening period of play in which the theme is not played out. Shawn's play with the rubber snake for twenty minutes would not be considered a theme even though that would be considered to be an unusually long time for a four-year-old to engage in such play. Although the play may be significant and an important occurrence in the developing relationship, the expression must occur more than once or twice to be considered a theme.

When Shawn came to the playroom for his second session and again played out the same scene of the rubber snake crawling around the dollhouse, sticking it's head into each window and door, and then slowly and deliberately crawling around the top of the dollhouse, the therapist suspected a theme. This suspicion was confirmed when Shawn repeated the same play in the third session. At this point the therapist learned that Shawn's home had been burglarized twice just a few weeks prior to his first play therapy session.

The theme may not always be readily recognizable because what is being played, the activity, or the toys being played with may be different each time, but the theme of the play or the underlying meaning of the play is the same. This was the case with Paul as described in the previous chapter. A theme of leaving and not leaving the security of home was evident in the scenes involving the airplane trip in which the people didn't fly away, the auto trip in which Paul stayed very close to the dollhouse, and his loading all the dollhouse furniture and fixtures into the truck and then quickly unloading and replacing the furniture in the dollhouse.

Such repeated play behaviors can indicate emotional issues the child is playing out. When the theme is no longer observable, that can be an indication the child has been able to emotionally move on to something else.

The Meaning of Termination

Termination is a harsh sounding term and seems so final that it does not at all convey what I would like to communicate about discontinuing regular contacts with children. The words "concluding" and "ending" could be used, but again these seem so final, as though the relationship is completely severed and will in no way continue to exist. Nothing could be farther from the truth. Child and therapist have shared, sometimes tentatively, sometimes painfully, sometimes eagerly, and sometimes in rocky ways, in developing and building a meaningful, sensitively caring relationship. Tender moments have occurred, times of great excitement, joy that could almost not be contained, periods of anger and frustration screamed out at the world, points of grand discovery, intervals of quiet being together when words or sounds were not necessary, and a season of shared understanding and acceptance. Such a relationship can never be terminated for it goes on and on as a part of those persons who have shared in it. Such important experiences live on in the persons who have experienced them and do not end just because someone decides not to meet on a regular basis again.

> The leaving of the old and the beginning of the new constitute the ever-recurring shifting of the scenes in human development. The old is terminated with full regard for the values and satisfactions that have accrued from it. If these values must, however, be measured and felt only in the circumstances in which they were experienced originally, then they cease to be growth-inducing influences and lose their positive meaning. Values from any life experience retain their positive meaning only as the individual is free to use them in the ever-recurring newness of living. This is not forgetting and repressing the old, but it is using the old to provide the structure of the new. (Allen, 1942, p. 293)

A single word seems so inadequate in attempting to describe accurately this part of the process which the therapist has been moving toward since the initial contact with the child. The therapist's purpose in being in the relationship has been to contribute to the child's development of self-responsibility, enhancement of self, and unfolding of self-directed change. That the child would no longer need the immediacy of this kind of relationship is then a natural development in the process of growth—not an ending, but rather an extending. If the therapist has been successful in truly making contact with the child on a significant emotional level leading to the sharing of the inner self of the child and the therapist, then a significant relationship has been established, and the ending of personal relationships can be difficult.

Reference Points for
Determining Termination

Since the child-centered play therapist has no predetermined individually tailored specific goals for children in play therapy, the question of when to terminate is not always easily answered as might be the case when in the judgement of the therapist a specific behavioral problem has been ameliorated. No specific goals have been established to point to as having been achieved, thus indicating readiness for termination. The therapeutic relationship has focused on the child rather than on a specific problem. Therefore, no empirical check points exist to utilize as reference points of success. Haworth (1964) suggested the following questions as guides for determining readiness for termination.

1. Is there less dependence on the therapist?

2. Is there less concern about other children using the room or seeing his therapist?

3. Can he now see and accept both good and bad in the same person?

4. Have there been changes in his attitude toward time, in terms of awareness, interest, or acceptance?

5. Has there been a change in his reactions to cleaning up the room: less concern if he formerly had been meticulous or interest in cleaning up as contrasted to earlier messiness?

6. Does he (or she) now accept self and own sex?

7. Are there evidences of insight and self-evaluation; does he compare his former actions or feelings with those of the present?

8. Is there a change in the quality or amount of verbalization?

9. Is there less aggression toward, or with, toys?

10. Does he accept limits more readily?

11. Have his forms of art expression changed?

12. Is there less need to engage in infantile (e.g., bottle) or regressive (e.g., water) play?

13. Is there less fantasy and symbolic play and more creative constructive play?

14. Has there been a diminution in the number and intensity of fears? (p. 416)

Change is best viewed in terms of a global nature, and these questions help the therapist to focus on the process of change, rather than the attainment of some specific objective which has been predetermined. Any attempt to determine whether or not sufficient change has taken place to merit consideration of discontinuing play therapy should focus primarily on examining changes in children. The following areas can be used as a basis for consideration of self-initiated changes within children.

1. Child is less dependent.

2. Child is less confused.

3. Child expresses needs openly.

4. Child is able to focus on self.

5. Child accepts responsibility for own actions and feelings.

6. Child limits own behavior appropriately.

7. Child is more inner directed.

8. Child is more flexible.

9. Child is more tolerant of happenings.

10. Child initiates activities with assurance.

11. Child is cooperative but not conforming.

12. Child expresses anger appropriately.

13. Child has moved from negative-sad affect to happy-pleased.

14. Child is more accepting of self.

15. Child is able to play out story sequences, play has direction.

Children will give cues in a general way about their readiness to bring the relationship to a close. Some children may begin to stand around in the playroom, no longer as interested in the toys. They may seem listless, uninvolved, and almost as though they are playing in slow motion. Children often express a general complaint of having nothing to do, they seem bored and wander around the room. At such times, some children will announce, "I don't think I need to come anymore." Such a statement is a declaration of the child's wholeness and ability to separate from the therapist and to rely fully upon self. This is a very positive affirmation of self. Sometimes children will compare present behaviors or reactions with their earlier different reactions thus noting the changes in self. The therapist may note a general change in the feeling-tone of the time together in the playroom. The time together just doesn't "feel" the same. Changes described by parents and teachers also should be considered as a part of the whole in a decision to end the play therapy relationship.

Procedures for Ending the Relationship

The age of the child and thus the child's developmental concept of the future, as well as the child's ability to comprehend and effectively participate in the verbal pursuit of abstractions imposed by words, will determine to a considerable degree the approach taken by the therapist to initiate the process of concluding the play therapy experience. In keeping with the child-centered philosophy, the child should be included in the planning necessary for ending this significant relationship. When the therapist determines the child no longer needs the play therapy experience or becomes aware of the child's readiness to discontinue the relationship, this should be responded to in the session with the same degree of sensitivity as would any other feeling or decision by the child. The child can be included in the decision regarding bringing the relationship to a close and the date for the last session by asking the child how many more times she feels she needs to come to the playroom. In school settings and some agencies, the end of the school year will dictate the ending of the relationship, at least for a three month period, even though the child may not be ready to terminate. With the exception of deciding how many more sessions are needed, the other termination procedures would still be utilized.

Discontinuing the relationship should be a smooth process, not abrupt, and should be accomplished with great sensitivity to the feelings of children. If the termination of the play therapy experience is not handled properly, children may feel rejected, punished, or a sense of loss. Actually, no guarantee can be given that the child won't experience some of these feelings no matter how well the ending is handled. That children may feel anxious about separation from this meaningful relationship and this now significant person in their life is understandable. These feelings are accepted and no effort is made to make the child feel better about leaving. To do so would discount the child's feelings of anxiety, hurt, anger, or whatever the child experiences about leaving the relationship. Leaving the door open for children to return if they feel the need to do so, by informing them that they can come back, sometimes helps children with the turning loose process.

Children will need time in the playroom to live out the ending of this important relationship just as they have lived out other significant parts of their lives. Therefore, the process for actual termination will need to be started two or three sessions prior to the final session. In the beginning of this relationship, the child needed time to discover and develop a way of being in the relationship. Now the child will need time to work through emerging feelings about ending this meaningful part of life and to explore feelings about no longer having this area of support. Through participating in the planning for ending the relationship, the child has the opportunity to discover what the ending of a meaningful relationship feels like.

During the process of preparing for ending, some children may regress temporarily for part of a session and demonstrate behaviors observed in earlier sessions. This may be the child's way of reexamining old behaviors and experiencing the satisfaction of being able to compare the present with the past. A child may mess up a picture being painted and then say, "Used to, that would have made me mad." One could speculate that the child's playing out of earlier behaviors could be a belated attempt to say, "I don't want to leave. Please let me continue to come here."

With some children, the therapist may want to consider a tapering off process for termination by moving from a once a week schedule to once every other week for the final two sessions. Another variation would be to schedule one last follow-up session a month after the last regular weekly contact. This determination should be based on the child's needs, not the therapist's need to know how things are going or the therapist's reluctance to turn loose. Once the process for ending the relationship has begun, children will need to be reminded of how many more times they will have in the playroom at the beginning and at the end of the remaining two or three sessions. For some children, a week is a long time to remember how many more times they will get to come to the playroom.

Children's Reactions to the Last Session

Trying to predict how a child will react in the final session is usually not possible. Some children approach the final session in a rather matter of fact way. They may not even make a comment about this being the last time they will be in the playroom. The therapist should suppress any urge to make a big deal out of the last session either through conversation or lingering good bye hugs. If initiated by the child, that would be appropriate. Otherwise, such activity should be recognized as the therapist's need and dealt with accordingly. Even the last minute is still the child's time, a time for the child's needs to be expressed and responded to by the therapist. Some children may indicate their reluctance to end the relationship by lingering at the door on their way out, commenting about the room, or thinking of a variety of things they want to tell the therapist.

Some children may be very angry about ending the relationship, as was the case with seven-year-old Brad. We had experienced twelve wonderful times together during which Brad had never been overly messy or aggressive. He had played very actively but in careful ways. In our last session, Brad entered the playroom, made a comment about "Yeah, this is our last one," and began to pull toys off the shelves and dump them in the middle of the floor. Although he said not one word during this process, he was obviously angry. He did not stop until he had emptied all the shelves. What a mess! With hardly a glance to take in the mess he had made, Brad began to replace the toys on the shelves and did not stop until the job was completed. That was quite a task and occupied most of the time left in the session. With ten minutes remaining, he prepared the most delightful and elaborate meal for both of us, commenting about what he was cooking and foods he liked. Time was then up, and he walked out of the playroom without a good bye or any verbal reference to that being the last time together in the playroom. Brad had eloquently communicated his mixed feelings about the ending of our relationship.

Some children are very open in sharing their feelings about ending the relationship as was the the case with seven-year-old Lori who quite graphically expressed the importance of the relationship with the therapist in the following conversation which occurred in the final session.

Lori: (While filling pots and pans with sand.) I have lots of friends. They'll be my friends forever! (Looking sideways at counselor) You're one of my friends.

Therapist: Sounds like you think we'll always be friends.

Lori: (With intense affirmative head nod.) Uh, huh! Even when you're not here.

Therapist: So, we'll still be friends even when I'm gone.

Lori: You can just talk to Jesus about me.

Therapist: Seems like it's real important for me to always remember you.

Lori: We'll have a secret code. (Writes phone number on a piece of paper, and puts four stickers on another paper.) Here. This is my number if you have an emergency. And, you can look at these pictures and say "Jesus" or "God," whatever you want, and we'll be connected.

Therapist: So, you figured out a way for us to always be connected—and friends.

Lori: Yup—(Affirmative head nod.)—always connected.

REFERENCES

Allen, F. (1942). *Psychotherapy with children.* New York: Norton.

Haworth, M. (1964). *Child psychotherapy: Practice and theory.* New York: Basic Books.

CHAPTER 16

FILIAL THERAPY: CHILD-PARENT-RELATIONSHIP TRAINING USING PLAY THERAPY SKILLS (CPR FOR PARENTS)

Many parents occupy time and space with their children but do not *know* or *understand* their children. Parents at all socioeconomic levels in our society today are under tremendous stress from economic and societal demands for time commitments required to maintain their standard of living and life style. These commitments take parents away from their children physically and emotionally and thus place great stress on children because parents are unable to fulfill their needs for emotional nurturing. That so many parents are unaware of their children's emotional needs and lack the skill necessary to interact effectively on an emotional level with their children is both frightening and depressing. Parenting is so much more than a biological happening. Children need time for emotional sharing with their parents, and parents need to know how to respond in facilitative ways if the necessary relationship is to develop. Unfortunately many parents are basically not acquainted with their children because they have not taken time to be *with* their children in such a way as to allow them to be the person they are. The nature of the parent-child relationship is of primary importance to the present and future mental health of children. Therefore, clearly if we are to significantly impact in positive ways the mental health of our future adult population, greater effort must be made to substantially improve the mental health of all children and not just those who obviously are in need of professional help. The skills of professionals in the helping professions must be brought out of hiding from behind closed office doors and must be given away through training to parents who are in the best position to profoundly impact the lives of future adults. A direct attempt by therapists to improve the adjustment of our future population is an impossible task. Therapists helping parents to become therapeutic agents in their children's lives seems to be the most efficient and perhaps the only way to significantly improve the mental health of the adult population of the future.

Parental Efficacy

How parents feel about themselves, their sense of adequacy as a person and a parent, significantly affects their interaction with their children and thus their children's development. Parenting is at best a difficult, stressful, and often frustrating process for even the most skillful and dedicated parent. When difficulty occurs in the parent-child relationship and things just are not going well, parents are susceptible to self-blame and doubt their adequacy as a parent. Research has shown that parents' sense of efficacy can have a profound impact on any number of the dimensions of children's development. Schaefer (1981) found that parents who scored high on internal locus of control had children who scored high on language and cognitive activities. Swick and Graves (1986) concluded that when parents have high internal locus of control and high interpersonal support, they seem to influence their children's development in positive ways.

The extent and pattern of parental involvement at home has been reported by Swick (1987) to be linked positively to children's self-image, optimism, and positive social relationships. Spivack and Cianci (1987) found that parent involvement resulted in their children demonstrating increased self-control and ability to manage their own behavior. Rohner (1986) reported the children of parents who were warm, accepting, and nurturing exhibited more positive social skills. Children who were experiencing difficulties with social skills had parents who were rigid, authoritarian, and cold. Swick, Gladstone, and Hayes (1988) noted that specific designed parent intervention plans helped increase parents' sense of control and improved children's behavior.

The dynamics of the relationship between parent and child most assuredly affects children's development, and a major factor in this relationship is the parent's attitude and perception of self as related to parental locus of control. Parent's perception of self affects their locus of control, which in turn, influences the direction and extent of parental guidance and involvement in their children's lives. Generally, when a child experiences some developmental difficulty or parents experience prolonged difficulty in their interpersonal relationships with their children, parents feel out of control, they believe they can do nothing, and they feel inadequate. Therefore, when parents ask for help or training, the sensitive therapist will convey faith in the parent's ability to grow in understanding and acceptance of the child and to have a positive impact on the child's development. Parents need assistance in learning skills which encourage the development of positive parent-child relationships. To assume that most parents already know what these skills are and how to utilize them is the wrong assumption because relatively little effort has been put forth in our society to teach parents how to interact with their children in effective ways.

Historical Development of Filial Therapy

Precedents for training parents to be therapeutic agents in their children's lives can be traced to the early part of the twentieth century. In 1909 Sigmund Freud (1959) successfully utilized the father of a five-year-old boy in the treatment of the child by instructing the father in how to respond during play sessions with the boy. The treatment was carried out by the father at home, and Freud contended the changes made in the child's behavior would have been impossible without the father's interaction. As early as 1949, Dorothy Baruch advocated planned play sessions at home for the purpose of enhancing parent-child relationships. A dramatic example of the effect of play therapy type home play sessions was reported by Natalie Fuchs (1957). With advice and encouragement from her father, Carl Rogers, she employed regularly scheduled special play times based on procedures suggested in Axline's (1947) writings and achieved significant results in helping her daughter overcome emotional reactions related to toilet-training. Moustakas (1959) provided one of the earliest detailed descriptions of these special play therapy type home play sessions between parent and child.

> Play therapy in the home is essentially a relationship between a child and his mother or father through which the child discovers himself as an important person, sees that he is valued and loved, and recognizes his irreplaceable membership in the family. It is a way through which the child opens himself to emotional expression and in this process releases tensions and repressed feelings . . . He learns to count on regular meetings with the parent once or twice a week for one-hour periods in which he is the center of the experience. A variety of play materials are made available to him at this time . . . The parent does not tell him what to do, but sits nearby watching him closely and showing interest and regard . . . In the play therapy relationship created in the home, the child finds that his parent really cares, wants to understand, and accepts him as he is. (pp. 275-277)

These earlier experiences of parents conducting special play sessions at home differed from filial therapy in that the parents did not receive regularly scheduled systematic training, close supervision, and the opportunity to discuss their experiences with peers in a group therapy type format.

Filial therapy was originally conceptualized by Bernard Guerney (1964) as a structured treatment program for children ages three through ten with emotional problems. Utilizing a small group format, parents are trained in the overall principles and methodology of client-centered play therapy. The structure of the therapeutic program is regularly scheduled parent-child play therapy type sessions at home in which the parent is the therapeutic agent, rather than a professional therapist.

Louise Guerney participated with her husband in the early research and development of filial therapy and has continued in her work at Pennsylvania State University to be one of the leading authors and proponents of this innovative approach to helping children.

The Process of Filial Therapy

As in child-centered play therapy, filial therapy is structured to enhance the relationship, in this case between the parent and child, with the parent serving as the therapeutic agent of change. Through didactic instruction, viewing of video tapes, and role playing, parents' sensitivity to their children is enhanced, and parents learn how to create a nonjudgmental, understanding, and accepting environment during which children feel safe enough to explore other parts of themselves as persons and other ways of relating to their parents. The setting for this new kind of environment is a required thirty minute special play time. Since the parents' only objectives are to be sensitive to their children, to understand, to accept, and to communicate these dimensions to their children, they develop a new perceptual awareness of their children and their potentialities. This new creative dynamic of empathic responding by parents becomes the creative process through which change occurs within the parent and child and between parent and child.

The relationship between parent and child is consistent during the special play times because the parent plays with the child in a consistently empathic manner. Thus, the child develops a new perception of the parent as an ally because the parent is constantly trying to understand the child's feelings, reactions, activity, expressions, and point of view. This acceptance of the child and the child's need for independence facilitates the child's acceptance of self and enhances the child's trust of the relationship. Since the parent does not initiate or direct play activities, the child is allowed to express fully his/her own developing creativity, resourcefulness, and in turn experience the accompanying responsibility. The power of this kind of freedom, within appropriate boundaries set by the parent, to direct one's self, to be creative, to be bossy, to be silly, to be somber, to be serious, to just enjoy the fullness of being alive at that moment without any fear of parental rejection or judgment is without a doubt, the most facilitative, growth enhancing experience that can be created. As the parent affirms and empowers the child, the child's self-esteem grows and develops.

The objectives of the play sessions as stated by Bernard Guerney (1969) are

> . . . first to break the child's perception or misperception of the parent's feelings, attitudes, or behavior toward him. Second, they are intended to allow the child to communicate thoughts, needs, and feelings to his parents which he has previously kept from them, and often from his own awareness. (This communication is mainly through the medium of play.) The children's sessions with their parents are thus meant to lift repressions and resolve anxiety-producing internalized conflicts. Third, they are intended to bring the child—via incorporation of newly perceived attitudes on the part of his parents—a greater feeling of self-respect, self-worth, and confidence. (p. 452)

Since parents are expected to demonstrate the skills they have been taught only during the limited time of the scheduled once a week play sessions, they are not threatened by the magnitude of having to change their approach completely. When parents are expected to practice a new approach or method of relating to their children twenty-four hours a day, they are likely to enter into the experience feeling defeated before they ever start because they know what is being asked is an impossibility. In the filial therapy approach there is no obligation to change completely. Therefore, parents are less likely to feel debilitating guilt when they fall back into old patterns of behavior outside the play sessions. What generally happens, however, is that parents spontaneously utilize their new skills outside the play sessions and then feel quite satisfied and encouraged by their own generalized use of empathic responding.

Selecting Parents

A modification of the original intent for filial therapy is that this training is, in most cases, appropriate for the parents of all children, not just children with adjustment problems.

Even in well adjusted, stable families, experiences occur which may result in temporary disruptions in parent-child interactions or emotional reactions on the part the child which make it essential that the parents be especially sensitive to the child's emotional reactions and needs (i.e., birth of an infant; stressful academic difficulty; difficult to manage child; night fears; moving from one home to another; death of a parent, sibling, or close friend; a parent who is too involved in work and absent from home; loss of a job or major change in parent income, involvement in an auto accident). These experiences can result in children being fearful, anxious, clingy, or they may withdraw or act out. Many parents do not know how to respond adequately in appropriate emotionally nurturing ways to such reactions or behaviors. Their natural tendency is to try to stop the behavior rather than to try to understand the child.

My experience has been that filial therapy is appropriate for most children, not just the emotionally maladjusted. Parents today are much more aware of their need to know more about relating effectively to their children. Almost as many parents are in my training groups because they want to be better parents as there are parents whose children are experiencing some kind of adjustment problem. Grandparents who had recently received custody or had adopted their grandchildren have enrolled in some of my groups "to learn some new ways of parenting." Several affluent families have sent their live-in nannies to learn how to conduct the special play sessions. Recently a young nanny in her early twenties was enrolled by the parents of a fourteen-month-old who were concerned that the nanny be sensitive to the emotional development and needs of their child. She did a superb job of responding empathically to the fourteen-month-old in their scheduled play sessions which were video taped for critique in the weekly parent group sessions. One six-month-pregnant mother-to-be signed up for the training because she wanted "to get an early start on practicing the special play techniques." She borrowed a friend's child to practice on during the training period and was one of the most excited parents in the group. A couple expecting for the first time enrolled in another group, and both parents-to-be had weekly play sessions in their own home with the children of a relative. The parents of a five-year-old girl sought out the training because they felt it was important for the father to build the relationship bond with his child before he began serving a jail sentence.

The reasons for wanting filial therapy training have been varied and have included many of the more typical child adjustment problems and parent-child relationship difficulties as well as children who were experiencing emotional difficulties. One of the most dramatic improvements occurred with a child who had been referred because she had been sexually abused by her father prior to the parents divorcing. The child was receiving medication for the occurrence of seizures which still occurred on the average of ten times a day. Suspected emotional factors were mentioned in the medical report. In the first five weeks following the initiation of twice-a-week play sessions at home, the mother reported the average number of seizures had declined to one a week and the medication had not been altered. Six months later the mother was still having the special play sessions with her daughter and the average number of seizures was less than one a week.

Louise Guerney (1976) has recommended screening out parents who are psychotic, mentally retarded, suicidal, or homicidal. She reports the typical parent in her training groups has been in the middle income category and has had at least a high school education. That also has been my experience. However, one of my most exciting projects has been the training of carefully selected helping professionals from the Dallas Hispanic community to organize and train groups of Hispanic parents in filial therapy. Four of these trainees were public school counselors, two were directors of day care centers, one was a nurse with previous mental health training, and one was a counselor in an agency. After a year of training, the more experienced trainees were assigned to lead a Hispanic parent group by themselves, and the other trainees were assigned to co-lead groups. Many of these parents were in the lower income category, did not have a high school education, and spoke only Spanish. Since these were inexperienced leaders, children considered to have difficult emotional problems were screened out. Two-hour weekly supervision sessions were continued with the trainees during the course of their training sessions with the parents, and video tapes were made for supervisory purposes. The first groups were just recently concluded, and information from follow-up parent interviews has been overwhelmingly positive.

Group Format

Filial therapy is a blending of didactic elements with timely exploration of feelings and emotional reactions in the group as parents interactively share feelings about themselves and their children. Therefore, skill and experience in group therapy as well as expertise in play therapy is essential for the professional contemplating employing filial therapy in a group setting. Therapists often have a tendency to get caught up in exploring feeling dimensions to the exclusion of the didactic material. Maintaining a sensitive balance is essential. Exclusive group therapy is not the order of the day. Parents also need to learn new skills of parenting.

Parent training groups consist of a combination of six to eight individual parents or couples. Ten parents in a group is too large for the necessary supervision and places too many restrictions on group interaction which is essential for the effectiveness of the group. Perhaps the best format would be to have groups composed of all couples or all individual parents. However, my experience has been that the vast majority of individuals seeking this kind of training are mothers and to place the occasional couple who wants the training on a waiting list until two other couples are located would result in an unnecessarily long wait. Sometimes months may pass before another couple shows up on the waiting list. One caution is that when couples are included in a training group, relationship problems may emerge in the sharing that goes on and the leader may need to work extra hard to keep the discussion focused on the training objectives.

Utilizing filial training is also possible with individual parents and couples, and many times may be the training mode of necessity for professionals in private practice when getting a group together for training is not possible. My preference is the group setting because of the group dynamics feature and the vicarious learning that is always available to parents. One of my most exciting adventures in filial training, though, was an all day training session with a couple who lived several hundred miles away and could not attend weekly training sessions. The couple brought their child which allowed me to demonstrate the concepts with their child and then supervise several of each parent's sessions in the playroom with their child. Each parent session was followed with feedback and additional training throughout the day.

Filial therapy provides a positive structure of interpersonal group support which enhances parents' perception of themselves as being worthwhile and capable. The group feeling that develops and group cohesiveness are important dimensions of the filial therapy process. Therefore, groups are closed with no new participants added after the second session. Parents meet once a week for two hours for ten weeks, which is a minimum for this kind of training and certainly a longer period of training, supervision, and support is needed by parents who have children with very difficult emotional problems. In private practice settings, keeping all members of a group coming for longer periods of time may be difficult because of the expense incurred. In some non-fee or reduced fee agencies, university settings, and elementary schools, committing to attend for fifteen or twenty sessions should not be a problem. Parents in Louise Guerney's (1976) groups attend for six to twelve months.

Structure and Content of the Training Sessions

The basic format is six to eight parents and the therapist sitting in a circle engaged in a discussion with lively interaction among parents. Lengthy lectures are avoided and as often as possible the focus is kept on the parents. In addition to the set training format, teaching points and training information are carefully introduced in connection with spontaneously expressed parent concerns or information presented about their children. This interspersing of information and attaching to points of concern results in the information being received and incorporated by the parents in a more meaningful manner. Solutions to concerns and new ways to respond to children often originate within the group. Homework assignments are given at each session to help maintain involvement between sessions. Parents are advised to take notes during the training sessions. The basic outline of the ten once-a-week two hour training sessions is as follows.

Session 1. Parents introduce self, describe family, and characterize child of focus (the child they will have special sessions with). To increase consistency, parents work with only one child during training. Special times of another nature, baking cookies, etc., are arranged for other children in the family. Initially, parents typically want to have play sessions with all their children and, when allowed to do so, soon find their schedules too hectic to maintain their original commitment and become inconsistent in carrying through with the special play times. All sessions are conducted by the same parent. Alternating sessions between parents interferes with the building of trust and the development of themes across sessions. Goals and objectives of the training are explained. Training focus is primarily on developing sensitivity to their children and empathic responding. Role playing is employed by the therapist. The homework assignment is to identify emotions of anger, happiness, sadness, and surprise in the child of focus and make a reflective response. Responses are to be written down for reporting to the group.

Session 2. Homework assignments are reviewed, empathic responding is elaborated on, therapist demonstrates empathic responding with a volunteer followed by viewing of a video tape of the therapist in a play session with a child. Parents are taken to the playroom where they role play in pairs taking turns being the parent and the child. Parents are given a list of toys (Play Doh, crayons, paper, blunt scissors, nursing bottle, rubber knife, dart gun, doll family, toy soldiers, car, Lone Ranger type mask, Tinkertoys, doctor kit, bandaids, play money, rope, transparent tape, Bobo, ring toss, small cardboard box with window and door cut in side doubles as doll house and container for toys). Therapist demonstrates each toy. Toys need not be new. To enhance the specialness of the play sessions, the toys may be played with only during the play time. This also helps children learn to delay gratification needs and provides the parent with an opportunity to practice being firm and consistent. The homework assignment is to put the toy kit together, select a time and an uninterrupted place in the home suitable for the play sessions. The child's room should be avoided because of all the other toys available there. Sessions may not be interrupted to answer the phone or door. This conveys importance to the child and communicates the child is special.

Session 3. Parents report on arrangements for their sessions. Play therapy skills are taught, role playing in the playroom is utilized, a second video tape is shown of the therapist with a child in a play session. In some settings where someone is available to look after the children, the therapist may want to use a live demonstration with one of the parents' children. The homework assignment is to help the child make a "Play Session—Do Not Disturb" sign to hang on the door and to have the first of their weekly play sessions. During the special play time, parents adhere to the following rules:

Don't

1. Don't criticize any behavior.

2. Don't praise the child.

3. Don't ask leading questions.

4. Don't allow interruptions of the session.

5. Don't offer information or teach.

6. Don't preach.

7. Don't initiate new activities. (These first seven are taken from Guerney, 1972)

8. Don't be passive or quiet.

Do

1. Do set the stage.

2. Do let the child lead.

3. Do track behavior.

4. Do reflect the child's feelings.

5. Do set limits.

6. Do salute the child's power and effort.

7. Do join in the play as a follower.

8. Do be verbally active.

Cleanup after the sessions is the task of the parent. Children may assist if they choose but may not continue to play after the time has ended. Timers are not allowed for keeping up with the time because this displaces responsibility. The parent is responsible for ending the session even though the child would like to continue. Thus the child learns the parent can be firm and will follow through. Parents are reminded to make notes about happenings in the play sessions immediately following the sessions. Parents are instructed to tell their children that the parents are going to a class to learn to play with their children. One parent volunteers to video tape their session at home or comes to the center to video tape. If someone is available to look after the child and a two-way mirror is available, live demonstrations by parents may be preferred. If these options are not available, demonstrations can be carried out in a corner of a room with the rest of the group watching from behind a bookcase or table, something to form a barrier of separation.

Session 4. Reports are given by each parent on the first session and areas of difficulty with suggestions offered by the therapist. Attention is given to the feelings parents experienced. A video tape of a parent play session is viewed with feedback given from the other parents in the group. An advantage of the video tape is that parents get to observe themselves, an experience which can produce tremendous insight. This experience usually produces considerable anxiety for parents, but the rest of the group is always extremely supportive and the anxiety quickly dissipates. One goal of the therapist while viewing the parent video tape is to always find responses and behaviors to support. Correction is kept to a minimum. Following the video tape, each parent reports on their play session. Since this has been the parents' first opportunity to practice the new skills they have acquired, usually they have so much they want to share about the experience that the time for specific training is minimal. Another parent is asked to volunteer to be video taped or to bring their child for demonstration before the group.

Session 5 through 9. These sessions follow the same general format. Brief reporting by the parents of their play session, interspersed with suggestions and instruction from the therapist along with group interaction on common problems and attention to parents' feelings. A parent video tape is viewed or a parent session is observed and discussed. Depending on the size of the group, in some training sessions two parent sessions may be observed. Homework assignments in which responses are written to typical happenings in play sessions are critiqued. Training and role playing of play session principles and skills are continued each session. Newly developed parental coping skills are identified to help parents develop a sense of personal power. Generalization of skills outside the play sessions typically occurs and is also encouraged for example by giving parents an assignment to make three therapeutic limit setting responses to typical happenings outside the play session. Parental concerns about long term and crisis related child problems not related to the special play times are dealt with. Sidetracking on discussions of minor child related problems is avoided.

Session 10. Parents report on their play sessions, parent session is viewed, and the last hour is spent with parents sharing their evaluation of the experience, how they and their children have changed. Parents share their perceptions of changes they have observed in other parents. Therapist shares notes of parents' original descriptions of their children as points of reference for parents to evaluate progress. This is usually a very rewarding time for the whole group. Parents and/or children needing additional help are scheduled for such help.

Research and Evaluation

Stover and B. Guerney (1967) conducted one of the earliest experimental studies of filial therapy. They evaluated the feasibility of training mothers in filial therapy techniques and found that the mothers trained in filial therapy significantly increased their reflective type statements and decreased their directive type statements, as compared to mothers without training. They also found that the children's behavior was affected by the positive changes in the mothers' behavior.

In a later study, B. Guerney and Stover (1971) reported that children of mothers trained in filial therapy improved significantly on a variety of measures of symptomatology and psychosocial adjustment as rated by their parents. Significant improvement was also noted on two evaluation measures completed by clinicians. Guerney and Stover concluded that as a result of playroom experiences children were able to work out their aggressive feelings, and to deal more realistically with their mothers in terms of conversation and sharing. They also concluded that mothers can be trained to acquire the skills necessary to reflect feelings, allow children self-direction, and demonstrate involvement in their children's emotional expressions and behaviors.

Stuttering problems have been ameliorated through the use of filial therapy as an intervention system. In such problems, the emotional climate in the family was found to be a significant factor affecting the incidence of stuttering. Changing the interactional environment of the child resulted in the therapeutic conditions necessary for alleviating stuttering problems (Andronico & Blake, 1971).

Gilmore (1971) investigated the application of filial therapy with children diagnosed as having learning disabilities and found that through this approach, using parents as therapeutic agents, learning disabled children's self-esteem improved significantly. Their academic and social functioning also increased significantly, and family interaction variables improved.

Long term changes in behavior as a result of the filial therapy experience are encouraging. L. Guerney (1975) surveyed forty-two former filial therapy participants one to three years after treatment termination. Responses to the questionnaire showed that only three of the forty-two children who had participated in the filial therapy program were receiving professional help at follow-up. Thirty-two of the parents reported continued improvement in their child since termination. Four parents reported their child to be the same, four rated their child as exhibiting decreased adjustment, and one parent described their child as worse.

Using children as their own control group, Sywulak (1979) found no changes in parents' ratings of their children's behavior at the conclusion of a four-month wait period. During the following four months, most of the children received special play sessions from both parents who were in filial training and showed significant improvement in adjustment. Also a marked improvement occurred in the parents' acceptance of the children during the same period of time.

A three-year follow-up of children in the Sywulak study (Sensue, 1981) revealed no significant reduction in adjustment two to three years later. Compared to a control group of normal children, the children who had received filial therapy were as well adjusted although they had tested as maladjusted prior to treatment. In addition, parents who had participated in the filial training had higher scores on acceptance of their children than the control sample.

Glass (1986) compared the effects of parents in filial therapy training with a control group and found significant differences in favor of the parents in filial therapy in the areas of exhibition of unconditional love, in awareness, and lessening of conflict in the parent-child relationship, and in parents' increased understanding of the meaning of their children's play. Although not statistically significant, parents in filial therapy showed greater changes in parental acceptance, respect for children's feelings, recognition of children's need for autonomy, increased self-esteem of parents and children, and closeness between parent and child.

REFERENCES

Andronico, M., & Blake, I. (1971). The application of filial therapy to young children with stuttering problems. *Journal of Speech and Hearing Disorders, 36,* 377-381.

Axline, V. (1947). *Play therapy: The inner dynamics of childhood.* Cambridge, MA: Houghton Mifflin.

Baruch, D.W. (1949). *New ways in discipline.* New York: McGraw-Hill.

Freud, S. (1959). Analysis of a phobia in a five-year-old boy. In *Collected Papers* (pp. 149-289). New York: Basic Books.

Fuchs, N.R. (1957). Play therapy at home. *Merril-Palmer Quarterly, 3,* 89-95.

Gilmore, J. (1971). The effectiveness of parental counseling with other modalities in the treatment of children with learning disabilities. *Journal of Education, 154,* 74-82.

Glass, N. (1986). Parents as therapeutic agents: A study of the effect of filial therapy. Unpublished doctoral dissertation, North Texas State University.

Guerney, B.G., Jr. (1964). Filial therapy: Description and rationale. *Journal of Consulting Psychology, 28,* 304-360.

Guerney, B.G., Jr., (Ed.). (1969). *Psychotherapeutic agents: New roles for nonprofessionals, parents, and teachers.* New York: Holt, Rinehart, and Winston.

Guerney, B.G., Jr., & Stover, L. (1971). Final report on filial therapy for grant MH18264-01, National Institute on Mental Health.

Guerney, L. (1972). *Play therapy: A training manual for parents.* Mimeographed Report.

Guerney, L.F. (1975). *Brief follow-up study on filial therapy.* Paper presented at the Eastern Psychological Association, New York City.

Guerney, L.F. (1976). Filial therapy program. In H.L. Benson, (Ed.), *Treating relationships* (pp. 67-91). Lake Mills, IA: Graphic Publishing.

Moustakas, C.W. (1959). *Psychotherapy with children: The living relationship.* New York: Harper & Row.

Rohner, R. (1986). *The warmth dimension: Foundations of parental acceptance/ rejection theory.* Newbury Park, CA: Sage.

Schaefer, E. (1981). Development of adaptive behavior: Conceptual models and family correlates. In M. Begab, H. Haywood, & H. Garber (Eds.),

Psychological influences on retarded development. (Vol. 1), *Issues and theories in development*. Baltimore, MD: University Park Press.

Sensue, M.E. (1981). Filial therapy follow-up study: Effects on parental acceptance and child adjustment (Doctoral dissertation, The Pennsylvania State University). *Dissertation Abstracts International, 42,* 148A.

Spivack, G., & Cianci, N. (1987). High-risk early behavior patterns and later delinquency. In J. Burchard & S. Burchard (Eds.), *Prevention of delinquent behavior*. Newbury Park, CA: Sage.

Stover, L., & Guerney, B.G., Jr. (1967). The efficacy of training procedures for mothers in filial therapy. Psychotherapy: *Theory, research, and practice, 4,* 110-115.

Swick, K. (1987). Teacher reports on parental efficacy/involvement relationships. *Instructional Psychology, 14,* 125-132.

Swick, K., Gladstone, D., & Hayes, J. (1988). In search of themselves: Special needs children in a preschool setting. Unpublished report on the Special Needs Learner Project, University of South Carolina's Children's Center, College of Education, University of South Carolina, Columbia.

Swick, K., & Graves, S. (1986). Locus of control and interpersonal support as related to parenting. *Childhood Education, 62,* 26-31.

Sywulak, A.E. (1979). The effect of filial therapy on parental acceptance and child adjustment (Doctoral dissertation, The Pennsylvania State University). *Dissertation Abstracts International, 38,* 6180B.

CHAPTER **17**

SELECTED
PLAY THERAPY
BIBLIOGRAPHY

These previous sixteen chapters contain some of my thinking and obviously my biases about the play therapy relationship. There are many other points of view and a wealth of information to be found in the literature. This selected bibliography of play therapy literature is provided to facilitate the student and practitioner's efforts to go further in exploring the richness of the field of play therapy as you strive to enhance your learning about self, children, and the dynamics of this exciting field of play therapy. An effort has been made to include references providing a cross sectional view of play therapy and encompassing a wide range of topics such as the play therapy realtionship, meaning of play, play therapy in special settings, group play therapy, play therapy with special populations, specific problem areas in play therapy, training, the play therapy process, and research.

Alexander, E. (1964). School centered play-therapy program. *Personnel and Guidance Journal, 43,* 256-261.

Allan, J. (1988). *Inscapes of the child's world.* Dallas, TX: Spring Publishing.

Allan, J., & Berry, P. (1987). Sandplay. Special Issue: Counseling with expressive arts. *Elementary School Guidance and Counseling, 21*(4), 300-306.

Allen, F. (1942). *Psychotherapy with Children.* New York: W.W. Norton.

Allen, F. (1939). Therapeutic work with children. *American Journal of Orthopsychiatry, 4,* 193-202.

Amster, F. (1943). Differential use of play in treatment of young children. *American Journal of Orthopsychiatry, 13,* 62-69.

Ariel, S., Carel, C., & Tyano, S. (1985). Use of children's make-believe play in family therapy: Theory and clinical examples. *Journal of Marital and Family Therapy, 11*(1), 47-60.

Avery, C. (1968). Play therapy with the blind. *International Journal for the Education of the Blind, 18,* 41-46.

Axline, V. (1971). *Dibs: In search of self.* New York: Ballantine Books.

Axline, V. (1950). Entering the child's world via play experiences. *Progressive Education, 27,* 68-75.

Axline, V. (1947). Non-directive therapy for poor readers. *Journal of Consulting Psychology, 11,* 61-69.

Axline, V. (1947). *Play therapy: The inner dynamics of childhood.* Boston: Houghton Mifflin.

Axline, V. (1948). Play therapy and race conflict in young children. *Journal of Abnormal and Social Psychology, 43,* 300-310.

Axline, V. (1955). Play therapy procedures and results. *American Journal of Orthopsychiatry, 25,* 618-626.

Axline, V. (1949). Play therapy: A way of understanding and helping reading problems. *Childhood Education, 26,* 156-161.

Axline, V. (1950). Play therapy experiences as described by child participants. *Journal of Consulting Psychology, 14,* 53-63.

Azarnoff, P., & Flegal, S. (1975). *A pediatric play program: Developing a therapeutic play program for children in medical settings.* Springfield, IL: Thomas.

Barlow, K., Strother, J., & Landreth, G. (1985). Child-centered play therapy: Nancy from baldness to curls. *School Counselor, 32*(5), 347-356.

Barlow, K., Strother, J., & Landreth, G. (1986). Sibling group play therapy: An effective alternative with an elective mute child. *School Counselor, 34*(1), 44-50.

Bender, L. (1955). Therapeutic play techniques: Discussion. *American Journal of Orthopsychiatry, 25,* 784-787.

Bender, L., & Woltmann, A. (1941). Play and psychotherapy. *Nervous Child,* *1,* 17-42.

Bernhardt, M., & Mackler, B. (1975). The use of play therapy with the mentally retarded. *Journal of Special Education, 9*(4), 409-414.

Bills, R. (1950). Nondirective play therapy with retarded readers. *Journal of Consulting Psychology, 14,* 140-149.

Bills, R. (1950). Play therapy with well-adjusted readers. *Journal of Consulting Psychology, 14,* 246-249.

Bixler, R. (1949). Limits are therapy. *Journal of Consulting Psychology, 13,* 1-11.

Bixler, R. (1946). A method of case transfer. *Journal of Clinical Psychology, 2,* 274-278.

Bradway, K. (1979). Sandplay in psychotherapy. *Art Psychotherapy, 6*(2), 85-93.

Carns, M. (1979). *The long-term effects of play therapy.* (DAI 40/03A). Unpublished doctoral dissertation: University of North Texas.

Cassell, S. (1972). The suitcase playroom. *Psychotherapy: Theory, Research & Practice, 9,* 346-348.

Clatworthy, S. (1981). Therapeutic play: Effects on hospitalized children. *Journal of the Association for the Care of Children's Health, 9*(4), 108-113.

Cox, F. (1953). Sociometric status and individual adjustment before and after play therapy. *Journal of Abnormal and Social Psychology, 48,* 354-356.

Crow, J. (1989). *Play therapy with low achievers in reading.* Unpublished doctoral dissertation: University of North Texas.

D'Antonio, I. (1984). Therapeutic use of play in hospitals. *Nursing Clinics of North America, 19* (2), 351-359.

Damme, S. (1965). Play therapy for asthmatic children. *Allergy and Asthma, 11,* 289-292.

DeMaagd, J. (1971). *Play therapy: Client-centered counseling for elementary school children.* Unpublished doctoral dissertation. Western Michigan University: Kalamazoo, MI.

Despert, J. (1948). Play therapy: Remarks on some of its aspects. *The Nervous Child, 7,* 287-295.

DeStefan, T. (1981). *Family therapy compared to individual play therapy in the treatment of young children for behavioral and emotional problems.* (DAI 42/10B). Unpublished doctoral dissertation: University of Northern Colorado.

Digby, M. (1975). The hospital play therapist. *Child Care Health and Development. 1*(4). 233-237.

Dittman, A., & Kitchener, H. (1957). Life space interviewing and individual play therapy: A comparison of techniques. *American Journal of Orthopsychiatry. 29.* 19-26.

Dorfman, E. (1958). Personality outcomes of client-centered child therapy. *Psychological Monographs. 72*(3). 1-22.

Dukes, E. (1938). Play therapy for problem children. *British Journal of Medical Psychology. 2.* 213-215.

Dupent, H., Landsman, T., & Valentine, M. (1953). The treatment of delayed speech by client-centered therapy. *Journal of Consulting Psychology. 18.* 122-125.

Eaker, B. (1986). Unlocking the family secret in family play therapy. Child and Adolescent. *Social Work Journal. 3*(4). 235-253.

Ellerton, M., Caty, S., & Ritchie, J. (1985). Helping young children master instrusive procedures through play. *Children's Health Care. 13*(4). 167-173.

Elliott, C., & Pumfrey, P. (1972). The effects of non-directive play therapy on some maladjusted boys. *Educational Research,* 14(2), 157-161.

Fine, P. (1982). Play and family therapy as core skills for child psychiatry: Some implications of Piaget's theory for integrations in training and practice. *Child Psychiatry and Human Development. 13*(2). 79-96.

Finke, H. (1947). *Changes in the expression of emotionalized attitudes in six cases of play therapy.* Unpublished master's thesis. University of Chicago.

Fishbein, C. *The relationship between age-related toys and therapeutic expression in non-directive play therapy.* Unpublished master's thesis: The Pennsylvania State University.

Fleming, L., & Snyder, W. (1947). Social and personal changes following nondirective group play therapy. *American Journal of Orthopsychiatry. 17.* 101-116.

Foley, J. (1970). *Training future teachers as play therapists: An investigation of therapeutic outcome and orientation toward pupils. Final report. (OEG-0-8080059-3722).* Washington. D. C.: Bureau of Research, Office of Education (DHEW).

Frank, L. (1955). Therapeutic play techniques: Play in personality development. *American Journal of Orthopsychiatry, 25,* 576-590.

Freud, A. (1928). *Introduction to the technique of child analysis.* New York: Disease Publishing.

Freud, A. (1964). *The psychoanalytical treatment of children.* New York: Schocken Books.

Froehlich, M. (1984). A comparison of the effect of music therapy and medical play therapy on the verbalization behavior of pediatric patients. *Journal of Music Therapy, 21*(1), 2-15.

Fuchs, N. (1957). Play therapy at home. *Merrill-Palmer Quarterly, 3,* 89-95.

Gaulden, G. (1975). *Developmental play group counseling with early primary grade students exhibiting behavioral problems.* Unpublished doctoral dissertation: University of North Texas.

Gibbs, J. (1945). Group play therapy. *British Journal of Medical Psychology, 20,* 244-254.

Ginott, H. (1958). Play group therapy: A theoretical framework. *International Journal of Group Psychotherapy, 8,* 410-418.

Ginott, H. (1959). The theory and practice of "therapeutic intervention" in child treatment. *Journal of Consulting Psychology, 23,* 160-166.

Ginott, H. (1960). A rationale for selecting toys in play therapy. *Journal of Consulting Psychology, 24,* 243-246.

Ginott, H. (1961). *Group psychotherapy with children: The theory and practice of play therapy.* New York: McGraw-Hill Books.

Ginott, H. (1961). Play therapy: The initial session. *American Journal of Psychotherapy, 15,* 73-88.

Ginott, H., & Lebo, D. (1963). Most and least used play therapy limits. *Journal of Genetic Psychology, 103,* 153-159.

Ginsberg, B. (1976). Parents as therapeutic agents: The usefulness of filial therapy in a community mental health center. *American Journal of Community Psychology, 4*(1), 47-54.

Ginsberg, B. (1984). Beyond behavior modification: Client-centered play therapy with the retarded. *Academic Psychology Bulletin, 6*(3), 321-334.

Goodman, J. (1962). Nondirective psychodramatic play therapy. *American Journal of Orthopsychiatry, 32,* 532-534.

Gorman, J. (1972). Dissociation and play therapy: A case study. *Journal of Psychiatric Nursing, 10*(2), 23-26.

Graham, B. (1975). Non-directive play therapy with troubled children. *Corrective and Social Psychiatry and Journal of Behavior Technology Methods and Therapy, 21*(1), 22-23.

Green, C. (1975). Larry thought puppet-play "childish." But it helped him face his fears. *Nursing (Jenkin town), 5*(3), 30-33.

Greenwald, H. (1967). Play therapy for children over twenty-one. *Psychotherapy: Theory, Research & Practice, 4*(1), 44-46.

Guerney, B. (1964). Filial therapy: Description and rationale. *Journal of Consulting Psychology, 28*, 304-310.

Guerney, L. (1976). The treatment of child abuse: Play therapy with a four-year-old child. *Journal of the American Academy of Child Psychiatry, 15*, 430-440.

Guerney, L. (1979). Play therapy with learning disabled children. *Journal of Clinical Child Psychology, 8*(3), 242-244.

Hambidge, G. (1955). Structured play therapy. *American Journal of Orthopsychiatry, 25*, 601-617.

Hannah, G. (1986). *An investigation of play therapy: Process and outcome using interrupted time-series analysis.* (DAI 47/06B). Unpublished doctoral dissertation: University of Northern Colorado.

Harnish, P. (1983). *The effects of children's perceptions of certain therapist expressed conditions on the process and outcome of non-directive play therapy.* (DAI 45/03B). Unpublished doctoral dissertation: University of Toledo.

Haworth, M. (1964). *Child psychotherapy: Practice and theory.* New York: Basic Books.

Hejna, R. (1960). *Speech disorders and nondirective therapy: Client centered counseling and play therapy.* New York: Ronald Press.

Hellersberg, E. (1955). Child's growth in play therapy. *American Journal of Psychotherapy, 9*, 484-502.

Hendricks, S. (1971). *A descriptive analysis of the process of client-centered play therapy. (DAI 32/07A).* Unpublished doctoral dissertation: University of North Texas.

Hindmarsh, W. (1979). Play diagnosis and play therapy. *American Journal of Occupational Therapy, 33*, 770-775.

Horne, D. (1979). Play therapy as part of an educational program for an atypical child: A case study. *Journal of Educational Therapy, 1*, 22-36.

House, R. (1970). *The effects of nondirective group play therapy upon the sociometric status and self-concept of selected second grade children. (DAI 31/06A).* Unpublished doctoral dissertation: Oregon State University.

Howe, P., & Silvern, L. (1981). Behavioral observation of children during play therapy: Preliminary development of a research instrument. *Journal of Personality Assessment, 45*, 168-182.

Hudson, W. (1975). Play therapy in the treatment of hebephrenia. *Psychotherapy and Psychosomatics, 26*(5), 286-293.

Hug-Hellmuth, H. (1921). On the technique of child-analysis. *International Journal of Psychoanalysis, 2*, 287-305.

Hyde, N. (1971). Play therapy: The troubled child's self-encounter. *American Journal of Nursing, 71*, 1366-1370.

Irwin, B. (1971). Play therapy for a regressed schizophrenic patient. *Journal of Psychiatric Nursing, 9*, 30-32.

Irwin, E., & Malloy, E. (1975). Family puppet interview. *Family Process, 14*, 179-191.

Irwin, E., & McWilliams, B. (1974). Play therapy for children with cleft palates. *Children Today, 3*, 18-22.

Jackson, L., & Todd, K. (1950). *Child treatment and the therapy of play. (2nd ed.).* New York: Ronald Press.

James, D. (1977). *Play therapy: An overview.* Oceanside, NY: Dabor Science Publications.

Jeffrey, L. (1984). Developmental play therapy: An assessment and therapeutic technique in child psychiatry. *British Journal of Occupational Therapy, 47*(3), 70-74.

Jernberg, A. (1979). *Theraplay: A new treatment using structured play for problem children and their families.* San Francisco: Jossey-Bass.

Johnson, M. (1988). Use of play group therapy in promoting social skills. *Issues in Mental Health Nursing, 9*(1), 105-112.

Jones, J. (1952). Play therapy and the blind child. *New Outlook for the Blind, 46*, 189-197.

Keith, D., & Whitaker, C. (1981). Play therapy: A paradigm for work with families. *Journal of Marital and Family Therapy, 7*(3), 243-254.

Klein, M. (1955). The psychoanalytic play technique. American *Journal of Orthopsychiatry, 25,* 223-237.

Klein, M. (l959). *The psychoanalysis of children.* (3rd ed.). London: Hogarth Press.

Knudsen, K. (1975). Play therapy: Preparing the young child for surgery. *Nursing Clinics of North America, 10*(4), 679-686.

Kraft, A. (1973). Are you listening to your child? How to bridge the communication gap through creative play sessions. New York: Walker.

Kramer, E. (1972). *Art as therapy with children.* New York: Schocken Books.

Kramer, E. (1977). Art therapy and play. *American Journal of Art Therapy. 17*(1), 3-11.

Kranz, P. (l972). Teachers as play therapists: An experiment in learning. *Childhood-Education, 49*(2), 73-78.

Kremberg, M. (l982). The doctor as toy-fixer: A combination of art and play therapy. *American Journal of Art Therapy, 21*(3), 87-91.

Kuhli, L. (1979). The use of two houses in play therapy. *American Journal of Orthopsychiatry, 49*(3), 431-435.

Landisberg, S., & Snyder, W. (1946). Non-directive play therapy. *Journal of Clinical Psychology, 2*(3), 203-214.

Landreth, G. (1978). Children communicate through play. *Texas Personnel and Guidance Journal, 6*(1), 41-42.

Landreth, G. (1982). *Play therapy: Dynamics of the process of counseling with children.* Springfield, IL: Thomas.

Landreth, G. (1985). Play therapy: Organizing the program. *Texas Association for Counseling and Development, 32,* 17-22.

Landreth, G. (l987). Play therapy: Facilitative use of child's play in elementary school counseling. Special issue: Counseling with expressive arts. *Elementary School Guidance and Counseling, 21*(4), 253-261.

Landreth, G. (1988). Lessons for living from a dying child. *Journal of Counseling and Development, 67*(2), 100.

Landreth, G., Allen, L., & Jacquot, W. (1969). A team approach to learning disabilities. *Journal of Learning Disabilities, 2*(2), 82-87.

Landreth, G., & Barkley H. (1982). The uniqueness of the play therapist in a child's life. *Texas Personnel and Guidance Journal, 10,* 77-81.

Landreth, G., & Hendricks, S. (1977). Play therapy is for public schools. *Texas Personnel and Guidance Journal, 5*(1), 61-63.

Landreth, G., Strother, J., & Barlow, K. (1986). A reaction to objections to play therapy. Special Issue: Counseling middle-grade students. *School Counselor, 33*(3), 164-166.

Landreth, G., & Verhalen, M. (1982). Who is this person they call a counselor who has a playroom? *School Counselor, 29,* 359-361.

Leal, M. (1966). Group-analytic play therapy with pre-adolescent girls. *International Journal of Group Psychotherapy, 16,* 58-64.

Lebo, D. (1952). The relationship of response categories in play therapy to chronological age. *Journal of Child Psychiatry, 2,* 330-336.

Lebo, D. (1955). The development of play as a form of therapy: From Rousseau to Rogers. *American Journal of Psychiatry, 112,* 418-422.

Lebo, D. (1955). The expressive value of toys recommended for nondirective play therapy. *Journal of Clinical Psychology, 11,* 144-148.

Lebo, D. (1955). Quantification of the non-directive play therapy process. *Journal of Genetic Psychology, 86,* 375-378.

Lebo, D. (1955). The relationship of play to play therapy. *Journal of Education & Psychology, 13,* 114-121.

Lebo, D. (1956). Age and suitability for non-directive play therapy. *Journal of Genetic Psychology, 89,* 231-238.

Lebo, D., & Lebo, E. (1957). Aggression and age in relation to verbal expression in non-directive play therapy. *Psychological Monographs, 71*(20), 449-461.

Leland, H., & Smith, D. (1965). *Play therapy with mentally subnormal children.* New York: Grune & Stratton.

Leland, H., Walker, J., & Taboada, A. (1959). Group play therapy with a group of postnursery male retardates. *American Journal of Mental Deficiency, 63,* 848-851.

Levy, D. (1939). Release therapy in young children. *Child Study, 16*(1), 141-143.

Levy, D. (1939). Release therapy. *American Journal of Orthopsychiatry, 9,* 713-736.

Linnell, A. (1976). *The effects of adult play therapy on therapist skill development and client change. (DAI 37/11B).* Unpublished doctoral dissertation: University of Northern Colorado.

Lowenfeld, M. (1935). *Play in childhood*. London: Gollancz.

Lowenfeld, M. (1938). The theory and use of play in the psychotherapy of childhood. *Journal of Mental Science. 84.* 1057-1058.

Lowenfeld, M., & Maberly, A. (1946). Discussion on the value of play therapy in child psychiatry. *Proceedings of the Royal Society of Medicine. 39.* 439-443.

McDermott, P., & McDermott, J. (1976). The treatment of child abuse. Play therapy with a 4-year-old child. *Journal of the American Academy of Child Psychiatry. 15*(3), 430-440.

Miles, M. (1981). Play therapy: A review of theories and comparison of some techniques. *Issues in Mental Health Nursing. 3.* 63-75.

Moreno, J. (1985). Music play therapy: An integrated approach. *Arts in Psychotherapy. 12*(1), 17-23.

Morris, M. (1978). Family play therapy: An extended treatment model. *Ontario Psychologist. 10*(4), 25-29.

Moulin, E. (1970). The effects of client centered group counseling using play media on the intelligence, achievement, and psycholinguistic abilities of underachieving primary school children. *Elementary School Guidance and Counseling. 5*(85), 85-95.

Moustakas, C. (1951). Situational play therapy with normal children. *Journal of Consulting Psychology. 15.* 225-230.

Moustakas, C. (1953). *Children in play therapy*. New York: McGraw-Hill.

Moustakas, C. (1955). Emotional adjustment and the play therapy process. *Journal of Genetic Psychology. 86.* 79-99.

Moustakas, C. (1955). The frequency and intensity of negative attitudes expressed in play therapy: A comparison of well-adjusted and disturbed young children. *Journal of Genetic Psychology. 86.* 309-325.

Moustakas, C. (1959). *Psychotherapy with children: The living relationship*. New York: Harper and Row.

Moustakas, C., & Schalock, H. (1955). An analysis of therapist-child interaction in play therapy. *Child Development. 26.* 143-157.

Myamoto, M. (1965). The meaning of silence in play therapy. *Psychologia. 8.* 191-196.

Myrick, R., & Haldin, W. (1971). A study of play process in counseling. *Elementary School Guidance and Counseling. 5*(4), 256-265.

Nelson, R. (1966). Elementary school counseling with unstructured play media. *Personnel & Guidance Journal, 45*(1), 24-27.

Nelson, R. (1967). Pros and cons of using play media in counseling. *Elementary School Guidance and Counseling. 2,* 143-147.

Nemiroff, M., & Annunziata, J. (1990). *A child's first book about play therapy.* Hyattsville, MD: American Psychological Association.

Newcomer, B., & Morrison, T. (1974). Play therapy with institutionalized mentally retarded children. *American Journal of Mental Deficiency. 78*(6), 727-733.

Nickerson, E. (1973). Recent approaches to and innovations in play therapy. *International Journal of Child Psychotherapy. 2*(1), 53-70.

Nickerson, E. (1973). Recent trends and innovations in play therapy. *International Journal of Child Psychotherapy. 2*(1), 53-70.

Noll, R., & Seagull, A. (1982). Beyond informed consent: Ethical and philosophical considerations in using behavior modification of play therapy in the treatment of enuresis. *Journal of Clinical Child Psychology. 11*(1), 44-49.

Oaklander, V. (1978). *Windows to our children. A gestalt therapy approach to our children and adolescents.* Utah: Real People Press.

Oe, E. (1989). *Comparison of initial session play therapy behaviors of maladjusted and adjusted children.* Unpublished doctoral dissertation, University of North Texas.

Orgun, N. (1973). Playroom setting for diagnostic family interviews. *American Journal of Psychiatry. 130,* 540-542.

Osterweil, Z. (1986). Time-limited play therapy: Rationale and technique. *School Psychology International. 7*(4), 224-230.

Oualline, V. (1975). *Behavioral outcomes of short-term nondirective play therapy with preschool deaf children. (DAI 36/12A).* Unpublished doctoral dissertation: University of North Texas.

Peck, M., & Stewart, R. (1964). Current practices in selection criteria for group play-therapy. *Journal of Clinical Psychology. 20*(1), 146.

Perry, L. (1988). *Play therapy behavior of maladjusted and adjusted children.* Unpublished doctoral dissertation: University of North Texas.

Raskin, N. (1954). Play therapy with blind children. *New Outlook for the Blind. 48,* 290-292.

Russo, S. (1964). Adaptations in behavioral therapy with children. *Behavior Research and Therapy, 2,* 43-47.

Sandler, J., Kennedy, H., & Tyson, R. (1980). *The technique of child psychoanalysis: Discussions with Anna Freud.* Boston, MA: Harvard University Press.

Schaefer, C. (1976). *The therapeutic use of child's play.* New York: Jason Aronson.

Schaefer, C., & O'Connor, K. (1983). *Handbook of play therapy.* New York: Wiley.

Schiffer, M. (1952). Permissiveness versus sanction in activity group therapy. *International Journal of Group Psychotherapy, 2,* 255-261.

Seeman, J. (1949). A study of the process of non-directive therapy. *Journal of Consulting Psychology, 13,* 157-168.

Siegel, C. (1972). Changes in play therapy behaviors over time as a function of differing levels of therapist-offered conditions. *Journal of Clinical Psychology, 28*(2), 235-236.

Sjolund, M. (1981). Play diagnosis and therapy in Sweden: The Erica-method. *Journal of Clinical Psychology, 37*(2), 322-325.

Slavson, S. (1952). *Child Psychotherapy.* New York: Columbia University Press.

Smathers, S., & Tirnauer, L. (1959). Speech-play therapy. *The Journal of Speech and Hearing Disorders, 24,* 59-61.

Solomon, J. (1938). Active play therapy. *American Journal of Orthopsychiatry, 8*(3), 479-498.

Solomon, J. (1948). Play technique. *American Journal of Orthopsychiatry, 18,* 402-413.

Solomon, J. (1955). Play techniques and the integrative process. *American Journal of Orthopsychiatry, 25*(3), 591-600.

Stollak, G. (1981). Variations and extensions of filial therapy. *Family Process, 20*(3), 305-309.

Subotnik, L. (1966). Transference in client-centered play therapy. *Psychology, 3*(1), 2-17.

Traill, P. (1945). An account of Lowenfield technique in a child guidance clinic, with a survey of therapeutic play techniques in Great Britain & U.S.A. *Journal of Mental Science, 91,* 43-78.

Ude-Pestel, A. (1977). *Betty: History and art of a child in therapy*. Palo Alto, CA: Science and Behavior Books.

Vinturella, L., & James, R. (1987). Sand play: A therapeutic medium with children. *Elementary School Guidance and Counseling, 21*(3), 229-238.

Wall, L. (1979). *Parents as play therapists: A comparison of three interventions into children's play. (DAI 39/11B)*. Unpublished doctoral dissertation: University of Northern Colorado.

Waterland, J. (1970). Actions instead of words: Play therapy for the young child. *Elementary School Guidance and Counseling, 4*(3), 180-187.

Weigle, H., & McNally, H. (1980). When a child needs counseling: How two children were helped through the use of non-directive play therapy. *Early Years Parent, 11*(4), 12-13.

West, J. (1984). Ending or beginning? A discussion of the theory and practice of termination procedures in play therapy. *Journal of Social Work Practice, 1*(2), 49-65.

Withee, K. (1975). *A descriptive analysis of the process of play therapy. (DAI 36/12B)*. Unpublished doctoral dissertation: University of North Texas.

Woltmann, A. (1955). Concepts of play therapy techniques. *American Journal of Orthopsychiatry, 25*, 771-783.

INDEX

INDEX

Change
    dimensions 323-5
    within children 328-9
Characteristics
    facilitative responses 183-208
Child
    elective mute, case of 310-8
    in waiting room 158-61
    initial encounter 158-61
    leading 206-7
    making contact 155-8
    manipulative, case of 299-310
    questioning techniques 170-8
    reactions to the last session
      331-3
    responding to the reluctant
      anxious 165-7
Child dying 293-8
Child Life Programs 39
Child's hour 153-82
Child-centered
    play therapy 55-84
Child-centered philosophy 9
Children
    acceptance 3
    adjusted 20-2
    communication through play
      10-13
    in play therapy 269-318
    like molasses 53-4
    like popcorn 53-4
    maladjusted 20-2
    principles for relationships 5-6
    resilient 51-3
    view of 49-54
Ching, play therapist 101
Chris, case of 87-8
Cianci, N. 337, 352
Cindy, case of 299-310
Clatworthy, S. 355
Clean
    asking the child 261-3
Communication
    play 10-13
Conference
    play therapy 35
Confidentiality 145-7
Conn, J.H. 41, 43, 313, 319
Contact
    with the child 155-8
Cooper, S. 132, 151

Corsini, R. 85, 355
Crow, J. 42, 43, 355

D

D'Antonio, I. 355
Damme, S. 355
de Saint Exupery, A. 70, 85
DeMaagd, J. 355
Dependence of the child 239-41
Despert, J. 355
DeStefan, T. 356
Development
    play therapy 25-42
Diatkine, R. 40, 43
Digby, M. 356
Dimensions
    change 323-5
    of relationship 180-2
Dimick, K.M. 33, 43
Dittman, A. 356
Dorfman, E. 265, 268, 356
Douglas, play therapist 101
Dudek, S. 42, 43
Dukes, E. 356
Dupent, H. 356
Dupent, J.J. 41, 43

E

Eaker, B. 356
Ekstein, R. 41, 44
Ellerton, M. 3
Elliott, C.D. 35, 41, 46
Emerson, R.W. 55
Enuresis 310-1
Evaluation 202-3
    filial therapy 349-50
Experiences
    play out 11
Exploration
    real life experiences 119

F

Family therapy
    play therapy techniques 36-7

Y

ABOUT
the
AUTHOR

GARRY LANDRETH

Dr. Garry L. Landreth is internationally known for his writings and work in promoting the development of play therapy as a procedure for understanding and assisting children in their process of growth. He received the distinguished appointment of Regents Professor in the Department of Counselor Education at the University of North Texas, and is founder and director of the Center for Play Therapy, the largest play therapy training program in the nation. He has worked extensively with children in therapy relationships and has conducted workshops focusing on play therapy and relationships with children throughout the United States, Canada, and in China.

His more than sixty publications include the books, *Play Therapy: Dynamics of the Process of Counseling with Children; Group Counseling: Concepts and Procedures,* and this text which is an exploration of his child-centered approach to play therapy. Garry is a licensed professional counselor and licensed psychologist in the state of Texas and is a member of the Board of Directors of the International Association for Play Therapy.

Garry has received numerous professional honors including the:

1985	Meadows Honor Professor Award
1986	President's Outstanding Teacher Award
1987	Toulouse Scholar Award
1987	Regents Distinguished Professor Award

He is a frequent keynote speaker at national and state conferences and gave the keynote address at the Southeast Asia Association for Counselors and Psychologists Conference. He has also been the featured speaker at several International Association for Play Therapy Conferences.